PHANTOMS OVER VIETNAM

US Navy F4 Phantoms
1965-1973
PART 1

PHANTOMS OVER VIETNAM

US Navy F4 Phantoms
1965–1973
PART 1

OSPREY
PUBLISHING

THE MILITARY
BOOK CLUB

First published in Great Britain in 2001 by Osprey Publishing,
Elms Court, Chapel Way, Botley, Oxford, OX2 9LP
Email: info@ospreypublishing.com

ISBN 1 84176 599 6

Editor: Sally Rawlings
Series editor: Tony Holmes
Page design by Tony Truscott and Mark Holt
Colour plates commentaries (Part 1) by Tom Chee, Brad Elward and Tony Holmes
Photo captions by Brad Elward and Tony Holmes
Cover artwork by Iain Wyllie
Aircraft profiles by Jim Laurier
Scale drawings by Mark Styling
Maps by Zaur Eylanbekov
Index by Alan Thatcher

Origination by Grasmere Digital Imaging, Leeds, UK
Printed in China

00 01 02 03 04   10 9 8 7 6 5 4 3 2 1

ACKNOWLEDGEMENTS - PART 1
The Editor wishes to thank the following individuals for the provision of text and
photographs included within this volume – Robert F Dorr, Peter Mersky, Angelo
Romano, Nick Stroud at Aerospace Publishing and Lt Don J Willis (Ret). Both
Authors and the Editor also acknowledge the important contribution made by Tom
Chee, who provided much of the material included within the Colour Plates
commentaries, and USAF Historical Research Agency archivist Archie DiFante at
Maxwell AFB. Finally, the Authors wish to thank the following naval aviators for
their input – Lt David Batson (Ret), Capt Roy Cash (Ret), Lt Cdr Jerry Beaulier
(Ret), Capt Eugene Lund (Ret) and Capt John Nash (Ret).

ACKNOWLEDGEMENTS - PART 2
The Editor wishes to thank the following individuals for their valuable photographic
contributions – Robert F Dorr, Capt John C Ensch (Ret) and his squadronmates at
VF-161, Michael France, Capt Jerry Houston (Ret), Dave Menard, Peter Mersky,
Michael Padgett, Angelo Romano and Nick Stroud. Both Authors and the Editor
acknowledge the contribution made by Tom Chee and Alan Howarth, who provided
much of the material included within the Colour Plates commentaries. Finally,
thanks to Adm Winston 'Cope' Copeland (Ret) for explaining why he was 'in hack'
in June 1972!

For a catalogue of all Osprey Publishing titles please contact us at:

Osprey Direct UK, PO Box 140, Wellingborough, Northants NN8 2FA, UK
E-mail: **info@ospreydirect.co.uk**

**Osprey Direct USA, c/o MBI Publishing, 729 Prospect Ave,
PO Box 1, Osceola, WI 54020, USA**
E-mail: **info@ospreydirectusa.com**

Or visit our website: **www.ospreypublishing.com**

CONTENTS

PREFACE

There are few knowledgeable individuals who would dispute that the McDonnell Douglas F-4 Phantom II played an instrumental role in prosecuting the air war over North Vietnam. This rugged, versatile jet, originally designed as a long-ranged interceptor, served quite well as a bomber and reconnaissance platform, and flew as the frontline fighter for all three United States military services during the war.

During the late 1950s, the Phantom II, as well as its complement of air-to-air missiles (namely, the medium-range, radar-guided AIM-7D Sparrow and the short-range, infrared-guided AIM-9B Sidewinder) were believed to be the way of the future, detecting, tracking and killing non-manoeuvring targets at great distances before the targets realised that they were even being hunted. But, as the war in Vietnam soon showed, those beliefs were still a long way from fruition, and are only now today, in the 21st Century, becoming a reality. Even so, beyond visual range (BVR) engagements are still not the norm, as today's conflicts often take place in congested littorals.

While the air war over North Vietnam was predominantly a bombing campaign that was designed to bring the North Vietnamese to the bargaining table, MiG fighters of the Vietnamese People's Air Force (VPAF) were an ever-present threat to US strike aircraft. Although widely believed to be a rather inept cadre during the early years of the conflict, the VPAF pilots honed their skills and improved their tactics during the course of the war.

Between 1965 and 1970, VPAF MiGs claimed eight US Navy fighter aircraft, five of which were F-4 Phantom IIs. In return, Navy F-4 crews downed thirteen MiGs (seven MiG-17s and six MiG-21s) and one Communist Chinese MiG-17 (the Chinese in turn also claimed an F-4 destroyed). Even considering the kills of Navy F-8 Crusader crews (see *Osprey Combat Aircraft 7 - F-8 Crusader Units of the Vietnam War* for further details), the overall kill ratio was a dismal 2.42 to 1, which compared poorly with the ratios seen in Korea and World War 2.

Part of this deficiency could be blamed on the fact that the Phantom II was still an aircraft in its infancy, and its performance envelope had yet to be fully explored. The same was true of the new, and in many cases complex, missile systems used by the F-4 crews. But part of the blame could equally be placed on the short-sightedness of the US Navy in failing to properly train its aircrews in air combat tactics - the art of dogfighting that had been discarded by the intercept community in favour of the new air-to-air missiles.

As Capt Frank Ault, former Commanding Officer of USS *Coral Sea* (CVA-43), and the person responsible for the now famous 'Ault Report', commented in the early 1970s, 'During my Tonkin Gulf tour in *Coral Sea*, air combat kills rose to about eight per cent of US combat losses, from a 1966 figure of three per cent. By 1968, this figure had reached 23 per cent. The numbers were worse than they appeared because we were losing two people and a four-million-dollar aircraft with every Phantom II shot down, versus a million-dollar, single pilot MiG.

'We knew from Phantom II versus Crusader and Phantom II versus MiG hassles that fighting a heads-up fight with a heads-down system was a loser. Worse than that, neither Phantom II nor Crusader pilots had much air-to-air combat training because of doubts that it was needed, and because the Navy was not willing to accept the higher possibility of accidents demonstrated by earlier experience.

'The Phantom II's problems were exacerbated by the conversion to a free-fall, lanyard-actuated Sparrow from earlier rail-launched weapons, and failure to periodically verify weapon system functional integrity. Consequently, we encountered air combat situations where neither the pilot nor his aircraft had ever fired the weapon(s) involved.'

Capt Ault's comments tell it accurately, and paint the background against which the 'MiG killer' of the *Rolling Thunder* years emerged.

This book details the story of the US Navy's F-4 Phantom II 'MiG killers' during the first phase of the Vietnam air war, from 1965 to 1970. These men fought under considerable political and tactical restrictions, and yet prevailed in the toughest of all air battles – man-versus-man. To some extent, it can be said that these men were even more heroic and ingenious than those who flew during the second major air phase of the Vietnam air war, as the 'MiG killers' of 1965 to 1970, equipped with poorly functioning weapons and outdated tactics, were pitted against an ever-growing, and aggressive, VPAF MiG force. Yet they prevailed.

INCIDENT AT HAINAN

On 9 April 1965 the carrier USS *Ranger* (CVA-61) was operating as part of Task Force 77 on *Yankee Station* in the Tonkin Gulf. While Navy carriers had been involved in Operation *Rolling Thunder* for a mere three weeks, *Ranger's* Carrier Air Wing Nine (CVW-9) had already seen its share of action, having participated in *Blue Tree* missions (pre-strike reconnaissance flights), and also having flown top cover for the 7 February *Flaming Dart I* strikes against Vit Thu Lu and 11 February *Flaming Dart II* retaliatory strikes against the Chanh Hoa barracks in southern North Vietnam.

Although the Navy's first encounter with VPAF MiGs had taken place just six days earlier (four F-8Es from VF-211 tangled inconclusively with a quartet of MiG-17s from the 921st Fighter Regiment near the Dong Phong Thong bridge), crews had nevertheless briefed heavily on the possibility of an engagement in the months leading up to this first encounter.

Also, given *Yankee Station's* proximity to Hainan Island, a Chinese possession just north of the 20th parallel, aircrews had been warned to keep a lookout for Chinese MiGs – particularly since the Chinese had 'claimed' a 30-mile 'no-fly' zone extending from its border.

At 0803 hrs on the morning of the 9th, two F-4B Phantom IIs from VF-96 launched from *Ranger* and headed north to perform a routine

VF-96 (along with sister-squadron VF-92) would complete more combat tours to Vietnam than any other F-4 Phantom II unit in the US Navy. This photograph was taken in late 1965, by which time the 'Fighting Falcons' were already participating in their second (of eight) cruises to Vietnam. 'Showtime 606' (BuNo 149426) is seen taxiying forward towards the waist catapults on the *Enterprise* (*via Aerospace Publishing*)

In the weeks immediately prior to the Hainan clash, VF-96 (and VF-92) had been flying fighter escort for RA-5C Vigilantes tasked with performing *Blue Tree* reconnaissance missions over North Vietnam. Here, F-4Bs BuNos 151439 and 151441 formate with their charge (a Vigilante from RVAH-5) for the benefit of the camera following the successful prosecution of yet another recce flight (*US Navy, Cdr K W Stecker*)

BARCAP (Barrier Combat Air Patrol) at 35,000 ft, some 25 miles off the coast of North Vietnam near the port city of Hai Phong. These jets were crewed by Cdr William F Fraser (the squadron CO) and Lt(jg) Christopher Billingsley (RIO) and Lt Don Watkins and Lt(jg) Charles R Hayes (RIO). Both F-4Bs were armed with two AIM-7D Sparrow IIIs and two AIM-9B Sidewinders, and each carried a 600-US gallon centre-line drop tank.

The third F-4B (BuNo 151425) that was due to participate in the BARCAP experienced an engine failure two-thirds of way through its catapult stroke and subsequently crashed into the Gulf. Its crew, Lt Cdr William E Greer and Lt(jg) Richard R Bruning (RIO), ejected and were swiftly recovered, leaving Lt(jg) Terry M Murphy and Ens Ronald J Fegan to launch (in BuNo 151403, call sign 'Showtime 602') in their place as replacement section leaders. Minutes later standby crew Lt Howard B Watkins Jr and Lt(jg) John T Mueller (RIO) departed CVA-61 to join Murphy and Fegan on BARCAP. The latter F-4s were equipped exclusively with Sparrow rounds.

There had been some delay in launching the standby jet, which was manned on the deck, but not in position to immediately take a catapult shot. Desperately trying to catch up with their section leaders as Murphy and Fegan sped north, Watkins and Mueller heard the pilot of 'Showtime 602' call 'Three in the con' (contrails).

A flight of three Chinese MiG-17s had been detected approaching the *Ranger*, and Murphy had been vectored in the direction of Hainan Island. He made the chilling call once the fighters had been visually acquired.

Still some way behind their section leaders, Watkins and Mueller were then jumped by a fourth MiG. The delayed 'cat shot' now meant that both Phantom II crews would have to fight it out alone, or at least until Fraser and Don Watkins arrived to lend a hand after being hastily called off their station to assist. At the same time that 'Howie' Watkins was bounced from behind by the single MiG, Murphy reported that he was being fired upon.

According to personal accounts, the US crews engaged the MiGs, firing two Sparrows (one went ballistic and the other suffered a motor ignition failure) and two Sidewinders (one was evaded by the target and

VF-96's 1964-65 *WestPac* aboard the *Ranger* lasted a staggering nine months, during which time the vessel spent 103 days on the line generating combat sorties. This photograph, taken in January 1965, features three jets from the unit performing a tight formation break for the camera. The third F-4B in this shot is none other than BuNo 151403, which was lost in action on 9 April 1965 during the Hainan clash. This historic photograph was taken by squadron CO, Cdr William F Fraser, who was flying lead during the engagement with the Chinese MiG-17s. F-4B BuNo 151438 was also lost during 1965 when, on the night of 28 December, its crew was forced to eject when they failed in their attempts to trap aboard the *Enterprise* during bad weather following an armed recce over Laos. With their fuel exhausted, pilot Lt Dean Forsgren and RIO Lt(jg) Robert Jewell had little choice but to abandon the fighter – both men were quickly recovered by the ship's plane guard helicopter (*US Navy*)

the second failed to make contact) at close quarters. In the ensuing melee, the crews lost track of Murphy and Fegan, and only realised they were missing when the three surviving jets rendezvoused and headed for nearby A-3B tankers diverted from the morning's *Rolling Thunder* strike.

Despite repeated radio calls, 'Showtime 602' could not be raised, and Murphy and Fegan were posted missing in action. At least one of the F-4 crews had heard Murphy transmit 'Out of missiles, RTB' (Returning to Base) during the course of the engagement, and as they were leaving the area, Watkins and Mueller saw a silver MiG-17 explode and crash, prompting them to call 'Good shooting, who got him?'

At the same time, the ship-borne GCI (Ground Controlled Interception) controller in *Ranger's* CIC (Combat Information Center), which had noticed 'Showtime 602' turn away from Hainan, also spied a second blip behind it. Moments later, the Phantom II disappeared from the radar plot. The official squadron report stated that at 0905 hrs, Murphy and Fegan 'did not check in with the flight leader'. An air search was conducted over an area of 7500 square miles for over two hours, with no luck.

The official reports are less detailed as to the last moments of Murphy and Fegan's short lives, although they do provide insight into Fraser and Watkins' actions upon joining the fray. Moreover, they lend credibility to Murphy's victory, given that none of the remaining crews involved in the engagement scored a hit.

VF-96's reports show that 'Showtime 603' (Fraser) and '610' (Don Watkins) were on station at 40,000 and 35,000 ft respectively. At 0855 hrs, '603' acquired one of the MiGs in boresight at six miles as it passed from left to right. At five miles the pilot illuminated the MiG with the Westinghouse AN/APQ-72 radar fitted in his Phantom II, and the RIO quickly secured a missile lock, then switched to MAP (Multiple Aim Point) mode to obtain auto track. '603's' pilot banked the Phantom II 30 degrees to the right, establishing a lead on the MiG, then placed the steering dot in the ASE (Allowable Steering Error) circle. At three miles, Fraser fired an AIM-7, and although lock-on was maintained, the missile failed to track and went ballistic, travelling wide and below the MiG.

Still keeping the original lock, 'Showtime 603' 'switched to heat and tracked (the MiG) optically (35 miles lead) and received tone'. The Sidewinder was fired at a range of 1.5 miles and initially tracked the MiG, which was in a shallow left bank. The MiG then broke hard left and slightly nose down, causing the Sidewinder to lose track and miss by some 50 ft. Later, '603's' crew commented that 'this missile should have been

BuNo 151438 is seen in happier times at Edwards AFB in May 1964 during a base open house. Although the '01' aircraft is traditionally assigned to the CO of the squadron, this particular Phantom II bears the name *LTJG TERRY MURPHY* on its forward canopy rail – perhaps he had flown the jet from VF-96's NAS Miramar home to the air force's primary testing facility. In April of the following year Murphy and his RIO Ron Fegan were almost certainly responsible for the F-4's first aerial victory, and just minutes later became the first crew to be lost in action in the McDonnell fighter interceptor. Their mount during the Hainan clash was BuNo 151403 (*US Navy via R Besecker Collection via Norm Taylor*)

able to intercept the target, but the missile did not appear to be turning as sharply as it was capable of, even at that high altitude'.

'Showtime 603' readied for another shot at the MiG, now at 47,000 ft and manoeuvring. Lock-on was achieved at 12 miles, then lost, and re-acquired at seven miles. At 3.5 miles, the crew fired a second Sparrow at the MiG, which was now flying straight and level, but the missile's rocket motor failed to ignite and the round dropped harmlessly into the sea.

The crew of 'Showtime 610' experienced the same frustrations as they pursued their own MiG-17;

'Our first run commenced as soon as the MiGs were spotted visually in the contrails. We acquired them on radar about 45 degrees left, 18 miles,

VF-96's first experience of operating in South-East Asia occurred almost two years prior to the Hainan incident when, between 2-5 May 1963, the *Ranger* conducted air operations in the South China Sea off Vietnam in response to the Laotian crisis. The first Phantom II-equipped unit to venture into these waters, VF-96 (and the rest of CVW-9) did not see action on this occasion, however. Looking forward from the island of CVA-61, two F-4Bs prepare to launch from the bow cats following the successful departure of a pair of F-8Cs from VF-91. Behind the Phantom IIs in the launch queue is an A-4C Skyhawk from VA-93 (*US Navy via Naval Aviation Museum*)

Seen in typical BARCAP configuration, this VF-96 F-4B carries two AIM-7D Sparrow IIIs in the rear centreline launch troughs, two AIM-9Bs on its shoulder pylons and a 600-US gallon centreline drop tank. Two of the four F-4s involved in the Hainan incident were identically configured to this jet (*US Navy via Peter Davies*)

and made a port turn to put them on a collision course. At this time the arm-safe switch was placed to "arm". The starboard missile armed since the port select light had blinked off. They (the MiGs) appeared to turn into us, and a forward quarter run developed. We switched to "10-mile" scale. In range occurred at eight miles and maximum blossoming at five miles, at which time we fired the Sparrow III missile on number seven fuselage station. The pilot felt a thud, but the missile was not observed, even after sharply banking the aircraft left and right. Apparently, the missile motor did not fire.'

'Showtime 610' made a second run at the MiG, the communist fighter being acquired at ten degrees left at a range of six miles, in a starboard turn. Pulling hard to starboard to match the MiG's turn, '610' fired at the MiG at 3.5 miles, but the missile dropped without the motor firing. Undaunted in their attempt, the crew drove hard on the MiG's seven o'clock position, and at 1.5 miles, and with good tone, triggered the starboard Sidewinder. As with the Sparrow, the AIM-9B failed to fire.

Switching to the port Sidewinder, the pilot fired into the MiGs now-ignited afterburner – the AIM-9B failed to track and missed wide. A final attempt was made with the starboard missile, but it again failed to fire.

The Chinese subsequently claimed that 'Showtime 602' had been destroyed by their Air Force, contending that the Phantom II crew had tried to turn with the MiG, bled off speed, and 'was caught in the MiG's gunsights'. Other reports suggest that the F-4 may have been downed by an errant AIM-7, which, given that similar incidents were not uncommon later in the air war, has not been completely ruled out.

The Hainan Island incident had provided both the first MiG kill of the war (although this was not officially acknowledged in order to avoid upsetting the Chinese) and almost certainly the first F-4 loss to a MiG. The type of MiG that downed Murphy and Fegan also remains a mystery, for certain theorists believe a MiG-19 or MiG-21 could have snuck up behind the fleeing Phantom II at high speed and hit it with a heat-seeking missile.

Although not publicised for years, the Hainan Island incident had a significant impact on the F-4 community, as it demonstrated the fundamental problem that would be encountered when attempting to fight a MiG on its own terms. Moreover, the engagement demonstrated the inherent unreliability of American air-to-air missiles – another problem that would continue to plague Navy and Air Force crews throughout the war.

As noted by the mission report prepared by the crew of 'Showtime 603', 'the performances of the missiles was most disappointing and frustrating. Three good runs were made that should have resulted in the missiles intercepting their targets. All indications available to the crew were that the weapons system should have been functioning perfectly'.

Hook retracted, VF-96's BuNo 150412 is seen on short finals to NAS Atsugi during the unit's 1964-65 *WestPac* on the *Ranger*. Situated on the outskirts of Tokyo, Atsugi, and its maintenance facilities, would play a vital role in supporting carrier air wings during their many months on the line in the South China Sea. This was particularly true during the early combat deployments, as VF-96 CO Cdr Bill Fraser remembers;

'McDonnell had not really learned yet how to properly seal the F-4 to prevent salt corrosion. Where there were dissimilar types of metals, like on the tail section, you got a good galvanic action. Where it got bad you could literally poke a pencil through it. We ended up having to send some of the F-4s to Atsugi to have replacement panels of aluminium made. I remember the hate and discontent when we turned those birds over to other squadrons on our return.'

Most units would leave one of their aircraft ashore at Atsugi to act as a spare in case of combat or operational attrition, and the facility also served as an arrival point for replacement airframes flown over from the US
(*via Aerospace Publishing*)

THE PLAYERS

When the war in South-East Asia turned 'hot' in April 1965, and the Vietnamese People's Air Force started to oppose American air strikes on targets in the North, the US Navy was in the midst of transition in both aircraft carrier types and naval aircraft.

The so-called 'large-deck' carriers assigned to the Pacific Fleet at the time included the *Kitty Hawk*, *Ranger*, *Constellation* and the Navy's sole nuclear-powered carrier, the USS *Enterprise* (CVAN-65), as well as the smaller *Coral Sea* and *Midway*. Five Atlantic Fleet carriers also participated in combat operations, namely USS *Franklin D Roosevelt*

USS *Kitty Hawk* steams off the coast of southern California at the start of its first *WestPac* to Vietnam in October 1965. Embarked are the nine squadrons of CVW-11, including F-4-equipped VF-114 and VF-213. This cruise would see the air wing suffer its greatest losses in combat, with no less than 20 aircraft being downed over enemy territory. Included in this number were no fewer than six Phantom IIs (*via Brad Elward*)

(CVA-42), USS *Forrestal* (CVA-59), USS *Saratoga* (CVA-60), USS *Independence* (CVA-62) and USS *America* (CVA-66). These vessels displaced as much as 89,600 tons (CVAN-65), and could handle up to 90 aircraft.

Each of these carriers operated air wings that controlled two fighter (VF) squadrons, equipped with the new McDonnell F-4B Phantom II. Only three vessels – *Midway*, *Kitty Hawk* and *Coral Sea* – briefly operated F-4s and F-8 Crusaders alongside each other, and such a mix had been abandoned by 1966.

When VF-114 participated in its first *WestPac* with the F-4B in 1962-63, it was the sole Phantom II unit within CVW-11. As this photograph of CVA-63 at anchor in Japan clearly shows, the fighter duties on this deployment were shared with F-8D-equipped VF-111, whose jets are chained down over bow cat one (*via Aerospace Publishing*)

F-4 PHANTOM II

By 1964, the F-4B Phantom II was fast becoming the primary US Navy fleet fighter, replacing the ageing F-8 Crusader, which had been introduced in 1956.

In the late 1950s, Navy fighter squadrons operated two fighter types – the F-8 for traditional close-in dogfighting and the F3H-1 Demon for missile interceptions. McDonnell's F-4 would eventually replace both aircraft.

Designed as a fleet defence interceptor to stop long-ranged Soviet bombers, the F-4 was built around a complex radar and weapons system featuring the Raytheon AIM-7 Sparrow III semi-active radar-homing missile. The jet's radar (the Westinghouse AN/APQ-72) provided range-to-target and bearing information displayed in 'B-scope' format, and provided the guidance for the Sparrow III missile system, then designated the AAM-N-6.

The Sparrow essentially rode a 'beam' of electromagnetic energy emitted from the AN/APQ-72 radar and reflected back to the missile from the target. Introduced in 1958, the Sparrow possessed a maximum head-on range of 13 miles, and carried a 65-lb warhead. Far superior to comparable weapons of the time, the Sparrow nevertheless suffered from the need to keep the F-4 aimed at the target aircraft while the missile tracked. AIM-7D/E Sparrows were responsible for 27 kills during the course of the war, and nine of the seventeen Navy F-4 kills during the 1965-70 time frame.

The Sparrow proved not nearly as effective as intended, however, primarily because of the operational restrictions placed on its use by the politically-imposed Rules of Engagement (ROEs). These required visual identification of the target before a missile could be launched, thus cancelling out the weapon's ability to knock down targets beyond visual range.

An early-production F4H-1 is waved off from its approach during VF-114's first carrier qualification period with the Phantom II aboard the *Coral Sea* in September 1961 (*via Aerospace Publishing*)

As tensions grew in South-East Asia, the US Navy was moving from McDonnell's F-3B Demon interceptor to its replacement, the F-4 Phantom II. Demon pilots were seldom involved in dogfighting or 'hassling', as pilots dubbed ACM, and this showed as they transitioned to the more manoeuvrable Phantom II and struggled to combat the infinitely more agile MiG-17 (*US Navy via Naval Aviation Museum*)

And because of the MiG's small size, it was generally not visible until just a mile-and-a-half away from the Phantom II, which put the communist jet within the Sparrow's minimum launch range, and the F-4 within the MiG's cannon range. The Sparrow was also susceptible to interference from 'ground clutter', and faired poorly against targets flying at altitudes below the launching Phantom II.

Complementing the Sparrow was the AIM-9B (AAM-N-7) short-range, infrared-guided Sidewinder,

which had already made its combat debut in the 1958 engagements between Taiwanese Air Force F-86Fs and Communist Chinese MiG-15s and MiG-17s over the Straits of Taiwan. The missile was credited with four kills during these large-scale clashes.

The Sidewinder was a creation of Bill McLean at Naval Ordnance Test Station China Lake, and dated back to the early 1950s. The Sidewinder was then a rear-aspect only missile that was most effective when launched within a 30-degree cone from a mile to a mile-and-a half back, where the missile's seeker head could home in on the enemy aircraft's hot exhaust.

As with the Sparrow, the Sidewinder was designed for intercepting non-manoeuvring bombers rather than nimble communist fighters. Experiences over the skies of North Vietnam soon proved that the AIM-9's envelope changed with the amount of g-forces placed on it by the host aircraft, which meant that it was not as effective in a 'rough and tumble' dogfight. Moreover, it could be defeated by 'getting low and turning sharply'.

The AIM-9B/F-4B combination had claimed just two MiGs for the Navy by the time the missile was replaced by the greatly improved AIM-9D in 1967. The new variant featured improved seeker coolant (high-pressure nitrogen), a new engine, longer range and a sleeker profile that caused less drag.

Of all the Sidewinder variants to see service in Vietnam, the AIM-9D (Sidewinder 1C) had the highest hit ratio. In 1968, it gave way to the AIM-9G, which touted one major improvement – the Sidewinder

The first US Navy Phantom II units to see real action in the Vietnam conflict were VF-142 and VF-143, embarked on the *Constellation* for CVW-14's 1964-65 *WestPac*. Both squadrons participated in Operation *Pierce Arrow*, on 5 August 1964, which saw retaliatory strikes on North Vietnamese PT boat bases following attacks on US Navy destroyers in the Gulf of Tonkin. While A-4s and A-1s bombed the targets, Phantom II crews flew TARCAP, guarding the strike aircraft en route to, and over, their targets. This F-4B is seen launching from 'Connie's' waist cat three, toting a live Sparrow round on its starboard shoulder pylon (*via Aerospace Publishing*)

AIM-9Bs on the shoulder pylons, AIM-7Ds in the aft missile troughs and a 600-US gal 'fixture' fuel tank on the centreline, this F-4B from VF-143 was photographed on a routine BARCAP mission off the 'Connie' during CVA-64's 1963-64 *WestPac* (*via Aerospace Publishing*)

Expanded Acquisition Mode (SEAM). SEAM slaved the seeker head to the F-4's radar, allowing the missile's seeker to be directed to the target. The seeker's azimuth was also expanded to 25 degrees in a circular scan. Provisions were also included for a visual target acquisition system (VTAS) helmet-mounted sight, which was trialled during the conflict and adopted in the mid-1970s.

Yet even with its armada of advanced and continually updated missiles, the Phantom II was lacking in one critical respect – it carried no internal gun. Although crews tried to remedy this serious oversight by adding a centreline gun pod (the SUU-23, housing the M61 Vulcan 20 mm six-barrelled Gatling gun fitted in the self-powered GAU-4 unit), it proved unworkable and was abandoned. With the pod fitted, the ubiquitous 'fixture' centreline drop tank had to be abandoned, resulting in two smaller tanks taking up vital space on the outer wing pylons. And the overall unreliability of the gun pod was further exacerbated by the shock of deck launches and recoveries. Despite these problems, a similar system enjoyed some success, and wider employment, with the USAF and Marines.

F-4 veteran and former Topgun instructor John Nash explained to the authors that the failure to include an internal gun was 'a tragic mistake';

'The F-4 needed an internal gun. The USAF had the better F-4 in the E-model (which had an internal gun). The Navy bought the Mk 4 (GAU-4) gun pod, which was "worthless", and that is an understatement. The NAVAIR civilians forbade us to go to Nellis and get 40 USAF SUU-16 gun pods for free when I was in VF-121/Topgun.

'Having an internal gun would have given the aircrews one more kill option. But as important as that, it would have changed the enemy's tactics. A gun would have added a significant threat that would have had to have been defended against by the MiGs. As it was, in an air-to-air engagement, a US Navy F-4 at 500 ft behind a bogie was *totally* ineffective without a gun.'

Although configurations were often mission-driven, F-4Bs could launch with up to four AIM-7 and four AIM-9 missiles and a 600-US gallon (2270 l) centreline tank. Odd configurations, such as six Sparrows, were sometimes carried, as were 370-US gallon (1400 l) wing-mounted tanks. F-4s flying BARrier Combat Air Patrols (BARCAP) were often configured with three AIM-9s, two AIM-7s and a centreline tank, whilst Phantom IIs flying MiGCAP (hunting for MiGs) typically boasted four AIM-9s and four AIM-7s, with between one and three external tanks.

The F-4B relied on two 17,000-lb (75.65-kN) maximum afterburner rated General Electric J79-GE-8 turbojet engines to power it off the carrier deck, with the assistance of the catapult. Although basically a good engine, the J79's primary drawback was that it left a long, black smoke trail when not operating in afterburner. This meant that Phantom IIs could be seen from many miles away, sometimes as far as 25 miles. 'Smoking engines get you shot, or shot at', noted John Nash.

MiG pilots used this deficiency to their advantage on many occasions during the *Rolling Thunder* campaign, conducting sneak attacks on F-4 formations. The problem was finally rectified in later models of the F-4J (from Block 37 onwards), and retrofitted into early Js and F-4Bs. However, some squadrons soldiered on with 'smoking' Phantom IIs until war's end, as John Nash explains;

'We had an "additive tank" that could inject something into the engine that was supposed to stop the smoking. However, I never saw any of the "stuff", and no one was concerned enough to get the programme going! Min-burner stopped the smoke trails, but burned gas faster – not the ideal remedy, but when no one cares enough to fix the problem, that's the only solution.'

Crews were wise to this problem, and devised several of their own ingenious 'fix-alls', including flying in minimum afterburner, then quickly changing altitude, and flying with one engine in idle and the second in minimum burner. Capt Jim Ruliffson, a former F-4 pilot and commanding officer of Topgun, also commented on these tactics;

With only a hint of the telltale smoke trails emanating from its J79 engines, a VF-213 F-4B powers away from the *Kitty Hawk* at the start of yet another combat mission in March 1968 (*via Robert F Dorr*)

'We trained in the States to go min-burner, which eliminated the smoke completely, when setting up head-on engagements. Over North Vietnam, though, we rarely had the "luxury" of knowing there was a bogie nearby, let alone in a position for a classic head-on pass, so nobody went min-burner to eliminate smoke trails.'

Flown by a crew of two (a pilot and Radar Intercept Officer, or RIO), the Phantom II was one of the first Navy fighters to be dual manned. Unlike the USAF, which at that time placed junior pilots in the flight control-equipped back seats of its Phantom IIs (these individuals were eventually designated Weapons Systems Operators, or WSOs, later in the war), the Navy used Naval Flight Officers (NFOs) who had been specially trained in navigation and radar operation. These men were NFOs by choice, rather than being junior pilots waiting their turn to move into the front seat. John Nash again;

'The RIO in the Phantom was totally indispensable. First, the aircraft was designed so it could not be fully employed in combat without a RIO. Second, a pilot would be downright stupid to get into a fight with more than one aircraft and not jump at the chance to use those extra eyeballs to stay alive.'

As the Phantom II was meant to be a successor for the F-100, F-104 and F3H-1 in the missile interception role, most of the crew training for the F-4 concentrated on the employment of these long-range weapons. While performing the intercept mission, RIOs spent the majority of their time 'head-down', studying their radar and working the AIM-7 system.

However, during close-in fights, where the Sparrow was essentially useless, RIOs best served the crew by watching for MiGs and surface-to-air missiles (SAMs). In fact, once the fight went 'visual', the RIO had the responsibility for all threats from the cockpit aft, while the pilot maintained the watch on the front section. As the conflict progressed, most MiG sightings were called by RIOs.

When the war began, the Navy's Phantom II squadrons were exclusively equipped with B-models, the first of which had joined the fleet with east coast-based VF-74 in July 1961 – VF-114 was the first deployable Pacific Fleet squadron, going to sea in September 1962.

The F-4B was the first definitive fleet defence model of the Phantom II, and the jet made its combat debut with VF-142 and VF-143 (from the *Constellation*) during the initial *Pierce Arrow* strikes of August 1964. Four years later, the F-4J joined the fray with VF-33 and VF-103 aboard the *America*, which was an Atlantic Fleet carrier that he been pressed into duty in Vietnam because of the escalation in hostilities. J-models (from VF-33 and VF-142) would claim MiGs in 1968 and 1970 respectively.

The F-4J offered a much improved AN/APG-59 radar and AWG-10 pulse-Doppler fire-control system (capable of detecting and tracking low and high altitude targets), as well as some aspects of the AN/ASW-25A datalink landing system that had been briefly ushered into fleet service by the rare F-4G when VF-213 embarked aboard the *Kitty Hawk* for a combat cruise in 1965-66.

The F-4J also featured uprated, and smokeless, J79-GE-10 engines, each offering 17,900-lb (80 kN) thrust in maximum afterburner. The improved Phantom II still lacked the internal gun requested by Navy aircrews, however.

The F-4B/J officially achieved a 2.8-to-1 kill ratio against VPAF MiGs during the 1965-70 time frame, claiming 14 MiGs (most historians now credit the jet with 16 kills, although the two An-2s downed during this period are not included in the ratio) to the F-8's 18 kills. Moreover, the Navy kill ratio as a whole – a disappointing 2.8-to-1 – was only slightly better than the 2.02-to-1 achieved by US Air Force fighter crews.

As explained later in the chapter on Topgun, the poor kill ratio was the result of inadequate training and a lack of appreciation by F-4 crews of the boundaries of the Phantom II's performance envelope. Many of the crews, and their aircraft for that matter, had never fired a live missile in training. Similarly problematic was the lack of ACM training resulting from the overconfidence placed in the effectiveness of new and developing missile systems.

During the late 1950s it was presumed that long-range air-to-air missiles such as the Sparrow, in conjunction with sophisticated airborne radar, would make dogfighting, and fighting with guns, a thing of the past. Indeed, this was the prevalent view in the F3H Demon community, and the mind-set had changed very little within Navy Phantom II squadrons by the early 1960s.

It was this mentality that the F-4B crews took with them to Vietnam, and which the founders of the Navy's Fighter Weapons School in 1968 sought to change, as the Americans faced the smaller, agile cannon-armed MiGs of the VPAF.

US TACTICS

US Navy fighters used a two-aeroplane basic fighting unit known as a section and employed an air-to-air formation known as 'loose deuce', which placed two aircraft flying abeam of each other with a separation distance of about one mile. From this position both crews could cover the other's rear quarter, or 'six o'clock', and provide mutual support.

The principal of loose deuce called for one aircraft (the 'engaged' fighter) to attack while the wingman (called the 'free' fighter) would manoeuvre with the engaged fighter, but far enough back to keep an eye out for other bandits or threats in the area. As the engaged fighter drove the bandit into a predictable flight pattern, the free fighter would call the shot.

This formation also gave Navy crews greater flexibility, as either aircraft could assume the engaged or free role. Moreover, both aeroplanes could operate at full power without fear of colliding with the other.

Loose deuce represented a departure from the standard intercept formation that saw the two Phantom IIs fly in a radar trail formation, separated by approximately three miles. The lead aircraft, known as the 'eyeball', would essentially serve as the spotter, calling the contact to the trailing Phantom II, which would then take a shot with a Sparrow. This separation preserved the requisite minimum distances needed for a successful AIM-7 launch, but proved unworkable in a close-in dogfight scenario within the Sparrow's parameters.

At the heart of the loose deuce formation was the ability to provide mutual support, both offensively and defensively. Mutual support, from a tactical perspective, is obtained when each aircraft can readily clear his counterpart's rear-aspect of aerial threats. And, while the military lead of the section never changes (always the senior aviator), the tactical lead is held by the aircraft with the best tactical position to see, evaluate and direct the flight.

The man with the initial contact (radar or visual) *has the lead* (be he the wingman or RIO), and calls a 'turn' on UHF, followed by a description of the bogie position and composition. In any event, the tactical lead must maintain sight of his wingman.

The loose deuce formation, which presented a variation of the famous 'Thatch Weave' developed during World War 2, was vastly different to the rigid 'fluid four' formation flown by USAF pilots. Fluid four was based on a four-aircraft flight split into two elements of two aeroplanes. In a dogfight, the two element leads, numbers 1 and 3, would engage the bandit in a similar fashion to the loose deuce, with the exception being that the two wingmen, numbers 2 and 4, served solely to protect their element leaders, numbers 1 and 3.

The wingmen flew as a 'welded wing' or 'fighting wing', staying within 1500 to 2000 ft behind their leader, and offset about 45 degrees. This formation worked fine when the aeroplanes were slower and propeller-driven, as in World War 2, but it was unworkable with the fast-moving jets of the 1960s. Welded wing pilots found they were so intent on staying in formation, and keeping from hitting their element leader, that they simply did not have an opportunity to look for other bandits in the area.

Fluid four flights also suffered from a 'single shooter' policy that meant that only the flight leader

A 'markingless' Phantom II from VF-21, off the *Midway*, drops cluster bomb units on suspected Viet Cong (VC) positions in seemingly featureless jungle in South Vietnam on 24 October 1965. At relatively low level the effect of these weapons would create a carpet of destruction across a wide area. Unfortunately, the chances of there being any VC in the vicinity by the time the bombing actually took place was slim. This photograph was taken by an RF-8A from VFP-63 Det A, the dedicated 'photo-bird' taking post-strike images for the mission debrief (*via Aerospace Publishing*)

could take a shot – the remaining fighters were along to protect the leader as he went after the MiGs. Naturally, this policy drastically reduced the offensive capabilities of the formation since only one of the four aeroplanes could shoot.

Jim Ruliffson remembers one situation where a USAF flight lead had expended all his missiles in pursuit of a MiG. When one of his wingmen called out that he had the MiG in his sights, and asked for permission to fire, the flight leader denied his request and ordered the flight to return to base!

Although designed as an interceptor, the Phantom II served in many roles, and was the first true multi-role/multi-mission aircraft. While the F-4B did not initially have an air-to-ground capability, it soon began flying flak suppression and strike missions once the US involvement in the conflict escalated. But the mainstay of the Phantom II missions were the TARCAP, BARCAP and escort missions, and later MiGCAP.

Most air wings alternated their fighter squadrons, either weekly or during line periods, between the strike/flak suppression and CAP/escort missions. This added flexibility reduced rearmament problems, and also created an equality in opportunity for crews to see MiGs. Fighter sweeps (air superiority) were not initially part of the Navy mission over South-East Asia.

The BARCAP and TARCAP missions were meant to provide early warning of attacking MiGs, and to serve as a buffer against the MiGs reaching the strike aircraft. BARCAP was usually flown by two F-4s (a section) flying in combat spread at 10,000 to 20,000 ft, and under the control of the *PIRAZ* (Positive Identification Radar Advisory Zone) destroyer.

If directed to investigate a contact, the Phantom IIs were to assume a two-to-three-mile radar trail formation where the Sparrow could be utilised if needed – TAR-CAP aircraft also flew in sections using a modified combat spread. Normal procedure called for the TARCAP to accelerate ahead of the main strike group and take up station in the area deemed most likely to be threatened by MiGs. Air speeds were typically around 400 knots.

MiGCAP was essentially a fighter sweep mission authorised from 1967 onwards in response to increased MiG activity. US aircraft were prohibited from attacking the

As the conflict continued, the relationship developed between the Phantom II and the drastically improved E-2A Hawkeye blossomed. Most air early warning squadrons had commenced operations with TF 77 flying the antiquated E-1B Tracer. However, by the time this photograph was taken (by an RA-5C from RVAH-11) in January 1968, virtually all the medium and large-deck carriers had traded up to the new E-2. This particular Hawkeye was assigned to VAW-114, which was in the process of conducting its second *WestPac* with the E-2 aboard the *Kitty Hawk* when 'snapped' by the 'Viggie'. The AEW aircraft is being escorted by VF-213 F-4B BuNo 153017 (*via Robert F Dorr*)

THE PLAYERS

19

MiGs directly, and were not authorised to strike VPAF bases until April 1967. Even then, the northernmost bases, including Phuc Yen, near Hanoi, were off limits. Trolling for MiGs was not an authorised mission, although some air wing commanders sought ingenious ways to 'set up' encounters where MiG engagements could occur. Capt Ault remembers during his time aboard the *Coral Sea* in 1966-67;

'I spent a lot of time with my CAG and the F-4 squadron COs figuring out ways to get into fights with MiGs. For example, one stratagem was double cycling a section of F-4s and "hiding" them in a valley north of Hai Phong in the hope of "jumping" a MiG following an exiting strike group. Although a target never showed up, planning for an engagement included a thorough assessment of our weapons systems, and revealed both strengths and weaknesses.'

MiGCAP forces used their own operating frequency, rather than that employed by the strikers, and were controlled by a surface ship such as *Red Crown* or *PIRAZ*.

AIR OPERATIONS OVER NORTH VIETNAM

When the air war began in March 1965, there was some confusion between the Navy and Air Force as to which service would control what sector. Although a plan was conceived that divided each day into three-hour time slots, with control thereof alternating between the services, this soon proved unworkable, and a system was devised in November 1965 whereby sections of North Vietnam were divided according to six geographic regions called Route Packages. Responsibility for each 'Pak' was assigned on a rotating week-to-week basis. This, too, proved unworkable.

Beginning in April 1966, responsibility for each Pak was permanently assigned. The Navy was responsible for Packages II, III, IV and VIA, while the Air Force operated in Packages I, V and VIB. Within Pak VIA was the major port of Hai Phong and the MiG bases at Cat Bi and Gia Lam. Pak VIB contained the North Vietnamese capitol of Hanoi, as well as the major MiG bases at Kep, Hoa Lac and Phuc Yen.

The infamous Thanh Hoa Bridge, which was the focus of numerous missions before it was finally destroyed in 1972, was located in Pak IV, as was the MiG base at Quan Lang. Pak VIA and B were regarded as the most dangerous of the Route Packages.

Task Force 77 (TF 77) carriers of the Seventh Fleet operated from two stations, namely *Yankee Station* in the north and *Dixie Station* in the south. *Dixie Station* was established in June 1965 at the request of Gen William C Westmoreland (US field commander in South Vietnam), who was impressed with the level of expertise demonstrated by naval air crews.

Located approximately 100 miles south-east of Cam Ranh Bay at 11 N, 110 E, *Dixie Station* served as the starting point for a carrier on deployment to Vietnam, and aircrews would often spend a week operating from here – where MiGs and SAMs presented no threat – so as to get reacquainted with air operations, and refine tactics, before heading north. The station was eliminated in August 1966 after being operational for 15 months, carriers instead being sent directly north to *Yankee Station* upon their arrival in-theatre.

Yankee Station began at a location just east of the DMZ, then slowly moved north as the war ground on, eventually reaching a point just 70 miles east of Hai Phong. From *Yankee Station* Navy aircraft launched missions against all Route Paks within their command.

Generally, three carriers were stationed 'on the line' at *Yankee Station*, although a fourth was later added. Each carrier operated 12-hour operational shifts from noon to midnight and then midnight to noon, with a third added during the day. Line periods ran in ten-day increments within each operational segment. Whilst three carriers were on station, a fourth vessel would be in port in either Subic Bay or Japan.

Carriers conducted 'cyclic ops' when on station, strikes being 'cycled' every 90 minutes (eight per twelve-hour period) against smaller, yet lucrative, logistical targets in Paks II, III and IV. Alpha strikes – the all-air wing assaults which became prevalent during the later years of the war – were directed primarily against larger strategic targets (Petrol, Oil, Lubricants (POL) stored, power stations and MiG bases) in Paks IV and VIA.

The proximity of the *Yankee Station* carriers from the shore – the distance usually varied between 70 and 100 miles – often drastically reduced North Vietnamese warning time in comparison with Air Force strikes launched from Thailand. Later in the war, this would lead to fewer MiG-21 attacks against Navy aircraft, as the VPAF lacked sufficient time to set up 'hit and run' attacks using their elaborate Ground Controlled Intercept (GCI) network. This partially explains why Navy F-4 crews saw more MiG-17s than their Air Force counterparts.

Supporting each of the carriers were two to four destroyer screens to protect against possible submarines or attacking aircraft. Beginning in April 1965, the Navy also established two permanent radar pickets in the northern Gulf of Tonkin between TF-77 and North Vietnam. In July 1966, Seventh Fleet began operating *a PIRAZ* ship, tactically called *Red Crown*, in order to locate and track all aeroplanes over eastern North Vietnam and the Gulf of Tonkin, vector naval aircraft and keep a look out for approaching MiGs. During the war, ship-based SAMs were responsible for seven MiG kills. *Red Crown* controllers were widely respected by Air Force and Navy flyers alike, especially from 1970 onwards.

Interestingly, there were four very different air wars fought over South-East Asia. In South Vietnam, the air efforts provided ground support for

Camouflaged in a 'snake' scheme of dark green and earth, this MiG-17F is seen parked on the flightline at Noi Bai alongside MiG-21s in 1972. The mainstay of the VPAF in the early years of the Vietnam War, the MiG-17 'Fresco' (built under-licence in China as the J-5) was a subsonic fighter derived from the MiG-15, featuring a 45-degree swept-back wing. Although it carried no missiles until late in the conflict, the 'Fresco' was heavily armed with two Nudelmann-Rikhter (NR-23) 23 mm and one Nudelmann-Surana (NS-37) 37 mm cannon, the former having the greater range (up to 5000 ft). While the 'Fresco' had a phenomenal rate of turn, especially at slow speeds (below 400 knots), it was limited to high subsonic speeds, despite its afterburning engine, and possessed a roll-rate of only 136 degrees. So superior was the MiG-17's turn rate that VF-21's combat manual stated specifically, 'The basic philosophy currently taught to all jet aircrews concerning the MiG-15 and MiG-17 fighters is don't, repeat, DON'T turn with them!' Both of these factors would later become important to Topgun instructors as they trained students (and fleet pilots) in how to combat the MiG-17 using the Phantom II's strong points (*via István Toperczer*)

US ground forces and ARVN troops fighting the Viet Cong and NVA regulars. Interdiction operations were flown in Laos against re-supply efforts along the Ho Chi Minh Trail, and Cambodia saw a combination of interdiction and ground support missions. In North Vietnam, however, the air war took the form of a series of strategic bombing campaigns, and it was in this sector that *Rolling Thunder*, and later *Linebacker I* and *II* operations, were conducted.

All US Navy MiG kills (aside from aircraft shot down by SAMs fired from ships) were claimed over North Vietnam by aircraft operating from carriers on *Yankee Station*.

Air operations over North Vietnam occurred in two stages – Operation *Rolling Thunder*, which ran from 3 March 1965 to 31 October 1968, and Operations *Linebacker I* and *II*, during 1972. *Rolling Thunder* was intended to be a slowly escalating strategic bombing campaign aimed at convincing the North Vietnamese to come to the negotiating table.

In *Rolling Thunder*, targets were highly regulated by Washington, and pilots subject to overly restrictive Rules of Engagements that prohibited them from attacking certain 'sensitive' targets in and around Hanoi and Hai Phong and, until mid-1967, most MiG bases. The *Linebacker* raids, on the other hand, had few restrictions, and proved quite effective.

The Navy F-4/MiG engagements during the *Linebacker* raids are covered in the companion volume to this publication, *Osprey Combat Aircraft 30 - US Navy F-4 Phantom II MiG Killers of the Vietnam War, Vol II, 1971-73*.

Other air operations conducted during the war included *Blue Tree* surveillance flights over North Vietnam, and *Barrel Roll, Steel Tiger* and *Tiger Hound* interdiction operations over Laos. *Proud Deep Alpha*, directed against North Vietnamese troops massing along the DMZ, lasted for five days in 1971, and Operation *Freedom Train* represented the initial US air response to the 1972 North Vietnamese invasion (the Easter Offensive) of South Vietnam.

ROLLING THUNDER BEGINS

On 13 February 1965, in accordance with a planned strategy, President Lyndon B Johnson consented to the start of the strategic bombing campaign against North Vietnam, code-named *Rolling Thunder*. However, because of poor weather, and talk of possible negotiations, the strikes were delayed for two weeks. Finally, on 2 March, *Rolling Thunder* commenced with an attack against an ammunition depot at Xom Bong, just south of the 20th Parallel.

The Navy flew its first missions on 15 March, with strikes from the carriers *Hancock* and *Ranger* against the ammunition depot at Phu Qui. Despite the growing number of sorties, no engagements with VPAF MiGs had yet occurred. Some had been seen following strike packages from the target area, but none were bold enough to engage US aircraft. A number of crews speculated that this period represented one of training for the MiGs and their GCIs.

This situation soon changed on 3 April, when four MiG-17s (see *Osprey Combat Aircraft 25 - MiG-17 and MiG-19 Units of the Vietnam War* for further details) attacked a Navy strike package from CVW-21 that had been sent to bomb the Dong Phong Thong Bridge. One F-8 Crusader was badly damaged in the engagement, and no communist jets were downed.

The strike package from the *Hancock* had been escorted by four F-4Bs from *Coral Sea*, although because of communications problems and a lack of mission co-ordination, the Phantom IIs did not realise that the strike formation was under attack until after the event, and therefore did not enter the fray.

Four F-4Bs from VF-151 'Vigilantes' are seen in diamond formation during work-ups for the unit's debut cruise with the Phantom II in 1964. VF-151 was involved in the *Coral Sea's* record breaking 1964-65 *WestPac* that saw the carrier depart its homeport of Alameda, California, on 7 December 1964, and return to its San Francisco base on 1 November 1965. During this time the vessel spent an astounding 167 days on the line in the Gulf of Tonkin – one of the longest in-action periods of any carrier during the entire Vietnam War. Then the sole Phantom II unit within CVA-43's embarked air wing (CVW-15), the 'Vigilantes' were conducting their first *WestPac* with the F-4B following their transition from the F-3B Demon in January 1964 – fighter duties were shared with F-8D-equipped VF-154. The unit was indirectly involved in the first MiG encounter of the Vietnam War on 3 April 1965, when four MiG-17s attacked a strike package from the *Hancock* that was sent to bomb the Dong Phong Thong Bridge. Four F-4Bs were performing a MiGCAP sortie high above the strikers when the mixed force of F-8s and A-4s was attacked by the VPAF fighters. Due to a lack of mission co-ordination between squadrons from different carriers, the strike package was not aware of the radio frequency on which the F-4s were operating, so were unable to call for assistance when the MiGs struck. Fortunately, no Navy aircraft were lost, although a solitary F-8 was forced to land at Da Nang after being hit by cannon fire from the MiGs. Despite seeing much action on cruise, and downing a MiG-17, VF-151 successfully completed the marathon deployment without losing a single jet, either in combat or operationally (*US Navy*)

The beginning of *Rolling Thunder* for the US Navy commenced on 15 March, with strikes launched against the ammunition depot at Phu Qui. Phantom IIs from the *Midway*, such as this VF-21 Alert jet 'spotted' over one of the waist catapults in June 1965, flew flak suppression and TARCAP for those strikes, but did not encounter any MiGs (*US Navy*)

More formation flying, this time from VF-21 in the spring of 1964. A year later, on 9 April 1965, *Freelancer 103* almost certainly claimed the US Navy's first MiG kill, but was then lost just minutes later. By then the jet was flying as *Showtime 602* with VF-96, embarked on the *Ranger*. VF-21 had completed a single *WestPac* (8 November 1963 to 31 May 1964) with CVW-2 aboard the *Midway* prior to the unit making its combat debut in April 1965 (*US Navy*)

The next day, MiG-17s downed two Air Force F-105Ds from the 355th TFW during a follow-up attack on the bridge.

FIRST MiG KILLS

While skirmishes continued into the spring, little in the way of air-to-air action ensued. However, on 17 June the air war erupted as two F-4B crews from VF-21 became the first American VPAF 'MiG killers' of the Vietnam War.

At about mid-morning, a 14-aeroplane strike package from the carriers *Midway* and *Bon Homme Richard* was heading inbound for a strike against the Thanh Hoa Bridge. Spanning the Ma River about 80 miles due south of Hanoi, the bridge provided a direct link between the port of Hai Phong and the mountain passes through which supplies went into South Vietnam via the Ho Chi Minh Trail.

TARCAP for the strike was provided by six F-4Bs, two of which were from VF-21. The Phantom IIs were to establish a six-aeroplane combat air patrol for the attacking Skyhawks, and protect them against any MiGs that attempted to intercept them. Squadron XO, Cdr Lou Page, and Lt John C Smith crewed F-4B BuNo 151488/NE 101, with Lt Jack E D Batson and Lt Cdr Robert Doremus flying F-4B BuNo 152219/NE 102 as their wing. Both jets were armed with two Sidewinders and three Sparrows, and carried single centreline tanks. The following account of this historic engagement comes from Lt Batson;

'About half of the missions we were flying at this time were *Rolling Thunder* strikes. Briefing was in the Air Intelligence Center as usual about two hours before launch. It was a large strike on a military target south of Than Hoa. The US Secretary of the Navy, Paul Nietze, was present. He came to our ready room for our individual squadron brief. Lou Page told him how we would shoot down MiGs.

'We launched, made a running rendezvous with the KA-3 tankers about 75 miles from the ship, and proceeded to our search area in the

vicinity of Ninh Dinh, north-west of Than Hoa. We began patrolling in a north-south pattern in basic search formation – one mile abeam of each other so that we could provide each other with protection from someone sneaking up on our tail. Using our powerful radar to look northward for targets, we listened to the strike group arrive on target, carry out their mission, and depart.

'As the strike group called "feet wet" (over the sea), Lou called for "One more sweep north". Up to then the flight was completely normal, except there was a significant amount of AAA, mostly from Ninh Dinh. As we rolled out of the turn, J C Smith spotted two radar contacts about 45 miles north. Rob Doremus spotted them almost immediately, also.

'We had observed a slight pattern of MiGs appearing late in our missions when our fuel was getting low. I think that we were all suspicious at this point. Lou called for me to move from the search position to the attack position – a three-mile trail and slightly below. We accelerated to approximately 500 knots for better manoeuvrability. The first aeroplane (Page and Smith) was to set up a head-on attack, having made a positive visual ID. Rob and I would manoeuvre for a head-on Sparrow shot.

'J C and Rob talked to each other regarding which radar targets to lock on to, and J C took the farther target, creating a slight offset to the head-on attack. This caused the MiGs to make a turn into the lead jet. When they banked, the very distinctive wing plan of the MiG-17 was visible.

'Lou fired at close to minimum range while shouting "It's MiGs!" I saw his missile fire, guide towards the formation and the warhead detonate. At first I thought it had missed, but then the outer half of the right wing came completely off the MiG and it started rolling out of control. I then put my full attention to the steering information on my radar scope, and I fired at minimum range. Just before firing, the steering dot moved up the screen, causing me to go into a slight climb to keep it centred.

'The missile (AIM-7) fired from the rail on the right wing and swerved under the nose of the aeroplane. I lost sight of the missile, but Rob saw it guide to a direct hit. Also, about this time one of the MiGs flew right by me. I think my missile hit either the Number 1 or Number 2 aircraft.

Amongst VF-21's principal 'customers' during its 1965 *WestPac* was VA-22 'Fighting Redcocks', one of two Skyhawk-equipped light strike units aboard *Midway*. Here, a pair of 'cock-marked' A-4Cs share deck space with *Sundown 101*, the assigned F-4B of VF-21 CO Cdr F A 'Bill' Franke. Following this successful 'MiG killing' cruise, the 'Freelancers' were considered by many naval aviators to be the premier West Coast F-4 unit in respect to the employment of air-to-air tactics. Living up to this accolade, 'Fighting 21' developed and authored the first written fighter tactics doctrine for the F-4B. The manual's summing up of the fighter squadron's mission over North Vietnam read, 'The primary function of Navy BAR-TARCAP and escort units is to provide warning of the approach of enemy aircraft. Secondarily, the fighter units provide protection as necessary until the attack aircraft can safely retire. Air superiority is not the aim of the fighter units' (*via Angelo Romano*)

VF-21's *Sundown 111* is within seconds of completing yet another uneventful BARCAP mission from the *Midway* in 1965, the jet's progress towards the carrier's modest deck area being closely monitored by the air wing's senior Landing Signals Officer (LSO). The sole Phantom II unit within CVW-2 at the time, the 'Freelancers' shared fighter duties with F-8D-equipped VF-111 (*US Navy*)

'My theory is that the first section did a wingover reversal to get behind Lou and J C. That caused my steering dot to climb as I chased them. The second section (at this point only one aeroplane) continued straight by me. The next phase of Lou's tactics was for us to disengage quickly. He was very concerned about trying to turn with a MiG-17 – our most likely foe – or MiG-19. We disengaged by lighting afterburner, climbing up through an overcast and rendezvousing. Then we reversed heading, re-established the "hunter" (search) formation and went back through the clouds looking for the rest of the MiGs. We saw smoke trails from our missiles, but no MiGs and one parachute.

Firmly clutching their 'coffee' cups, filled with scotch, a relaxed Lt Jack Batson (far left) and Cdr Lou Page join Lt Cdr Robert Doremus and Lt J C Smith in VF-21's Ready Room for an impromptu mission debrief. This photograph was taken soon after the crews had trapped back aboard the *Midway* following their history-making 17 June engagement with VPAF MiG-17s. Note the bullet bandoleers around the waists of Batson and Doremus (*US Navy via Naval Aviation Museum*)

'By this time we were below bingo fuel, so we headed back to *Midway*. Along the way we were offered refuelling, but we declined because if something went wrong we might not make it – we had just enough fuel to land. I was actually showing 400 lbs (sufficient fuel for just three minutes of flying) at the top of the glide slope. After landing, I taxied by our CO, Cdr Bill Franke, who was jumping up and down with his hands over his head. After shut down, Rob came up from the back seat, shook my hand, and said "Four more to go"!

'Lou was escorted up to the Flag bridge where he was congratulated by Secretary Nietze. To get to our ready room, we had to pass through the F-8 (VF-111) ready room, where they were yelling and cheering. Our own ready room was packed. Someone handed me a coffee cup. It

Secretary of the Navy Paul H Nietze congratulates Cdr Lou Page following his 'MiG killing' mission. Standing behind the VF-21 XO is Rear Adm William F Bringle, Commander Task Force 77. Note that Page is still wearing his harness and g-suit – he had stepped out of his F-4 literally minutes prior to this photograph being taken (*via Peter Mersky*)

was full of scotch! Lou quieted everybody down and gave a brief review of what happened. Then we were taken to Air Intelligence (I still had my "coffee" cup), where we told the Admiral and others what had happened. It was an amazing experience. We were told to get some clothes and get ready to go to Saigon, where we were to participate in the daily Press briefing, dubbed the "Five O'Clock Follies".'

Following the briefing, the men stayed as guests of Gen Westmoreland at his private home. All four duly received the Silver Star Medal for their gallantry. Unfortunately, just a little over a month later, on 24 August, Lt Cdr Rob Doremus' Phantom II (BuNo 152215/NE 112, flown by VF-21's CO, Cdr Franke) was hit by a SAM during a follow-up attack on the Thanh Hoa Bridge, and he spent the remainder of the war as a PoW. This was VF-21's sole combat loss during the entire deployment.

J C Smith, meanwhile, went on to become one of the first instructors, and later commanding officer, at the Navy's Fighter Weapons School.

The first two F-4 kills of the war were a proud moment for the Navy,

Above and top
Having returned to the *Midway* following their debrief in Saigon, the victorious crews pose with their F-4Bs 24 hours after downing their MiGs. The top photo features Lt Dave Batson and Lt Cdr Robert Doremus, and the bottom shot Cdr Lou Page and Lt J C Smith. Note squadron CO Cdr Bill Franke's name stencilled on the canopy rail behind XO Page's head

although they tended to prolong the thought that the Phantom II could be successfully employed against the MiG without dogfighting. The incident, after all, was a classic non-manoeuvring intercept, for which the Demon and early Phantom II crews had trained.

As a postscript to this action, Lt Dave Batson was finally awarded a second MiG kill from this engagement some 32 years later following the declassification of documents relating to the 17 June shoot downs. He had always maintained that a third MiG had been damaged by ingesting debris from its wingman after his Sparrow had exploded. Indeed, shortly after the engagement the two VF-21 crews had heard that only one of the four MiGs that they had encountered had returned to base.

The official documentation, and the backing of Batson's second kill theory by his then Carrier Air Group (CAG) CO, Cdr Bob Moore, was enough for the third MiG to be officially classified as destroyed. The VPAF, on the other hand, stated that the third MiG lost on this day had flown into mountains in the area because of poor weather, and that two F-4s had also been shot down during the course of the engagement.

Just as in previous conflicts, in Vietnam successful aircrew were quick to praise their groundcrews for providing them with serviceable aircraft that proved capable of doing the job when required. Cdr Page and Lt J C Smith pose for a group shot with the sailors specifically tasked with arming and maintaining *Sundown 101* (*via Peter Mersky*)

Bottom page 29
This VF-151 jet, seen formating with an RA-3B from VAP-61 during a spring 1965 combat sortie, later scored a MiG-17 kill with VF-51 on 11 June 1972 (*Don J Willis*)

Sundown 107 overflies CVA-41 with its hook down, prior to breaking hard left into the landing circuit. Note that both the carrier and its plane guard destroyer are in the process of turning into wind prior to commencing the recovery cycle. Photographed on *Yankee Station* in June 1965, this aircraft has a typical CAP load-out of two AIM-7 Sparrows (fuselage) and two AIM-9 Sidewinders (wing stations) (*US Navy via Peter Mersky*)

MORE MiG KILLS

Three days after VF-21's MiG-killing exploits, another squadron within *Midway's* CVW-2 celebrated the destruction of a 'Fresco', although this time the engagement was hardly a typical fighter-versus-fighter action. VA-25's Lt Charlie Hartman proved the folly of leaving guns out of the F-4 when he downed a MiG-17 at low-level over Mai Chau, in Hoa Binh Province, with the quartet of 20 mm cannon fitted into the wings of his piston-engined A-1H (BuNo 139768).

Proving that this was no one-off, a second MiG-17 would fall to the guns of the venerable Douglas Skyraider on 9 October 1966.

The next US Navy Phantom II MiG kill was not scored until 6 October, when a *Coral Sea*-based F-4B of VF-151 (operating as part of CVW-15) downed a single MiG-17 during a BARCAP mission. Flying *Switch Box 107* (BuNo 150634), Lt Cdr Dan MacIntyre and RIO Lt(jg) Alan Johnson were covering a strike against a bridge near Kep airfield.

As they set up their CAP orbit at 2500 ft (the clouds were between 3000 and 4500 ft), Johnson picked up multiple contacts on his radar that were 18 miles away, and closing. At first, it appeared that the blips might be F-8s, as they were known to be in the vicinity with the strike group, and had been seen on Johnson's scope earlier in the mission. But the three-ship line astern formation was a dead-ringer for VPAF MiGs.

At about eight miles Johnson achieved a missile lock on the second MiG, and at three miles MacIntyre established a visual ID, calling 'three MiG-17s on the nose', crossing from right to left at about 1000 ft above his Phantom II. MacIntyre slid in behind the trailing MiG as it crossed and fired a Sparrow, sending the 'Fresco' earthward streaming smoke.

When MacIntyre turned his attention to the remaining MiGs, he saw the lead jet, now turning behind him for a shot, off to his left. The second MiG, however, was virtually in front of MacIntyre's F-4B, and he was closing on it fast. Knowing that the lead 'Fresco' would not fire with one of his own just ahead of MacIntyre, he darted after the trailing MiG, closing on him with

Fuelled and armed, three F-4Bs from VF-151 await their crews aboard the *Coral Sea* in early April 1965. CVA-43 was nearing the end of its second period (of six) on the line when this shot was taken from 'Vulture's Row' by VAP-61 aircrewman Lt Don J Willis (*Don J Willis*)

BuNo 150634 was the mount of Lt Cdr Dan MacIntyre and Lt(jg) Alan Johnson when they downed their MiG-17 on 6 October 1965. It is seen in the US prior to the 1965 *WestPac* – note its unusual intake warning marking (*via Angelo Romano*)

close to 200 knots of overtake. MacIntyre and Johnson's Phantom II rolled directly over the MiG's canopy in full afterburner, before the former pulled a hard barrel roll left and started to converge on the lead MiG inside his turn. The trailing MiG, apparently shaken by this audacious manoeuvre, headed for Phuc Yen.

As MacIntyre completed his turn, he rolled out behind the departing MiG and savoured his next shot – one that would give him two kills for the day. But the lead MiG had now turned his attention to MacIntyre's wingman, and was in pursuit. Although longing for the second MiG, MacIntyre knew that his wingman was in trouble, and he turned his F-4 around. The lead MiG quickly moved into position on MacIntyre's wingman and entered into a turning battle, firing his 37 mm cannon at the helpless Phantom II.

At first, MacIntyre was above the MiG and unable to break through the ground-clutter for a lock. When he finally reached the MiG's altitude, and Johnson's radar obtained a Sparrow lock, the aggressive VPAF pilot broke off his attack and headed for China. MacIntyre followed for a while, but was unable to secure a missile lock, so he broke off the fight and joined up on his wing, who was returning to the carrier.

1965 finally came to an end with a 37-day bombing halt, known as the Christmas bombing pause, that continued to 30 January 1966. During the year, three VPAF MiGs had been officially shot down by F-4B crews, and no Navy Phantom IIs had in turn been lost to Vietnamese fighters.

THE YEAR OF UPS AND DOWNS

1966 saw the Navy experience little MiG activity until the late-spring. The Air Force, on the other hand, had fought a number of engagements,

This spotless VF-151 F-4B was photographed on the tarmac at NAS Miramar in September 1964. The unit had yet to undertake a *WestPac* with the McDonnell fighter when this shot was taken, although its work-ups were well underway aboard the *Coral Sea*. As with a number of the Phantom IIs supplied to the 'Vigilantes' in early 1964, this particular airframe had initially seen operational service with the USAF (as 62-12194). One of 29 F4H-1s loaned to the Air Force in 1962, this jet served with the 4453rd Combat Crew Training Wing at MacDill AFB, Florida, until early 1964, when it returned to Navy service with VF-151 (*US Navy via Naval Aviation Museum*)

VF-151 returned to the Gulf of Tonkin in 1966, this time aboard the *Constellation*. Parked on the Miramar ramp between sorties, this F-4B was assigned to the unit CO, Cdr J O Ward. Again, the 'Vigilantes' completed their second combat tour without suffering any losses through enemy action, although this time two aircraft and four aircrew were killed in operational accidents (*via Brad Elward*)

The *Enterprise* moves slowly beneath the Golden Gate Bridge on 21 June 1966 to signal the end of its *WestPac,* which had started from Alameda on 26 October 1965. Chained down in the centre of the flightdeck, these F-4Bs display an interesting mix of markings. The aircraft wearing *MARINES* titling had been issued to VF-92 and VF-96 three days after their final line period had come to an end on 5 June. It was standard procedure for Navy F-4 units coming off *Yankee Station* at the end of their *WestPac* to swap their 'low time' jets for 'high time' examples from land-based Marine Corps squadrons in-theatre – these particular jets came from MCAS Iwakuni-based VMFA-323. BuNo 152219 (NG 603) was the F-4B used by VF-21's Lt Batson and Lt Cdr Doremus to down a MiG-17 on 17 June 1965 (*via Brad Elward*)

VF-161's distinctive fin markings in 1966 (*via Peter Davies*)

resulting in six MiG kills being claimed between 23 and 30 April – the most significant of these occurred on 26 April, when a 480th TFS/35th TFW F-4C crew destroyed the first VPAF MiG-21.

The small, sleek fighter had begun arriving in North Vietnam in late 1965, although it did not make its combat debut until early 1966. The Navy would have to wait until 9 October to claim its first 'Fishbed', when the CO of VF-162, Cdr Dick Bellinger, 'bagged' one with a Sidewinder whilst flying F-8E BuNo 149159 off the *Oriskany*. That same day the 'Fishbed' may have claimed its first Navy Phantom II kill in the shape of VF-154 F-4B BuNo 152093 off the *Coral Sea*. Its crew (Lt Cdr Charles Tanner and Lt Ross Terry) maintain that they were hit by AAA, although the Vietnamese tortured them until they confessed that they had been downed by a MiG.

Returning to the summer, June 1966 had seen some of the heaviest MiG fighting to date, beginning on the 12th when F-8Es from VF-211 mixed with MiG-17s, downing one confirmed and one probable (the second aircraft was confirmed destroyed, but never officially credited to pilot, Cdr Hal Marr, who also downed the other 'Fresco').

Two days later the Navy scored another probable kill when an F-4B from *Ranger's* VF-143 was scrambled to intercept an approaching bogie. The crew locked onto the contact and fired a Sparrow, and moments later the blip 'disappeared' from the RIO's radar screen. Unfortunately for the crew, no wreckage was found and confirmation could not be made.

MiG activity continued on 21 June, when four F-8Es from VF-211 were jumped by four MiG-17s north-east of Hanoi. Two MiGs were shot down at the cost of one F-8 destroyed (BuNo 149152, flown by Lt Cdr Cole Black) and one damaged. This date marked the first loss of a US Navy fighter in air-to-air combat against the VPAF.

VF-161's FIRST MiG

On the morning of 13 July Air Wing 15, embarked on the *Constellation*, launched an *Alpha* strike against the Co Trai railroad and highway bridge. VF-161 was assigned CAP duties for the flight, and duly launched four F-4Bs. As the strike force was retiring from the target area, the Phantom II crews decided to make a final sweep. As they did so, they received an urgent call from two Skyhawks that had been flying an 'Iron Hand' (SAM suppression) mission. They were being chased by a gaggle of MiGs.

The four F-4s quickly engaged six MiG-17s, and Lt William 'Squeaky' McGuigan and Lt(jg) Robert Fowler (flying BuNo 151500/NL 216) emerged from the dogfight with a single Sidewinder kill to their credit. In the wake of the shoot-down, the following message was sent to CTG 77.8 from the Commander, Seventh Fleet;

'I am pleased to see that again the MiGs were visually detected before they attacked our fighters. This, and the repeated return to home plate with undamaged aircraft, is proof positive our pilots are flying heads-up missions.'

Lt William McGuigan and Lt(jg) Robert Fowler pose on the wing of their assigned F-4B (BuNo 151009) the day after they had downed a MiG-17 on 13 July 1966 in BuNo 151500. BuNo 151009 was shot down by AAA on 22 October 1966, and although its pilot, Lt Cdr E P McBride, was killed, his RIO, Lt(jg) E U Turner, was recovered alive. This was the sole Phantom II lost by VF-161 on cruise (*via Peter Mersky*)

A VF-114 F-4B heads for a 'three-wire' on the *Kitty Hawk* in late 1966. During CVW-11's first line period aboard CVA-63 on the 1966-67 *WestPac*, both VF-114 and VF-213 fitted the Mk 4 gun pod to the centreline station of their jets, and relied on two external wing tanks on the outboard stations in place of the centreline store. However, as noted by VF-114's records, 'the gun pod proved undesirable, and during the remainder of the deployment the 600-gal centreline tank configuration was standardised for both fighter and attack missions'

'Good show *Rock River 216*.'

The next two Navy MiG kills were claimed by Cdr Dick Bellinger in an F-8E on 8 October and by Lt(jg) William Patton in an A-1H just 24 hours later. The Navy's Phantom II force had to wait until the evening of 20 December for its next aerial successes, which took the form of two slow-moving Antonov An-2 biplane transports that were detected by *Red Crown* as they flew along the North Vietnamese coast.

No fewer than six Phantom IIs were lost in combat by CVW-11 during its first Vietnam deployment, aboard the *Kitty Hawk*, in 1965-66. The last of these was this particular jet, BuNo 152257, which was struck by AAA over Laos on 18 May 1966 – the carrier pulled out of the Gulf of Tonkin four days later. The crew of 'Black Lion 113', Lt Cdrs C N Sommers (pilot) and W K Sullivan (RIO), were successfully recovered (*via Robert F Dorr*)

Left
Amongst the 22 Phantom IIs deployed on the *Kitty Hawk* in 1965 were a handful of datalink equipped F-4Gs assigned to VF-213. Externally identical to a standard F-4B, these jets stood out due to their experimental Olive Drab camouflage which was trialled during the cruise. Neither the datalink system or the camouflage proved overly successful, and the surviving G-models were reconfigured as standard F-4Bs and resprayed in gull grey and white at the end of the deployment (*via Robert F Dorr*)

VF-213's 'An-2 killing' F-4B BuNo 153019 drops a full load of 500-lb Mk 82 'iron' bombs over South Vietnam early in its 1966-67 WestPac (*via Aerospace Publishing*)

The only confirmed non-MiG kills claimed by the Americans during the Vietnam conflict (VF-31's Cdr Sam Flynn almost certainly 'bagged' a third An-2 in 1972, although he was never officially credited), the An-2s were swiftly despatched by single AIM-7E Sparrow rounds fired from the alert F-4Bs launched off the *Kitty Hawk*.

The crews involved in this one-sided action were Lt Denny Wisely (who would claim a MiG-17 in April 1967, and eventually attain the rank of rear admiral) and Lt(jg) David Jordan from VF-114, flying BuNo 153022/NH 215, and VF-213's Lt David McCrea and Ens David Nichols in BuNo 153019/NH 110. This engagement brought the year-end tally to 11 kills for the Navy.

1966 had seen a marked increase in the tenacity and aggression displayed by attacking MiG pilots, as well as the deployment of more fighters by the VPAF. The communist pilots were now working closely with GCI units at Phuc Yen and Bac Mai, and were demonstrating that they could 'sneak up' on US strike packages virtually undetected. The VPAF had also recognised that it was more important to concentrate on the bombers, forcing them to jettison their loads, than it was to tangle with the American fighters.

Indeed, it was becoming clear that the MiGs had settled into a pattern of attack that would continue throughout the war – MiG-17s intercepting fighter-bombers primarily at low-altitudes, while MiG-21s attacked aircraft at high-altitudes. Moreover, by December, the MiGs were actively contesting all US strikes in and around Hanoi and Hai Phong, and their attacks had forced approximately 20 per cent of all strikes into Pak VI to jettison their loads before reaching their targets.

34

1
F-4B BuNo 151403/NG 602 of Lt(jg) Terrence
M Murphy and Ens Ronald J Fegan, VF-96,
USS *Ranger*, 9 April 1965

2
F-4B BuNo 152219/NE 102 of Lt Jack E D
Batson and Lt Cdr Robert B Doremus, VF-21,
USS *Midway*, 17 June 1965

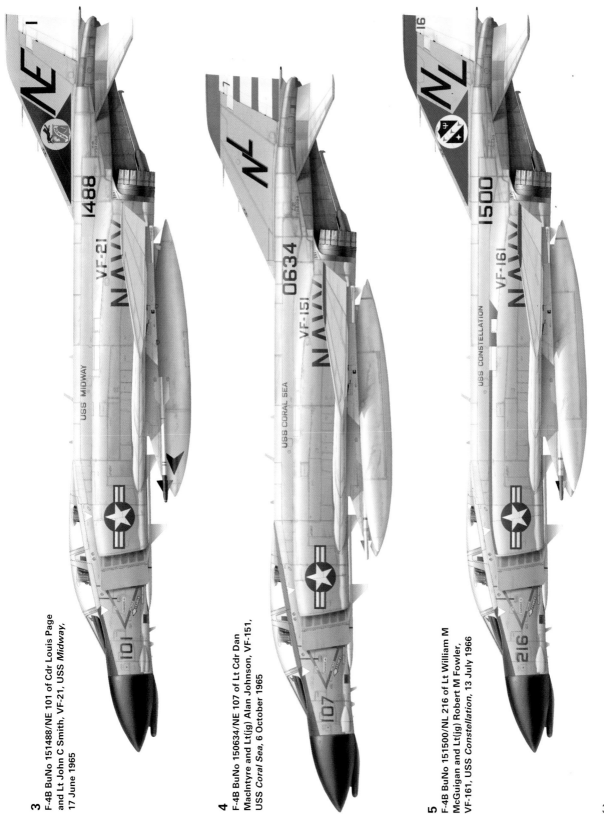

3
F-4B BuNo 151488/NE 101 of Cdr Louis Page
and Lt John C Smith, VF-21, USS *Midway*,
17 June 1965

4
F-4B BuNo 150634/NE 107 of Lt Cdr Dan
MacIntyre and Lt(jg) Alan Johnson, VF-151,
USS *Coral Sea*, 6 October 1965

5
F-4B BuNo 151500/NL 216 of Lt William M
McGuigan and Lt(jg) Robert M Fowler,
VF-161, USS *Constellation*, 13 July 1966

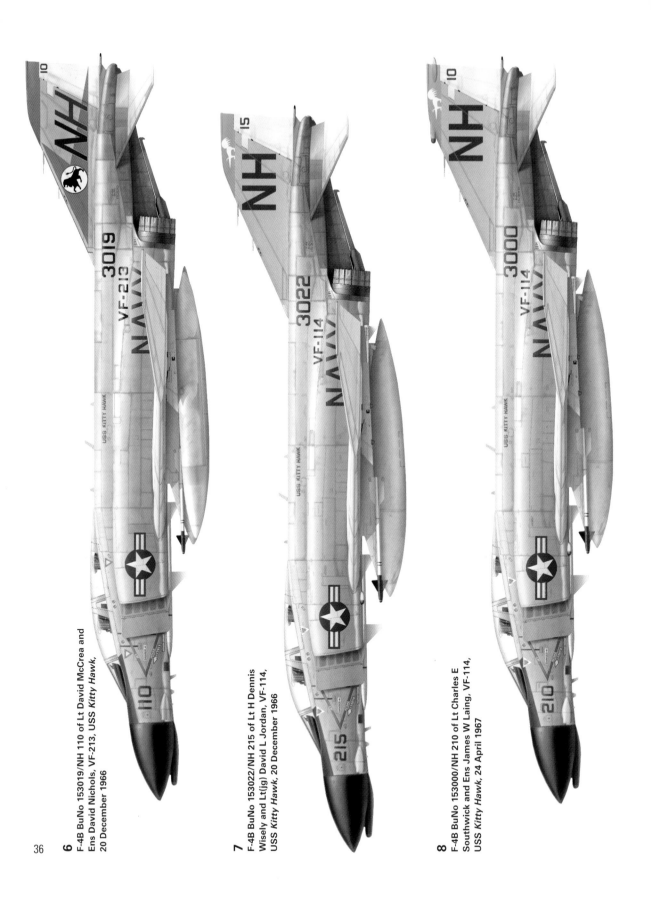

6
F-4B BuNo 153019/NH 110 of Lt David McCrea and
Ens David Nichols, VF-213, USS *Kitty Hawk*,
20 December 1966

7
F-4B BuNo 153022/NH 215 of Lt H Dennis
Wisely and Lt(jg) David L Jordan, VF-114,
USS *Kitty Hawk*, 20 December 1966

8
F-4B BuNo 153000/NH 210 of Lt Charles E
Southwick and Ens James W Laing, VF-114,
USS *Kitty Hawk*, 24 April 1967

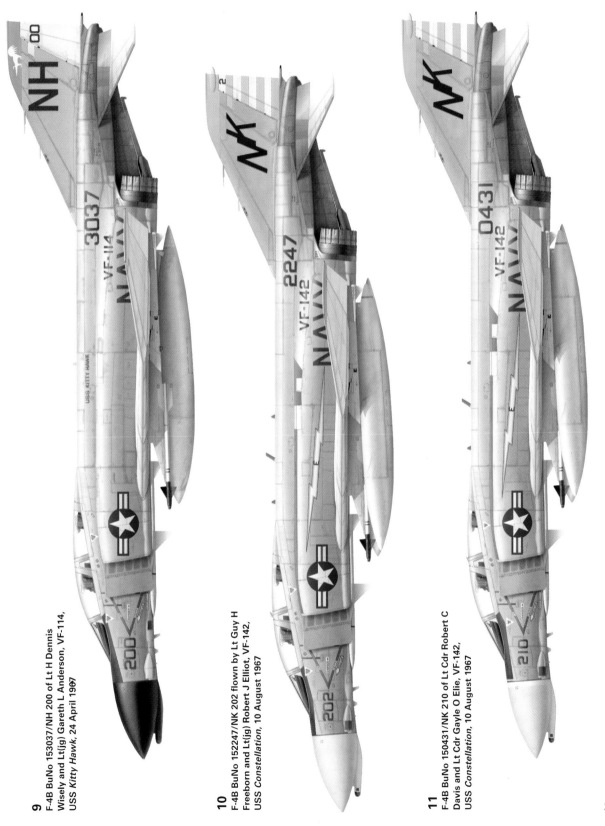

9
F-4B BuNo 153037/NH 200 of Lt H Dennis
Wisely and Lt(jg) Gareth L Anderson, VF-114,
USS *Kitty Hawk*, 24 April 1967

10
F-4B BuNo 152247/NK 202 flown by Lt Guy H
Freeborn and Lt(jg) Robert J Elliot, VF-142,
USS *Constellation*, 10 August 1967

11
F-4B BuNo 150431/NK 210 of Lt Cdr Robert C
Davis and Lt Cdr Gayle O Elie, VF-142,
USS *Constellation*, 10 August 1967

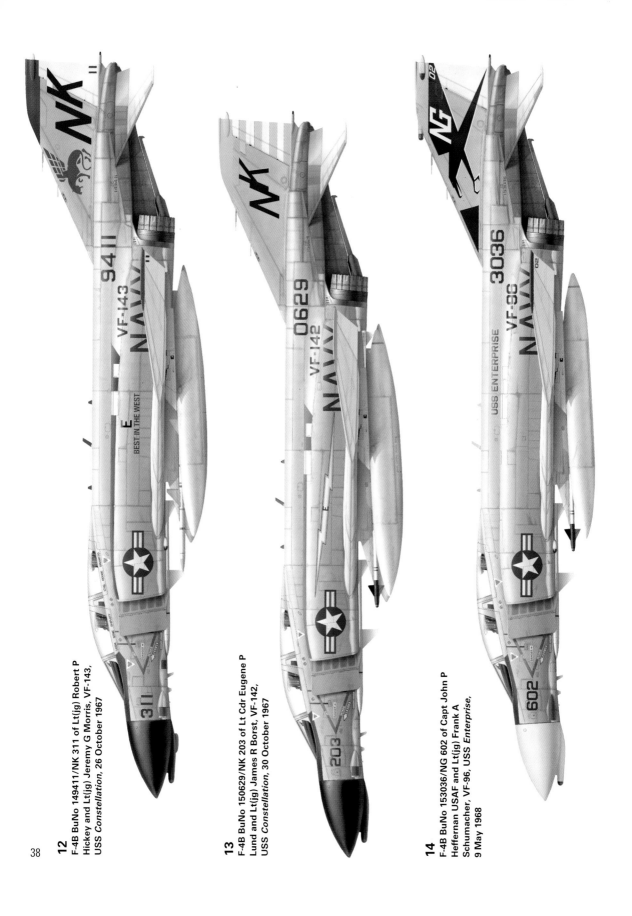

12
F-4B BuNo 149411/NK 311 of Lt(jg) Robert P
Hickey and Lt(jg) Jeremy G Morris, VF-143,
USS *Constellation*, 26 October 1967

13
F-4B BuNo 150629/NK 203 of Lt Cdr Eugene P
Lund and Lt(jg) James R Borst, VF-142,
USS *Constellation*, 30 October 1967

14
F-4B BuNo 153036/NG 602 of Capt John P
Heffernan USAF and Lt(jg) Frank A
Schumacher, VF-96, USS *Enterprise*,
9 May 1968

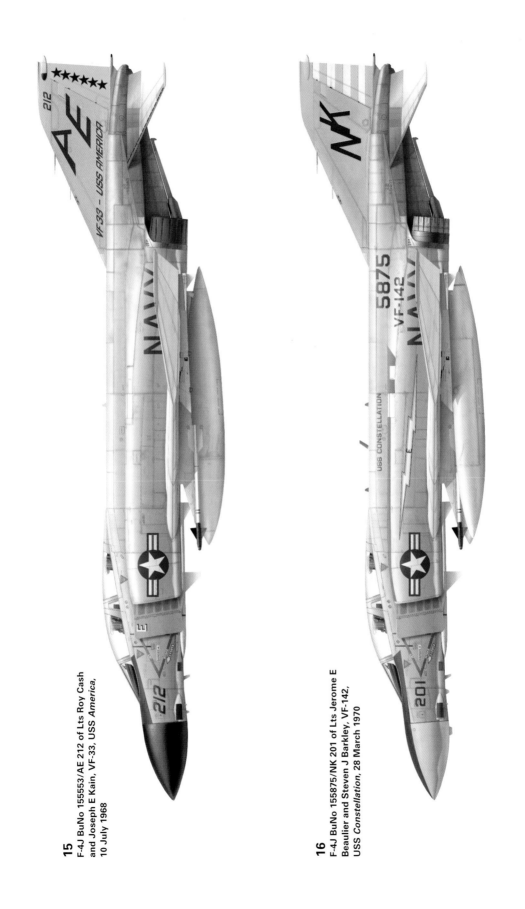

15
F-4J BuNo 155553/AE 212 of Lts Roy Cash
and Joseph E Kain, VF-33, USS America,
10 July 1968

16
F-4J BuNo 155875/NK 201 of Lts Jerome E
Beaulier and Steven J Barkley, VF-142,
USS Constellation, 28 March 1970

1

4

2

3

6

5

7

8

9

10

11

12

13

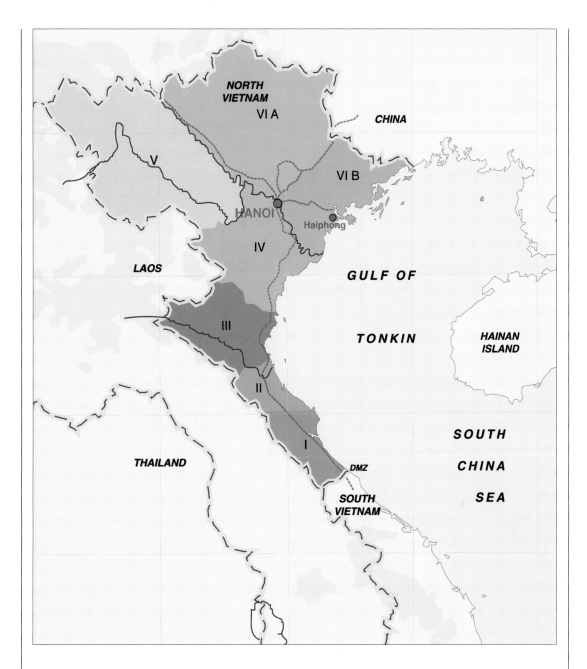

Map 1

The various geographic regions of North Vietnam were divided into Route Packages, called 'Paks' or 'RPs', and control assigned to a specific service. The Navy controlled operations in Paks II, III, IV and VIA, and the Air Force air operations in Paks I, V and VIB. The two stations from which Navy carriers operated during the war stretched along the length of the Vietnamese coast. *Yankee Station* was located north of the DMZ, and stretched up to Hai Phong. As many as three carriers (part of Task Force 77) would be operating in these waters at any one time. Further south, *Dixie Station* was typically serviced by only one carrier, and was eventually disestablished in August 1966 as more Air Force units moved into neighbouring Thailand and South Vietnam.

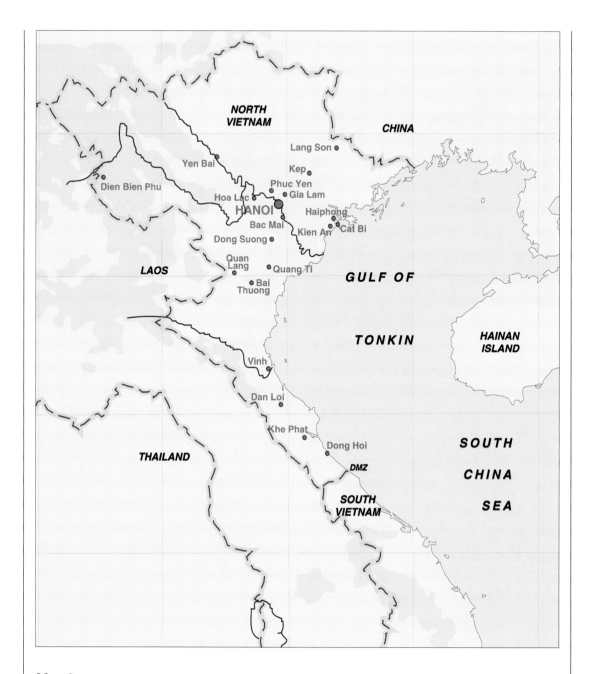

Map 2
The major VPAF MiG bases are highlighted in this map. Kep, Gia Lam and Phuc Yen were the initial airfields used by the communists, but many more were constructed as the war progressed. MiG bases were off-limits to US fliers for political reasons until March 1967.

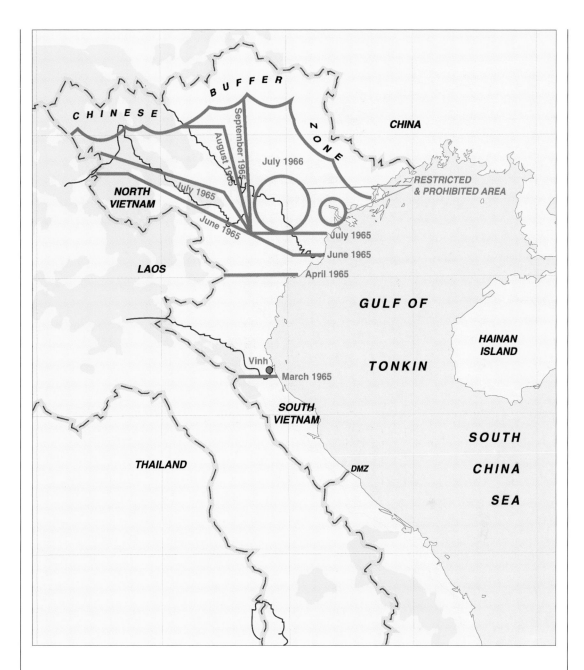

Map 3

Rolling Thunder air operations were focused against North Vietnam. Other missions, such as *Barrel Roll*, *Steel Tiger* and *Tiger Hound*, were conducted in Laos in order to interdict the supply of provisions and materials from North Vietnam to the Viet Cong. *Rolling Thunder* strikes progressively moved north, eventually covering all of North Vietnam except the protected and restricted areas around Hanoi and Hai Phong, and the 30-mile buffer zone near Communist China.

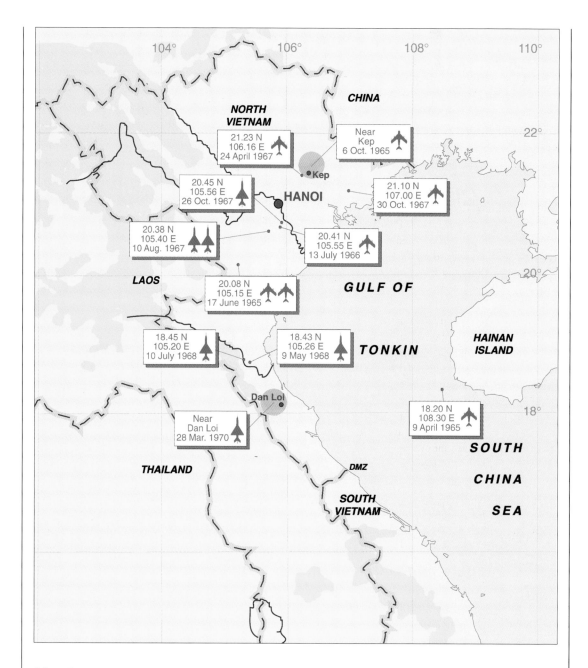

Map 4

This map shows US Navy F-4 MiG kills from 1965 through to 1970, including the Communist Chinese MiG-17 downed by VF-96 on 9 April 1965. The two An-2s downed on 20 December 1966 are not included.

AN INTENSE YEAR

Although by the end of 1966 both the Air Force and the Navy enjoyed a relatively good MiG kill ratio, a more in-depth analysis of combat over Vietnam led to the conclusion that something was amiss. US missiles were performing poorly, and the MiG-21 was scoring a disproportionate number of kills in comparison with the F-4.

Despite the growing MiG threat, American attacks against VPAF bases remained strictly prohibited. This restriction prompted a scheme implemented by the USAF to entice the MiGs up for a big fight. In January 1967, under the code-name Operation *Bolo*, Air Force F-4Cs from Thailand flew simulated F-105 profiles and successfully lured no fewer than 11 MiGs into a series of engagements. Using both Sidewinders and Sparrows, the Phantom II crews (all from the 8th TFW) downed seven MiG-21s without loss on 2 January, followed by two more four days later through the employment of a similar feint.

This rout of the VPAF MiG-21 force, coupled with unusually foul weather, saw communist 'Fishbeds' refrain from combat until mid-April, when new fighting began in earnest.

Despite the decimation of the MiG-21 unit, the MiG-17s of the 921st and 923rd Fighter Regiments continued to take the fight to the Americans in February and March. Indeed, the 'Fresco' pilots demonstrated a new confidence in combat, routinely trying to get the US fighters to come down and fight closer to the ground, where American missiles were least effective, and where the MiG-17's superior turning qualities could be used to their advantage.

At this time the infamous 'wagon wheel' formation emerged, which saw MiG-17s flying in a circle at low-altitude, where they could offer each other mutual protection. Ground clutter effectively rendered the AIM-7 useless, and the AIM-9's effectiveness was also greatly reduced because of the effects of low-altitude firing on its engagement envelope – at sea level the Sidewinder had a range of only 4000 ft, and a firing cone of only 30 degrees off the bandit's tailpipe. These tactics were complemented shortly thereafter by positioning AAA and SAM defences near the 'wheels' to further hamper American attempts to intercept the MiG-17s.

As the weather lifted in late April, MiG engagements rose dramatically, and some of the fiercest aerial battles of *Rolling Thunder* took place, resulting in the downing of nine MiGs by USAF F-4Cs and F-105Ds and two by Navy F-4Bs. This increased activity, and the MiGs' growing aggressiveness, led the Johnson administration to approve attacks on key VPAF bases, including Kep and Hao Lac.

VF-114 claimed the Navy's first MiG kills of 1967, and this particular F-4B played a major part in securing this success. Crewed by Lt Dennis Wisely and Lt(jg) Gareth Anderson, the jet downed one of two MiG-17s destroyed on 24 April. It is seen here at Miramar in July 1967, shortly after completing the final two months of *Kitty Hawk's* 1966-67 *WestPac* – BuNo 153037 had been assigned to the 'Aardvarks' on 8 April as an attrition replacement. As VF-114's designated CAG aircraft, *Linfield 200* was entitled to wear a traditional multi-coloured marking somewhere on its fuselage. However, the unit restricted its embellishment to additional titling (which reads *COMMANDER ATTACK CARRIER AIR WING ELEVEN*) on the spine above the *USS KITTY HAWK* stencilling. Note the storeless triple ejector rack beneath the port wing of BuNo 153037 (*US Navy*)

Linfield 200's RIO for the 24 April 1967 MiG-17 shoot down was Lt(jg) Gareth L Anderson of Kane, Pennsylvania. On his first *WestPac*, the young naval aviator had little time to savour his rare MiG kill for he was shot down by a SAM in *Linfield 204* (BuNo 153004) near Hanoi on 19 May. Both Anderson and his pilot, Lt(jg) J C Plumb, ejected safely and were quickly captured (*via Peter Mersky*)

Linfield 200's pilot on 24 April 1967 was Lt 'Denny' Wisely, who had already downed an An-2 earlier in the cruise. His MiG kill made him the Navy's first two victory naval aviator, and he would keep this distinction until May 1972. Like Anderson, Wisely was also shot down in May 1967, falling to AAA (in BuNo 153040/NH 213) on the 21st. However, both he and his RIO (fellow 'MiG killer' Ens James W Laing) were rescued (*via Peter Mersky*)

As would be expected, the attacks on Kep provoked some of the most ferocious aerial engagements experienced by American aircrews to date. Located approximately 37 miles north-east of Hanoi, Kep was one of five major MiG bases in North Vietnam.

On 24 April, jets from the *Kitty Hawk* launched and headed across the Gulf towards Kep. VF-114's Phantom IIs were providing the MiGCAP for the strike, with two of the F-4s being crewed by Lt Charles Southwick and Ens James W Laing (in BuNo 153000/NH 210) and Lt Denny Wisely and Lt(jg) Gareth L Anderson (in BuNo 153037/NH 200).

As the MiGCAP approached Kep, the crews encountered heavy AAA and SAMs, and several of the escorting F-4s were hit by flak, forcing them to return to the carrier. Southwick and Laing also felt a 'thud' at this early stage of the mission, but dismissed it as the impending action neared.

With the bombers in the process of dropping their ordnance, a call came that there were MiGs in-bound down the Red River valley. Southwick, who was now heading back towards the carrier, pulled his Phantom II around and immediately saw several MiG-17s heading straight at him. He called 'tally ho' as the MiGs roared by, and started a horizontal turn.

Southwick refused to play his foes' game by continuing his flat turn, and instead pulled his fighter up into a climbing vertical loop, then dropped down into the 'Fresco' wagon wheel at high speed. He saw one MiG on his right, then another flashed by on his left, exposing its underside as it turned. Southwick then entered the wheel after the MiG. Hearing the Sidewinder growl, he launched an AIM-9D which powered into the MiG's right wing. The communist jet smoked at first, spewing out fuel, then careened towards the ground.

When Southwick had entered the wheel and closed on his target, the wingman of the latter jet gave chase. About that time, Wisely and Anderson joined the fray. Wisely later stated that there were 'MiGs everywhere', and he recalled seeing them chasing an A-4 and an A-6. As he followed his own target, he also noticed that Southwick had a MiG on his tail, and it looked as if it was about to shoot. Wisely shouted 'pull up', and Southwick responded, pulling his F-4 into a left barrel roll. The MiG's missile passed harmlessly by. Wisely then triggered his own missile, which destroyed the MiG-17.

After Southwick rolled out, Laing noticed a warning light in the cockpit, indicating that they were low on fuel. He soon realised that the 'thud' he had felt earlier in the mission was likely to have been shrapnel from an exploding AAA shell. Apparently, the shot had severed fuel lines, and the Phantom II was unable to transfer fuel from its wing tanks, which were still full. With Wisely and Anderson escorting them, the crew of *Linfield 210* headed for the Gulf, where their chances of being rescued were much greater than if they had to eject over land.

Five or so miles out, both engines shut down through fuel exhaustion, and the Phantom II plunged into the water. Both crewmen ejected, and were rescued after just 30 minutes in the water.

The VPAF claimed credit for downing *Linfield 210*, the 923rd Fighter Regiment's Mai Duc Toai, Le Hai, Luu Huy Chao and Hoang Van Ky sharing in the victory

Denny Wisely's MiG kill was significant for the Navy, for he had been involved in the December 1966 engagements with the An-2 'Colts'. With two victories to his name, he was now the leading Navy VPAF killer. Indeed, it would not be until the second major phase of the air war in 1972 that the Navy would see another pilot or RIO with more than one official kill.

As an indication of the escalation of the air war in the spring of 1967, Wisely, Laing, Southwick and Anderson – flying with different crews – were all shot down in May. Southwick (in BuNo 153001/NH 201) went down near Thanh Hoa on the 14th after his jet had suffered an idle engine stall as a result of ingesting gas from its own Zuni rockets. The damaged Phantom II continued on after the crew had ejected, coming to rest upright on a riverbank – three Alpha strikes were subsequently launched in a futile effort to destroy the aeroplane before it was taken away. Southwick and his RIO, Lt D J Rollins, were made PoWs.

Anderson and his pilot, Lt(jg) J C Plumb, were shot down by a SAM near Hanoi in BuNo 153004/NH 204 on the 19th, and again both crewmen were captured. Finally, on the 21st, Wisely and Laing (in BuNo 153040/NH 213) fell to AAA, although on this occasion both men were rescued. Following the completion of his tour with VF-114, James Laing went on to become an instructor initially at VF-121 (the Pacific Fleet F-4 crew training unit) and then Topgun, specialising in ACM radar operation and RIO training.

Aside from VF-114's 'MiG-killing' successes on 24 April, sister-squadron VF-213 was also 'mixing it up' with VPAF fighters on this day. Towards the end of their flak suppression run north-east of Hanoi, seven F-4Bs encountered heavy SAMs and AAA. One of the Phantom IIs – 'Black Lion 115' – was then jumped by three MiG-17s, the pilot describing his assailants as 'silver MiGs with red star insignia'. The lead MiG fired eight bursts 'in runs from all over the clock, above, level and below'. The F-4 pilot in turn tried to engage, but his missiles failed, so he turned with the MiGs until he was able to break free and head for the carrier.

April and May 1967 saw the highest number of all-service MiG-kills of the entire *Rolling Thunder* campaign. A total of 38 MiGs was claimed to have been destroyed (11 in April and 27 in May), and such a tally would not be seen again until May 1972, when 27 kills were claimed during the initial *Linebacker* operations. The Air Force were credited with 30 of the 38 victories, these being shared between F-4C and F-105D crews. Of the eight kills attributed to Navy jets, five were claimed by F-8C/Es, two by the F-4B and one by an A-4C.

The successes of April and May were followed by a noticeable downturn in MiG activity, reduced levels of AAA and fewer SAM

The second aircraft involved in the 24 April 1967 MiG clash was *Linfield 210*, alias BuNo 153000. The aircraft is seen here on short finals to NAS Atsugi on Saturday, 19 November 1966, CVW-11 sending 36 of its aircraft on a shore run to the naval air station on the outskirts of Tokyo for a 48-hour R&R break. By the time CVA-63's *WestPac* had come to an end six months later, six of these aircraft had been lost in combat and one written off in an operational accident. Amongst the former was BuNo 153000, which suffered serious AAA damage on its 'MiG killing' mission on 24 April. Its crew, Lt Charles Southwick and Ens James W Laing, coaxed the big fighter back out to sea, but with no hydraulics, they could not lower the undercarriage for landing and were forced to eject. Note the fin-top AN/APR-30 Radar Homing and Warning System (RHAW) antennas fitted to this jet (*via A Romano*)

The next MiG kills for 1967 were claimed on 10 August when two MiG-21s were downed by a pair of F-4Bs from *Constellation's* VF-142. One of the aircraft involved in this action was *Dakota 210* (alias BuNo 150431), which is seen here at Da Nang following a diversionary landing. This shot was taken prior to the jet 'bagging' its MiG (*US Navy*)

attacks. Many observers believe that this was caused by the failure of the VPAF's supply system to keep up with the increased operational tempo. This inactivity lasted through June and July, for many MiGs had fled to China to regroup due to the persistent attacks on the southern-most air bases. Those fighters that remained in the north had taken up temporary residence at Phuc Yen and Gia Lam, which were still off limits to US jets.

Indeed, there were only five MiG kills in June, all of which fell to either USAF F-4C/Ds or F-105Ds. On 21 July a further four MiGs were claimed by F-8s (three by VF-24 and one by VF-211) off the *Bon Homme Richard*. By the end of that month only seven MiG-21s and twenty-eight MiG-17s remained in North Vietnam. However, in early August the MiGs returned, and F-4B crews began to 'mix it up' in Paks IV and VI.

TWO TO VF-142

At 1145 hrs on 10 August 1967, two F-4Bs from VF-142 launched from the *Constellation* to provide BARCAP for a large two-carrier Alpha strike heading for the Phu Ly transhipment point. The crews involved were Lt Guy Freeborn and Lt(jg) Robert Elliot (on only his ninth combat mission) in F-4B BuNo 152247/NK 202 (formerly an F-4G that had been reconverted back to B-model specification following an experimental deployment with VF-213 in 1965-66), and Lt Cdrs Robert C Davis and Gayle O Elie in F-4B BuNo 150431/NK 210.

The following account of this engagement comes from Lt Freeborn;

'I had been an F-4B Tactics Instructor with VF-121 for over two years, and the Training Officer in VF-142 prior to this cruise. Squadron activity in 1967 was, "Fly, eat, drink, play cards, man the Alert 5 watch, and curse the politicians for putting us in a war they wouldn't let us win.'

After tanking, the two Phantom IIs reached their CAP station just west of Nam Dinh and began a left orbit pattern at approximately 22,000 ft.

'The engagement was planned by us based on the environment – i.e. positive radar or radio control and thin cloud layers at 22,000 ft. We were BARCAP for the strike group, and held station just below the cloud layer, instead of the normal 15,000-18,000 ft, for the surprise element, which worked just as we had planned.'

As Guy Freeborn mentioned, the Phantom II crews were trying a new tactic on this mission that emphasised greater radar/radio control over BARCAP forces. Moreover, by taking advantage of the cloud layer, the BARCAP hoped to catch the MiGs as they broke through the clouds – VPAF fighters typically attacked from above the cloud under GCI control, and VF-142 hoped to intercept them as they dived down after the Navy fighter-bombers. The tactic worked well, and on this occasion the BARCAP encountered MiG-21s, which the Navy had rarely seen up to this point in the war, as the VPAF preferred to use to MiG-17s to oppose the northern Route Packs. Freeborn again;

'We were very familiar with the MiG-21's capabilities and tactics. We just hadn't seen many. They were mainly into "hitting the strike elements and running for home", with not much dogfighting capability. The feedback from USAF crews who had met the MiG-21 the previous year mostly confirmed this. They seemed to like the three-aeroplane formation, with one up front and two trailing the lead aircraft. They also liked to attack in multiple passes.'

As the *Constellation* strike group was exiting the target area, MiGs appeared, but they had yet to be seen by the Phantom II crews, despite their attempts to locate them. Finally, the communist fighters were spotted about 15 miles astern, and as the Phantom IIs turned left to engage, Freeborn noticed two objects directly above them. Coming through the clouds were two silver MiG-21s, heading north at 22,000 ft, and about 400 knots. As luck would have it, the MiGs did not see the F-4Bs.

The Phantom IIs moved into position behind the MiGs, ready for the shot. Davis and Elie took the MiG on the right, but when they triggered two Sparrows, they refused to fire. Davis then switched to Sidewinder and shot off a missile.

Back in more familiar surroundings on the steel deck of the 'Connie', BuNo 150431 serves as a backdrop for a group shot of the pilots and RIOs involved in the 10 August 1967 'MiG killing' mission. *Dakota 210's* crew, Lt Cdrs 'Swede' Elie (RIO) and Robert Davis, are standing closest to the fuselage, while further along the wing are Lt Guy Freeborn (pilot) and Lt(jg) Robert Elliot. The latter pair used *Dakota 202* (BuNo 152247) to claim their MiG-21 (*via Angelo Romano*)

At that same time, Freeborn loosed off a Sidewinder that tracked and exploded just left of the MiG, sending it down streaming smoke and fuel. Davis's first AIM-9 missed, and his second went ballistic. He quickly executed a high yo-yo manoeuvre and settled in behind the MiG Freeborn had just 'winged', which was now at 14,000 ft and in a left bank. Davis fired a third and then a fourth Sidewinder, destroying the MiG.

Freeborn, now agitated that Davis had 'plunked' his already damaged MiG (his mission tape later revealed the pilot exclaiming 'The bastard shot my MiG!' to his RIO seconds after the enemy fighter exploded), turned on the latter's original target, which was ahead and about 1000 ft below him. Getting a good heat tone in his headset, he squeezed off a Sidewinder, but it misfired and remained on the rail. He then quickly shot off a second missile, which tracked, wiggled for a moment, then ploughed into the MiG, creating a huge fireball.

These two kills represented the first Navy Phantom II victories against the new MiG-21 (VF-162's Cdr Dick Bellinger had been the first naval aviator to 'bag' a 'Fishbed', in his F-8E, on 9 October 1966). Although both were the result of nearly textbook engagements, the most disturbing aspect was that it took nine missiles to achieve the kills. Thus, while American crews were finding the upper hand tactically, poor weapons reliability was robbing them of the opportunity for a quick kill, and placing them in jeopardy in extended dogfights. Guy Freeborn remembers;

'My choice of missile for close-in fighting was always the Sidewinder. Bob Davis and "Swede" Elie fired two Sparrows with no good guidance. Their kill was also Sidewinder. Reliability of the missiles was a major issue then. The gun pod didn't work well and was too limited, so nobody wanted it. What we really wanted were built-in guns like those fitted to the Air Force's F-4Es.'

From January to the end of July 1967, Air Force and Navy units claimed a total of 55 MiGs shot down, with a further 30 destroyed on the ground. Of these kills, 12 were credited to the Navy, nine of which were

Recovery completed, the bow area of CVA-64 is full of recently-landed Phantom IIs and A-4s that will soon be re-spotted by the deck handlers. Most of the F-4s will be towed aft to the stern, which has traditionally been 'fighter country' aboard US Navy carriers. Chained down in the centre row of jets, sandwiched between two F-4Bs from VF-143, is VF-142's BuNo 152247 – Freeborn and Elliot's 'MiG killing' Phantom II. Toting an AGM-45A Shrike anti-radiation missile secured to its starboard wing hardpoint, the A-4C in the foreground has just returned from an uneventful *Iron Hand* SAM suppression sortie (*via Angelo Romano*)

scored using the new AIM-9D. Despite these heavy losses, the MiG force returned in strength during the remaining five months of 1967.

And through the employment of new harassing tactics during the course of September, the VPAF succeeded in its aim of drastically increasing the number of 'forced jettisons' of bombs from US aircraft prior to them reaching their intended targets. So heavy were the MiG attacks that President Johnson finally authorised strikes to be flown against the northern air base at Phuc Yen, leaving only the facility at Hanoi International Airport untouched.

These attacks took place on 24-25 October, and resulted in the destruction of a single MiG-21 in the air and another eight on the ground. Heavy VPAF fighter activity also led to the employment of dedicated MiGCAP sorties, where F-4Bs patrolled in search of fighters, rather than providing escort during TARCAP missions.

MiGCAP was employed by the F-4 units on the 'Connie' during the vessel's last two line periods of its 1967 *WestPac*. According to VF-143's end of cruise records, 'crews enthusiastically welcomed the advent of a fighter-sweep type tactic, referenced to as a MiGCAP, directed against an increasingly aggressive enemy Air Force'. The report continued;

'With increased MiG activity during the months of September, October and November, it was evident that TARCAP was insufficient to counter the threat. The TARCAP were on strike frequency, and used solely to protect the striking forces. This frequency, plus the "Bandit" calls on guard, made it virtually impossible for any close control to counter the MiG activity. Hence the idea of a MiGCAP was generated. Those aircraft were a distinct separate unit, flown in one or two sections, under the close control of a surface ship utilising a frequency other than the strike frequency.'

MiGCAPs during CVW-14's cruise were controlled by the northern SAR ships because of their advanced ECM and interrogation gear.

MiGCAP stations were established to provide the maximum coverage in areas most likely to encounter MiGs. Because of the frequency of MiG orbital patterns, two permanent MiGCAP stations were established and referred to as stations 'A' and 'B'. CVW-14's F-4s, operating from these stations, destroyed three MiG-21s and one MiG-17 during the latter half of 1967. VF-143's report also described in some detail how these MiGCAPs operated;

'The MiGCAP briefed with the main strike force, effected a rendezvous overhead with the tanker, refuelled approximately 2500 to 3000 pounds, and then departed separately for pre-briefed CAP stations. After the rendezvous on departure frequency, the MiGCAP switched to Strike Control, checked their SIF (Selective Identification Facility) gear and then checked in with PIRAZ Control.

'They then shifted frequency to Primary BARCAP Control, giving the controlling ship their state, weapon and armament status, and the station where they would hold feet dry. The controlling ship would then have the MiGCAP shift to a primary or secondary frequency different from the strike frequencies, thus allowing them to give full control to the fighters without disturbing the strike network. This close control was the first positive movement to make use of the full capabilities of the F-4. It was felt that with MiGCAP on their station, along with TARCAP near the strike force, the MiG threat to the force was minimised to a low degree.'

MiGCAP demonstrated to the VPAF that the US Navy was taking the threat posed by its MiGs seriously, and proved its worth during the late October engagements.

MiGCAP SUCCESS

On 25 October *Constellation* and CVW-14 returned to *Yankee Station* for their final line period of the cruise. Their arrival coincided with a period of poor weather, which hampered flying operations. However, the following day dawned clear, and a strike was launched against the army barracks at Van Dien, in Pak IV.

At a point between Hanoi and Thanh Hoa, a section of orbiting MiGCAP F-4Bs from VF-143 were vectored by *Harbormaster* (the ship-based *PIRAZ* GCI in the northern Gulf of Tonkin) towards a group of contacts believed to be MiGs. As the Phantom IIs sped towards their prey, clearance was given for the crews to fire without them having first obtained a visual identification of their targets.

Fortunately, the section leader's radar failed just as he was about to shoot, and his wingman's AIM-7 also refused to launch as he achieved missile lock. The wingman's Sparrow and Sidewinder shots also failed to acquire. As the formations merged, and to the horror of the two crews, it became clear that their 'MiGs' were actually other F-4Bs from VF-143!

A few moments later, the intercepting crews were directed to yet another contact believed to be MiGs. After receiving their vector, the lead

Posing for the cameras at Tan Son Nhut AFB, in South Vietnam, 24 hours after downing their MiGs, Lt Cdr Davis and Lt Freeborn employ the traditional 'hand talk' associated with fighter pilots reliving their experiences out of the cockpit. Both crews had been flown ashore from CVA-64 within hours of scoring their MiG-21 kills in order to brief the Press on how they had achieved their success. A photo session was also conducted before the 'MiG killers' returned to the 'Connie' to resume fighting the war. Both men are wearing baseball caps and shirts adorned with VF-142's 'Ghostrider' emblem (*via Peter Mersky*)

Hook down and 'in the groove' for landing, *Dakota 213* closes on the deck of CVA-64. During its 1967 *WestPac*, VF-142 logged most of its flight time providing CVW-14's strike aircraft with BARCAP, TARCAP and MiGCAP protection, as well as escorting RA-5Cs on photo-recce missions (*US Navy*)

A gruelling *WestPac* behind them, pilots and RIOs from VF-143 pose in front of the CO's jet on the eve of the 'Connie' returning to NAS North Island on 4 December 1967. All 11 of these men completed more than 200 combat missions during the course of the deployment. Standing at the extreme right is RIO Lt James Souder, who participated in the MiG-killing mission of 26 October 1967. Indeed, if his aircraft had not been plagued by intermittent radar and weapons system failure, Souder and his pilot, Cdr D K Grosshuesch (the unit CO, dubbed *THE HEAD DOG* on the canopy rail of *Tap Room 301*), would surely have downed a second MiG-21 to add to the 'Fishbed' destroyed by Lt(jg)s Robert Hickey and Jeremy Morris. VF-143, along with sister-squadron VF-142, had seen much action during the course of 'Connie's' 1967 *WestPac*, and although four MiGs had been downed, and hundreds of sorties completed, both units had paid a heavy price for this success. VF-143 had lost its CO, Cdr W P Lawrence (along with RIO Lt(jg) J W Bailey), to AAA on 28 June, while VF-142 had seen four of its jets destroyed in action. Fortunately for the 'Pukin' Dogs', its downed crew survived as PoWs, although VF-142 had had two naval aviators killed (*via Peter Mersky*)

section pilots, Cdr D K Grosshuesch and Lt(jg) Robert P Hickey Jr, conducted a visual search for the MiGs, while their RIOs, Lt James B Souder and Lt(jg) Jeremy G Morris respectively, focused on their radars. Souder's scope became inoperative, and Morris took over the intercept, directing his pilot (in BuNo 149411/NK 311) into a firing position. Hickey manoeuvred and fired an AIM-9D, which went ballistic and missed.

Meanwhile, Souder's radar had come back on line, and he immediately resumed control of the intercept, locking up the bandit and vectoring the section to a position on the MiG's six o'clock where the Phantom IIs could use their Sparrow IIIs. Although Grosshuesch could now visually identify the bandit as a MiG-21, he was powerless to shoot it down as his weapons system had now malfunctioned, so he ordered his wingman to fire. Hickey then engaged, firing an AIM-7 which tracked then struck the MiG's port wing. The 'Blue Bandit' pitched up and entered a flat spin.

Both Hickey and Morris received a Silver Star for their efforts, and Hickey went on to become an admiral – he was also bestowed with an award for gallantry from the Republic of South Vietnam. James Souder, who was later promoted to lieutenant commander, was shot down (along with his pilot, Lt Cdr A J Molinare) in F-4J BuNo 153025 of VF-51 on 27 April 1972 by an R-3S 'Atoll' that had been fired from a 921st Fighter Regiment MiG-21, flown by Hoang Quoc Dung.

On 29 October, a section of *PIRAZ*-controlled F-4Bs from VF-143 were vectored from their BARCAP station to intercept a MiG-21 some 25 miles south-east of Hanoi. The Phantom II intercepted the MiG and fired an AIM-7E at a distance of four miles. The missile exploded harmlessly about one-and-a-half miles short of the target, and the MiG executed a rapid 'split-S', before heading to Hanoi on the deck. The Phantom IIs returned safely to their carrier.

The next day VF-142's Lt Cdr Eugene P Lund and Lt(jg) James R Borst were flying MiGCAP in another of the unit's ex-F-4Gs (BuNo 150629). Working in the northern patrol station north-west of Hai Phong, the transcript of what happened next comes from 'Geno' Lund's debrief tape;

'We were on the northern MiGCAP station, which is over the ridge north-west of Hai Phong. We went "feet dry" just west of Cam Pha at 270 degrees at 18,000 ft, and we tracked down the northern ridge. About abeam of Hai Phong we got our first "Bandits" call, not from *Harbormaster*, but on *Guard* frequency. About a minute later *Harbormaster* came up and said he had an "unknown" – not a bogie – at 270 degrees and about 50 miles.

'Shortly afterwards he called it a bogie and commenced a vector from 270 degrees to 330 degrees. Shortly after that he confirmed that we were cleared to fire on the bogie, which was now at 353.60 degrees. He called it at "angels ten", and I suggested that it was climbing. He then said that there appeared to be a pair of bogies, and continued to give us vectors. Things got down to about ten miles, and we had got a lock-up on our radar at about fifteen miles. It appeared to be two bogies, from the scope. I more or less neglected any other vectors from *Harbormaster*, and we drove on in.

'At three to four miles I already had it in range, and I got a tally-ho (visual sighting) on *four* MiG-17s flying a finger-four formation in two sections – one section which we were locked onto, and another about 2000-3000 ft astern, all at about 18,000 ft. My range was about mid-range (for the AIM-7), and the missile (AIM-7) commenced to guide absolutely beautifully and impacted on the number two MiG, who was on the left wing of number one. It hit just aft of the cockpit, and he blew up and entered a flat spin. I never saw a 'chute ("Biff" Borst added later in the debrief, "Geno said 'We nailed it', and I looked out and saw a MiG-17 with its tail on fire spinning into the ground").

'At that juncture the second section broke left and the first section broke right. I came up in a high yo-yo to the right. My wingman (Lt(jg) Ron C Ludlow, with Lt(jg) Bruce L Hardison as his RIO, in BuNo 150629) was on my right, and he crossed over. I came back down and committed towards the second section, with my wingman hanging in there. A couple of times when I lost sight of them, he was able to take them on a lot better than I was. They appeared to be pretty aggressive, but I don't think they fired anything at us. I certainly didn't see any guns or missiles.

'Shortly after a couple of high-g turns (with the MiG leader), I think I picked up one section of them dead ahead (two aircraft circling at 5000 ft), slightly down at (estimated) three to four miles. I told James Borst to "go boresight", which he did and he locked up immediately at about three miles. The dot was in the centre (of his scope), and they were above mid-range – about a mile or so – so I fired again.

'The missile (AIM-7E) left the launcher, and about 100 to 200 ft from the aeroplane it exploded and broke up into all kinds of pieces. I felt a jarring sensation in

Lt(jg)s Bob Hickey and Jeremy Morris enjoy their first breaths of sea air following a successful 'MiG killing' mission on 26 October 1967. Hickey and Morris were the only 'all-nugget' (first tour naval aviators) crew to down a MiG during *Rolling Thunder*. Both men received the Silver Star for their success on this mission (*via Peter Mersky*)

Visibly elated, Lt(jg) Hickey carefully climbs down from the cockpit of his Phantom II, secure in the knowledge that he has just joined the elite band of US Navy 'MiG killers' (*US Navy*)

The highs and lows of aerial combat. The victorious Lt(jg)s Morris and Hickey talk through the mission with the nearly victorious Cdr Grosshuesch and Lt Souder in VF-143's ready room. The latter pair were robbed of success by equipment failure (*via Peter Mersky*)

the aeroplane – I didn't know if it was jet wash or not. Apparently the right engine had stalled, and I didn't know it.

'From that time on the aeroplane was sluggish. I'd gone into full burner on both engines and performed another high yo-yo to get back on (the MiG). I zipped past one, canopy to canopy, at about 20 ft, and this one I determined to be a camouflaged, olive drab MiG-17. I didn't get a shot at him because he was head-on. I almost got a shot on one more run through. I picked him up again dead ahead at about three miles, but I had about 80 degrees (of turn) to go to get on his tail. I was coming down at him at 30 degrees down, but I couldn't get a "growl" on my Sidewinder because of the aspect. It was a good Sidewinder, but we couldn't get a lock-up on him.

'We met a couple more times, and that's when I looked down and figured out why the jet was so sluggish. The right engine was at idle, and the TOT (Turbine Outlet Temperature) was about 300 degrees, with fuel flow at about 500 lbs, although the throttle was at full afterburner.

'I figured I had a stall, so I pulled it back to idle and started moving the throttle up to 70 to 80 per cent, but I got a heavy rumble in the aeroplane and the rpm dropped off, so I figured I had a fire in the right engine. Utility pressure was down about 1200 lbs, so I figured I had taken a hit from the fire or from the engine itself, and I had better get out of there, so I put full afterburner on the left engine.

'Unfortunately, my wingman's radar malfunctioned, so he could not fire an AIM-7, and since he was a good wingman, supporting me, he was unable to position himself for a Sidewinder shot.

'My wingman had reported that the three remaining MiGs had descended to the south-east towards Phuc Yen. We passed Kep airfield and still had three bogies ahead of us at about ten miles, but they descended in a south-easterly direction. I wanted to get out as quickly as I could, as I wasn't sure what else was going to happen to the aeroplane.'

As Lt Cdr Lund proceeded out at 400 kts and 18,000 ft, his wingman gave BuNo 150629 a thorough look-over, and reported hydraulic fluid all over the underside of the Phantom II. This confirmed his cockpit readings – zero hydraulic pressure, a speed brake warning light and 'the full utility failure routine'. On most Navy F-4s, the hydraulics powered around 27 crucial systems, ranging from the aileron power controls to the chaff dispenser door. 'Geno' Lund continues;

'I came out of burner, started heading south and called for a tanker. I had about 6500 lbs of fuel – barely enough to make it, but I could take another 1000 lbs. Then I realised I couldn't stick my probe out, and couldn't have tanked if I had wanted to. I determined that I could make the ship with about 3500 lbs, going 80 miles out, single-engined at about 300 kts.

The final MiG kill of CVW-14's lively *WestPac* in 1967 was claimed by VF-142's Lt(jg) 'Biff' Borst (RIO) and Lt Cdr 'Geno' Lund on 30 October. They failed to make it back to the the 'Connie' under their own steam, however, as their F-4B was critically damaged during the encounter with the MiG-17 when a recently-fired AIM-7E prematurely exploded just in front of their Phantom II (*via Peter Davies*)

'My wingman looked me over again and reported several holes in my starboard forward Sparrow missile well. He didn't say whether or not they had been caused by cannon fire – they seemed to be ragged holes, which could indicate they came either from the missile motor or fire from the missile as it exploded back down the aeroplane.

'I called the ship and requested a straight-in approach. I'd "dirty up" at about five miles, and I would need assistance after the arresting gear since I wouldn't have any brakes. At eight miles from the ship I attempted to lower the landing gear. Nothing. I pulled both the gear and flap circuit breakers, pulled the gear handle out, and the indicator remained "Up, up, up". My wingman checked, and the doors hadn't even cracked open.'

Repeated attempts and recourse to the emergency pneumatic flap handle failed, suggesting holes in the pneumatic lines also, although the gauge showed 3000 psi. The pair were advised to eject. Fuel was down to 600 lbs, and at one mile from the ship, at 5000 ft;

'Biff and I went through pre-ejection. We lowered our seats, knee-pads off, sat flat in the seat, rudder pedals fully forward, visors down. Biff went first, and I watched him in the rear view mirror. I then pulled the handle and got quite a jolt – a definite shock, then further jolts from the drogue 'chute. I could see a big splash in the water where the aeroplane had gone in.'

Removing his face mask, 'Geno' decided to wait until he was closer to the water before dropping his seat bucket, and he then fell among the parachute lines. Looking up, he saw 'Connie's' rescue helicopter above him. Both men survived the experience unharmed and fought on, although 'Biff Borst was later killed in an ACM accident flying an A-7 Corsair II after he had earned his pilot's wings and transferred to the attack community.

PHANTOM IIs DOWN

In November, renewed US strikes against the MiG bases – especially Phuc Yen – again sent many of the VPAF fighters into neighbouring China seeking refuge, and by month's-end only four MiG-21s and twelve MiG-17s were reportedly still in-country. Despite being seemingly 'on the ropes', the VPAF struck back hard on the 19th when a pair of Phantom IIs were downed by MiG-17s from the 923rd Fighter Regiment as they were vectored in to attack jets detected near Hai Phong's Kien An airfield.

The F-4Bs (BuNos 150997/NL 110 and 152304/NL 115), both from VF-151 off the *Coral Sea*, were jumped by unseen MiG-17s flown by Le Hai and Nguyen Dinh Phuc just as the engagement began, and were downed by missiles – the VPAF also erroneously claimed a third Navy Phantom II destroyed on this day. Lt Cdr C D Clower and Lt(jg) W O Estes (in NL 110) and Lt(jg)s J E Teague and T G Stier (in NL 115) all became PoWs, and Teague later died in captivity.

1967 ended on a heavy note, with fighter activity at a high and US Air Forces faced with a more aggressive and more successful MiG-17 and MiG-21 pilot cadre. Moreover, it had become evident that the North Vietnamese GCI units had improved as well, for VPAF controllers were now able to co-ordinate two pairs of MiG-21s, and were starting to integrate MiG-17s with the 'Fishbeds'.

THE END OF THE BEGINNING

Early 1968 saw limited, but nevertheless aggressive, attacks by VPAF MiGs, which also began to show an interest in US electronic warfare aircraft as well. On 14 January, a USAF EB-66C was shot down over Laos by two 921st Fighter Regiment MiG-21s (flown by Nguyen Dang Kinh and Dong Van Song), and a Navy EC-121 was pursued as it left its patrol station over the Tonkin Gulf just days later.

This pattern continued into February, when a MiG-21 came within 25 miles of an EB-66C orbiting over central Laos. Moreover, of the attacks that did occur, many were in the southern regions of North Vietnam and Laos, where MiGs had traditionally not ventured.

The MiG-21 pilots had also changed their tactics, for they had abandoned their solitary 'shoot-and-scoot' attack runs for multiple passes on targets. The 'Fishbeds' were now also operating in larger flights, and

VF-114 'Aardvarks' would complete four Vietnam deployments during *Rolling Thunder*, and six cruises over the course of the entire conflict. This jet carries four AIM-7Es and two AIM-9Ds, denoting that it was photographed during a MiGCAP or BARCAP mission whilst on *Yankee Station* in 1967-68. Proving that operational flying could be just as hazardous as combat, BuNo 153043 was lost in a mid-air collision with fellow VF-114 jet BuNo 153003 on 15 April 1968. All four crewmen were successfully rescued (*US Navy via Naval Aviation Museum*)

As with all of its Vietnam War *WestPacs*, VF-114 made its 1967-68 deployment aboard *Kitty Hawk* with VF-213. To split the burden of flying multi-role missions, and to allow some degree of specialisation, each F-4 squadron alternated sortie profiles by flying as strike aircraft for one half of the line period and as fighters for the remainder. This also minimised armament reconfiguration problems. The versatility of the Phantom II is clearly shown in this photograph, *Black Lion 104* carrying a mix of Sparrow and Sidewinder missiles, as well as 12 500-lb Mk 82 bombs (*US Navy*)

At some point during VF-114's 1967-68 *WestPac*, the unit added a black-trimmed orange stripe to the fuselage of its F-4Bs. All embarked Phantom IIs within CVW-11 also boasted a full suite of AN/APR-30 RHAW antennae on the fin tip and beneath the AAA-4 infrared sensor on the underside of the radome. Note that the auxiliary engine bay cooling door is open in this photograph of *Linfield 205*, taken in March 1968. CVW-11's efforts on this cruise earned *Kitty Hawk* the first Presidential Unit Citation awarded to a carrier during the Vietnam War. This honour was bestowed on the ship for spending 90 consecutive days on the line (*via Aerospace Publishing*)

On *Yankee Station* with CVW-11 and the *Kitty Hawk* in 1968 was CVW-9 and the *Enterprise*. VF-92 shared the fighter duties with VF-96 on this cruise, and lost three jets on deployment – one to a MiG-21 and two operationally, including this machine on 2 June 1968. The crew were recovered (*via Brad Elward*)

on one occasion no less than four MiG-21s were joined by four MiG-17s. Overall though, air operations were greatly restricted for much of February because of persistently poor weather.

And in the engagements that did take place, the Air Force claimed all the kills, although the price it paid for the five victories scored (exclusively by F-4Ds) was three aircraft shot down – an F-105D, an F-4D and an F-102A, all of which were claimed by MiG-21s from the 921st Fighter Regiment.

On 31 March, just a little more than three years after *Rolling Thunder* strikes had commenced, President Johnson announced that he was halting all air strikes north of the 20th latitude. Shortly thereafter, the line was moved further south to the 19th Parallel. This cessation shifted the bulk of American air power southward, beyond the range of both GCI units and MiGs, as well as most of the North's SAM sites.

Following the bombing halt, the VPAF immediately began to move its MiGs back into North Vietnam from their bases in China, where they had been hiding from the *Rolling Thunder* assaults on their bases. These fighters now turned their attention to the Navy strike packages, as the only Paks within the permitted bombing areas were Paks I, II and III, of which the latter two were controlled by the Navy.

To counter the renewed MiG threat, the Navy implemented a plan calling for all strike aircraft to leave the area when MiGs were sighted in order to give the F-4 crews a chance to launch their AIM-7s at greater ranges, and without the need for a visual ID. In addition, the Navy

Silver Kite 214 taxies in at an undisclosed base in South Vietnam after diverting ashore due to bad weather over the Gulf of Tonkin in early 1968. The efforts of both CVW-9 and -11 were often stymied by cloud over the target areas during this period (*via Brad Elward*)

VF-92's sister-squadron within CVW-9 was VF-96, which debuted its distinctive 'Black Falcon' marking on the 1968 deployment. Arguably the most famous squadron emblem in naval aviation during the Vietnam War, it had been designed by VF-96 RIO Lt(jg) John E Wohlfiel between the 1967 and 1968 *WestPacs*, and applied to the unit's F-4Bs at Miramar prior to embarking on the *Enterprise* on 3 January 1968 for the unit's fourth wartime *WestPac*. Officially approved by the Chief of Naval Operations on 7 March 1969, it remained in use until VF-96 was disbanded in 1975. The Phantom II at the extreme right of this photograph is BuNo 153036, which Capt John Heffernan (USAF) and Lt(jg) Frank Schumacher used to down a MiG-21 on 9 May 1968 (*via Angelo Romano*)

intended to use communications jamming aircraft to disrupt VPAF GCI units attempting to warn MiGs of impending Phantom II intercepts.

These tactics, combined with the fact that the MiGs were now operating at the limit of their GCI and SAM network, were believed sufficient to alter the air war in favour of US forces. Also significant was the fact that Navy aircraft were much closer to their own GCI, and could now rely on American SAMs for protection. Indeed, on 23 May a MiG had been downed by a Navy Talos missile launched from the cruiser USS *Chicago* (CG-11) – one of seven fighters claimed by Navy SAMs during the war.

Despite these advantages, the Navy faced a tough time, and in most cases, its failings could be attributed to poor weapons performance. For example, on 7 May 1968 five F-4Bs from VF-92 (embarked on the *Enterprise*) engaged a section of MiG-21s and fired two Sparrows. Both rounds missed, but in the ensuing fight F-4B BuNo 151485/NG 210 was lost to an AAM fired by the 921st Fighter Regiment's Nguyen Van Coc. The Phantom II's crew, Lt Cdr W M Christensen (pilot) and Lt(jg) W A Kramer, were both recovered.

Two days later, two VF-92 Phantom IIs again engaged three MiG-21s, firing four Sparrows. Although it is believed the crews scored one 'probable' and one 'possible' kill on this occasion, no official confirmation was forthcoming.

A KILL AT LAST

Although VF-92 had seemingly missed out on both 7 and 9 May, sister-squadron VF-96 did at last register a kill for CVW-9, although this still remains unconfirmed by the Navy to this day.

On the morning of 9 May, two F-4Bs launched from *Enterprise* and established their ForceCAP (Task Force Combat Air Patrol) orbit off the southern SAR east of Hon Matt, along a north-west to south-east axis. In the lead jet (BuNo 153036/NG 602) was USAF exchange pilot Capt John P Heffernan and RIO Lt(jg) Frank A Schumacher, with Lts Robert H Clime and Eugene L Sierras in the second fighter (NG 611).

Soon after arriving on station some 35 miles off the North Vietnamese coast, the crews received a message from *Loveland* (the fighter controller), who reported 'MiGs south Bullseye heading south 50, number uncertain'. Shortly thereafter, *Loveland* called 'three Blue Bandits', but instructed the crews to hold missiles and position while the area was 'sterilised'. At about 1017 hrs they were given a 'vector to bogie' and were 'cleared to fire'. The two Phantom IIs headed to the coast, gaining speed and dropping their centreline tanks.

Its deck crammed full of A-4E/Fs, A-6As and EKA-3Bs, CVAN-65 cruises through the Gulf of Tonkin in 1968. CVW-9 lost 11 aircraft in combat and four operationally during its 100 days on the line on this deployment. Of this number, four were F-4Bs
(*via Angelo Romano*)

The initial vector to the bogies was 270 degrees, 611 establishing an immediate 'lock' at 12 miles and calling contact to 602, which now became the wing jet. By this time the F-4s were speeding towards the MiGs at a speed of Mach 1.2 and a height of approximately 12,000 ft. Closure was now around 850 kts overtake.

At four-and-a-half miles Lt Clime fired a Sparrow missile, which drifted downward. Capt Heffernan then loosed off a second AIM-7E, which was observed to track in a straight path toward the target. Once the missiles had fired, Lt Sierras looked up and saw the sun, while Clime saw 'a burst of grey smoke' directly where the missile had been, but had lost visual on the round because of a 'thunderbumper' (high clouds) in the area, and the sun into which the aircraft was heading.

While the RIO was trying to locate the missile, the Phantom II's AN/ALQ-51 (missile track breaker) repeat light had come on, telling the pilot to 'break right'. Clime then triggered chaff, consuming a total of 19 bundles. As the F-4 pulled from ten to fifteen degrees off, the RIO saw an 'instantaneous blossom and then break lock'. The Phantom II's defensive turn meant that the jet was now heading away from the target area.

Minutes after the first MiG had been engaged, Clime and Sierras had an encounter with a second fighter. Just before the crew had fired its first AIM-7, Heffernan had started to descend, crossing to the other side of 611. From below, Clime saw both launches, and noted that 'the first

VF-96's CO for its 1968 *WestPac* was Cdr Joseph M Paulk, and *Showtime 601* (BuNo 153022) was 'his' aircraft. This photograph was taken prior to the unit's MiG kill in May, as two victory symbols were painted in the small black triangle at the fin root in the wake of this success. The second marking denoted the Chinese MiG-17 downed by VF-96 in April 1965 (*via Peter Mersky*)

This photograph graphically illustrates the bad weather encountered by carriers on *WestPac* in 1968, CVAN-65 shuddering through mountainous waves en route to the Japanese port of Sasebo from Pearl Harbor in mid-January. The 'Big E' subsequently spent several weeks on the hastily-created *Defender Station* in the Sea of Japan following the seizure of the naval 'spy' ship USS *Pueblo* (AGER-2) by the North Koreans on 23 January 1968. The carrier finally commenced *Rolling Thunder* operations from *Yankee Station* on 22 February (*via Peter Mersky*)

missile seemed to stay level and the second appeared to guide well straight along the aircraft axis'.

As Heffernan broke away from his wingman because of the missile threat warning, Schumacher picked up a second contact and 602 fired off another Sparrow at just over five miles. While the missile was in flight, both the pilot and RIO observed a 'wing flash' from the sun. The pilot saw a second flash, followed by a fireball and black smoke. A second contact was then picked up at 13 to 15 miles. 'About 15 seconds later, with lock-on at 11 miles head-on noted (and) 1600 knots closure', the crew attempted to fire a missile, and the EPU (electrical pulse unit, which supplies internal power to the missile) ignited, but the Sparrow failed to fire or leave the launcher.

The crews' post-mission report noted that, in their best estimate, and because of the missile's performance, visual, and radar cues, Heffernan's second shot 'was a kill'. Indeed, through electronic intelligence, VF-96 confirmed that of the three MiG-21s airborne at this time, only two radar contacts remained after the second Sparrow round had detonated.

VF-96's 'Class of '68' pose for the squadron's cruise book photograph towards the end of CVAN-65's *WestPac*. 'MiG killers' Lt(jg) Schumacher and Capt Heffernan can be seen in the front row, third and fourth from the right respectively. Squadron CO, Cdr Paulk, is crouched immediately behind the VF-96 *MiG KILLERS* sign, whilst the creator of the 'Black Falcons' emblem, Lt(jg) Wohlfiel, is standing at the extreme right. Note the MiG silhouettes in the black triangle on the tailfin of *Showtime 607* (*via Peter Mersky*)

Heffernan and Schumacher's *Showtime 602* was transferred to the Marine Corps at the end of CVW-9's 1968 *WestPac*, and it would see out the rest of its military service with the 'Flying Leathernecks'. Initially flown by VMFA-323, the fighter completed two combat tours with VMFA-115, flying from Chu Lai and Da Nang. Seen here in more peaceful times at Misawa AFB, Japan, in August 1974 (the unit was then based at Naha, on Okinawa), the veteran Phantom II was rebuilt as an F-4N in 1975-77 and then issued to reserve-manned VMFA-321. It was finally written off in an accident on 21 January 1981 (*Norm Taylor*)

Debuting the F-4J in combat, VF-102 experienced a frustrating *WestPac* deployment on the *America* in 1968. The unit frequently encountered MiGs but failed to down a single example through persistent radar, fire control or missile failure. To make matters worse, the squadron CO, Cdr W E Wilbur, and his RIO, Lt(jg) B F Rupinski, were shot down by an 'Atoll' missile fired from a MiG-21. Wilbur was subsequently captured but Rupinski was killed (*via Peter Davies*)

Despite this information, some post-war histories have listed this claim as a 'probable' (the USAF, for example, does not include Capt Heffernan in its official list of 'MiG killers'), while others have speculated that the MiGs could have been Chinese fighters, which might explain why the crew did not receive any medals for this shoot-down.

On 16 June, the pattern of engagements typified in May continued as two VF-102 F-4Js from USS *America* (CVA-66) encountered a pair of 921st Fighter Regiment MiG-21s over Do Luong. Four Sparrows were fired but no hits were registered. VF-102, however, had BuNo 155548 downed by an 'Atoll' missile fired by Dinh Ton, and although squadron CO, Cdr W E Wilbur, ejected and was captured, his RIO, Lt(jg) B F Rupinski, was killed. Wilbur and Rupinski had suffered radio failure at a crucial point in the engagement, thus failing to hear a missile warning shouted by their wingman.

Further unsuccessful missile launches took place on several other occasions during June and in total, F-4s from the *Enterprise* and *America* launched over 17 AIM-7s in three engagements without registering a hit.

The vast number of missile failures, and difficulties with ACM, as highlighted by the problems experienced by the Phantom II crews on station during the early summer of 1968, were the result of many factors. Here, ex-Topgun instructor Jim Ruliffson explains his view of the weaknesses in the F-4 community as a whole during the *Rolling Thunder* years, his comments reflecting the tenure of many of the actions during 1968;

'I've always contended that the F-4 was easy to fly in a mediocre way, but very difficult to fly well in ACM. Contributing to this theory were the following factors. Firstly, early lieutenant and above transition pilots came from the Demon (F3H) community, where they had flown an interceptor instead of a fighter, and been trained with the attendant focus on interception, where 30 degrees of bank was an unusual attitude.

'Secondly, the early Navy and Air Force Phantom IIs (F-4B/J and F-4C/D, respectively) had no internally-mounted gun, and the missile envelopes were narrow, hard to recognise visually, and were "foreign" to previous experience.

'Thirdly, no one understood the technical aspects of missile employment. Manoeuvring to either AIM-9 or AIM-7 envelopes was WAY more complicated than lining up for a guns kill, although doing this in an F-4 presupposed an unsuspecting and non-manoeuvring target.'

VF-33's SOLE MiG KILL

Following the mixes between MiGs and F-8s during late June and early July (which resulted in two kills for the older Navy fighter), the last Phantom II fighter engagement of *Rolling Thunder* took place on the afternoon of 10 July, when four MiG-21s were detected as they raced south to harass Navy strike forces.

Twenty-four hours earlier, MiG-17s had attacked an RF-8 reconnaissance aeroplane and its escort, resulting in a Crusader kill for Lt Tony Nargi of VF-111 Det 11 (embarked in the *Intrepid*).

On the 10th, and pursuant to the Navy's new policy, all friendly aircraft were cleared from the area, and the Phantom IIs went searching for the quartet of MiG-21s. The victorious pilot, Lt Roy 'Outlaw' Cash (whose famous uncle was just about to release his legendary *Johnny Cash at Folsom Prison* recording), describes the engagement;

'We had been on *Yankee Station* since the end of May, with one visit to Cubi Point in late June, so we were back after a "July 4th" break at the Cubi "O Club". On 10 July 1968, I was scheduled for a MiGCAP as wingman to Maj Charlie Wilson (callsign "Rootbeer 202" as I recall), a USAF exchange pilot who had been in the squadron for about a year, and had joined us on our Mediterranean cruise the year before – his RIO on this sortie was Lt(jg) Bill Williams. I made the whole Med cruise, so I was fairly experienced both in the aircraft and the squadron.

'Our jets were brand new F-4Js (Cash flew BuNo 155553/AE 212), our Med cruise F-4Bs of the previous year having been traded in for them in early 1968.

'Charlie and I (with Lt Joseph 'Ed' Kain as RIO) launched mid-afternoon at around 1500 hrs and were assigned a MiGCAP station about 15 miles off Vinh, clear of the beach but close enough to "Buster" feet dry if needed. We determined soon after launch that Charlie's radar was marginal to non-existent, so it was agreed that if we took a vector for bandits I would assume the lead. We quickly established CAP station, then about 45 minutes to one hour into the flight, our controller, *Raider* (on the cruiser USS *Horne* (CG-30)), called us over to cipher frequency to alert us to impending MiG activity.

Sharing the fighter responsibilities with VF-102 aboard the *America* in 1968 was VF-33. This photograph shows the unit's 'CAG bird' at rest aboard CVA-66 during the carrier's Yokosuka portcall in August. The 'Tarsiers' had certainly deserved a break from the fighting, as in July the unit had flown 524 sorties and accumulated 917.9 flight hours – 178 sorties and 327.8 hours were flown at night. Exposed to 'MiGs, missiles and AAA' on a near-daily basis, VF-33 lost three jets (and one crewman) and VF-102 two machines (and also one crewman) in combat (*via Aerospace Publishing*)

'Basically, the information boiled down to the fact that MiGs were about to launch and sortie down to attack the A-7s on their strike missions below the "no-bomb" line just north of Vinh.

'*Raider* kept us apprised of the increasing activity and MiG communications (our ECM and "spy" planes had picked up good info on the MiGs, apparently), switching us back and forth from clear to cipher frequencies. We told *Raider* that in the event we were vectored, we wanted to fly a specific attack profile, and they concurred. That profile was as follows – we would vector west at high speed and low altitude to gain a position south-west of the approaching MiGs so as to be able to vector north-west with the afternoon sun over our left shoulders. That might provide surprise, and put us in a position so the bandits could not see us well – coming out of the sun.

'The MiGs' tactics at this point in the war were to dash in over the "no-bomb" line, shoot at the A-7s and retreat north before fighters could be vectored for them.

'The MiGs finally launched and started south. *Raider* vectored us west, we jettisoned our centreline tanks, armed missiles and hit the deck. We went down to 1500 ft and got to the karst ridgeline just as the MiGs headed south and crossed the line. We were vectored north-east, turned and pointed to the area they were coming from, and immediately got a PD (Pulse-Doppler) radar contact – at 32 miles, as I recall. We were still low, and the MiGs were at around 5000 ft.

'On cipher we were told that they were two "blue bandits", which identified them as MiG-21s (MiG-17s were "red"), and there were no other known bandits in the area. Also, we were told that the MiGs' communications were being jammed by our EA-3 ECM bird, sitting just off the coast. That meant they probably would not know we were coming. Great sport!

'We continued at low level at a speed of 550 kts, with smoke off (the anti-smoke device on the F-4J diminished the amount of smoke emitted by the J79s), in combat spread formation, with Charlie at my three o'clock position so that he could look through me at "bad guy" country. He still had no radar. Since the MiGs had been "positively" ID'ed, I asked for "clearance", meaning clearance to fire. To my utter amazement *Raider* responded "Roger, contacts are two blue bandits – you are cleared to fire!"

'Ed and I were ecstatic, since it was normal to have to gain VID (Visual ID). I checked that the switches were armed and ready, and made sure that the missiles indicated good. We were loaded with two AIM-7E Sparrows and four AIM-9G Sidewinders. I reviewed in my mind procedures for switching from "radar" to "heat", and we kept on tracking.

'We maintained radar contact continuously, down to 20 miles, and we checked everything again, keeping Charlie up to speed on the situation. He was to maintain visual lookout for other bandits who might be hiding in the weeds. At 12 miles I reconfirmed "clear to fire" with *Raider* and began looking intently for any sign of bogies. At eight miles I called "tally ho two, on the nose". What I really saw were two glints from the bright sun behind us on the silver fuselages of the MiGs, not the aircraft themselves, but from eight miles I never lost sight of them.

'Locked on, dot in the centre, MiGs head-on – it looked good for Sparrow shots down the throat. At five to six miles the missile launch circle began to expand, indicating maximum range, expanding to mid or optimum range. At four miles the circle reached its largest diameter, indicating that the optimum firing parameters had been met. I fired off two Sparrows and called "Fox one, Fox one". The Sparrows appeared to guide, heading for what looked like an imminent kill.

'The range on radar suddenly appeared to freeze at three-four miles, and I watched as the MiGs, now fully in sight and looking like aeroplanes and not sun glints, began a lazy left turn away from us . . . and the missiles! Guess what the Sparrows did? They saw the decreasing Doppler, and by the time they got to the MiGs the missiles were looking at a belly-up, beam aspect. They exploded harmlessly at the wingman's two o'clock position, about 100 yards away.

'Until the Sparrows exploded, the MiGs did not know we were there. The wingman, apparently startled by the Sparrows, broke into the explosions, but then turned back left to stay with his leader. He then apparently realised I was quickly approaching a good six-seven o'clock firing position, and again broke hard into me, by this time rapidly closing to a firing position. The MiGs were only flying at about 350 kts, so the wingman quickly came into me and was just as quickly inside minimum range.

'I had switched to heat and fired off a Sidewinder, but the aspect was almost 90 degrees off at less than 1000 ft, so the AIM-9 missed. However, it scared him so badly he continued his descending right break, hit the deck and headed north out of the fight.

'Meantime, I was performing a high-g left barrel roll to get in behind the leader who, by this time, had figured out the programme and was breaking right into me. My wingman broke left over the top of me and spotted two more MiG-21s down in the weeds, about three miles away. Simultaneously, *Red Crown* (USS *Long Beach* (CGN-9)) broadcast, "Heads up 'Rootbeers'. You got two more bandits west".

'I was too busy to respond, and Charlie was telling me he saw them too, so I continued turning, and with my energy, combined with the MiG leader's bad position and slow speed, I quickly attained the six o'clock at about 1500 to 1800 yards and fired an AIM-9G. I watched it guide and impact the tail area of the MiG, blowing the empennage completely off. The pilot obviously knew he was had because almost simultaneously with the impact I saw his 'chute. It appeared he had ejected either just before impact, or as it occurred.

'Meantime, Charlie had called out something to me about breaking. I didn't hear it, but what he said was, "'Outlaw', break left . . . I mean RIGHT!" (I got to hear it on the tape later). One of the MiGs hiding in the weeds had fired off an "Atoll", well out of range, and I was vaguely aware of its smoke trail corkscrewing lazily across the sky, well away from me.

'I broke back to where the other MiGs were coming from and saw them hit the deck about two-three miles away. They turned tail and ran. As soon as they were tail-on they disappeared, vanished – couldn't find them, visually or on radar, so I called to Charlie to "Unload, unload. Bug out, bug out!" and we headed for the water. We called "feet wet", and *Raider* called and confirmed, "Splash one blue bandit, Rootbeers". I responded with something like, "You betcha *Raider*. I got that son of a gun".

'We hit the tanker, took on enough gas to get to the ship, and I performed the best rendition of a victory roll I could imagine. The ship and Air Wing crews swarmed me after landing in much the same way depicted in the movie *Top Gun*, when "Maverick" and "Iceman" return to the ship after shooting down the bad guys. It was a neat feeling to be a hero for the day – in fact, hero for the cruise.

'I gave up smoking as a result of that kill. I had told some of the guys jokingly, "If I shoot down a MiG today I'm going to quit smoking". I suppose God said, "Oh yeah? Let's see if you really mean it". I haven't smoked since.'

This engagement was important from the standpoint that it illustrated how the Navy's engagement philosophy 'should' work if all of the tactics developed earlier in the year came together. The GCI jamming was excellent, and played an important role in confusing the MiGs by severing them from their guidance.

Clearing the area also permitted the Phantom II to employ its BVR weapon, the Sparrow III, without fear of inadvertently hitting a friendly. Had the Sparrow functioned properly, the kill would have been textbook. This engagement was also significant because it represented not only the squadron's first MiG kill, but also the first aerial kill for an F-4J, and for an Atlantic coast-based fighter squadron.

But the successes of the 10 July engagement were short-lived, and the Navy's troubles continued in August when, on the 17th, two F-4s from VF-142, embarked on the *Constellation*, were fighting it out with a pair of MiG-21s. The lead Phantom II crew settled into a firing position, only to discover that their missile would not launch. The MiG then lit its afterburner and soared off, but another 'MiG' appeared in the distance, head-on.

The second 'MiG' fired a missile, hitting the F-4B (BuNo 151404/NK 206) flown by Lt(jg) Mark Gartley and Lt Bill Mayhew. The Phantom II went down and its crew were delivered into North Vietnamese hands for the remainder of the war. It is believed that the other 'MiG' was in fact an F-4, and possibly Gartley and Mayhew's wingman. If this was indeed the case, then the missile that downed them was an AIM-9D.

The summer of 1968 had proven more than a little frustrating for the Navy's deployed Phantom II units. They had launched dozens of AIM-7Es and managed just one unconfirmed hit. The AIM-9D was enjoying marginally better success, but crews were still having problems defining its firing envelope – particularly in the heat of combat or in a high-g environment.

From an aircraft perspective, the Navy had lost two Phantom IIs to MiGs and officially 'bagged' just one VPAF fighter in return (although VF-96's 9 May kill was almost certainly a definite, despite the Navy failing

Lts Roy Cash Jr and Joseph E Kain Jr pose with their suitably-decorated F-4J (BuNo 155553) several days after their MiG-21 kill on 10 July 1968. The caption for this official US Navy photograph read;
'A star of a different kind was added to this Phantom on board the aircraft carrier *America* in the Tonkin Gulf. Two proud aviators, pilot Lieutenant Roy Cash Jr., Memphis (left) and Radar Intercept Officer Lieutenant (junior grade) Joseph "Ed" Kain Jr., Haverton, Pa, downed a North Vietnamese MIG-21 during an engagement west of Vinh on July 10.
'The MIG symbol is now displayed on the aircraft, *America's* bridge and the staterooms of the Phantom crew. The MIG kill was the first for Fighter Squadron 33, Carrier Air Wing Six and the USS AMERICA, ALL on their first deployment to the Tonkin Gulf. AMERICA is home ported in Norfolk; VF-33 is from Oceana, Virginia'
(*US Navy via Peter Mersky*)

to confirm this), and a couple of possible/probables. To make matters worse for the F-4 community, the austere F-8 had faired considerably better, claiming five MiGs destroyed for no losses in six engagements.

USAF F-4Ds had also enjoyed mixed results in 1968, losing three Phantom IIs (as well as an F-102A and an F-105D) to MiGs, while striking eight VPAF fighters from the sky. More importantly, however, all of the confirmed USAF MiG to Phantom II kills were by 'Fishbeds'.

On 1 November 1968, the air campaign known as *Rolling Thunder* came to an end with the announcement by President Johnson that he was suspending all air attacks against North Vietnam in exchange for assurances from Hanoi that they would respect the DMZ, stop supporting insurgency operations in the South, and engage in peace talks. US Air Forces continued to fly *Blue Tree* reconnaissance missions throughout 1968 and 1969.

In all, over one million sorties were flown as part of *Rolling Thunder*, delivering 500,000 tons of munitions and costing the lives of 382 pilots and 289 airmen, and placing a further 702 in North Vietnamese PoW camps or on the Missing in Action (MIA) list.

In air-to-air combat, Navy F-4 crews had claimed 13 VPAF MiGs (including the 9 May 1968 MiG-21 'kill' by VF-96), seven of which were MiG-17s and the remaining five MiG-21s, plus two An-2 cargo aircraft, at the cost of five Phantom IIs. The F-4, despite the touting of many that it was the supreme fighter, trailed the F-8 by five kills, and posted an F-4-to-MiG kill ratio of just 3.25 to 1.

TOPGUN

s the *Rolling Thunder* aerial campaign ground to a halt in 1968, an event was unfolding back in the United States that would change the face of naval aviation. As the statistics on the air war were amassed and digested, few could argue that the Navy F-4 crews had performed to a historical par.

Each year of the air campaign saw an ever greater number of aircraft lost to MiG activity, rising from a low of one per cent in 1965 to three per cent in 1966 and eventually reaching twenty-two per cent by the end of 1968. While this rise can in part be attributed to improved anti-SAM and anti-AAA tactics, it nevertheless signalled that there was a serious problem.

Despite the air combat experiences gained in World War 2 and Korea, the Navy as a whole had abandoned the art of dogfighting and placed too much faith on technology to supplant raw aerial skills. Certainly the F-8 community had its 'gunfighters' who still understood the art of ACM, and the value of manoeuvring to an enemy's six o'clock position. But the F-8 community was shrinking and the aircraft on its way out as more squadrons transitioned to the F-4 and the *Essex*-class carriers, capable of operating only Crusaders, were retired.

Perhaps the first sign of this trend towards a reliance on missile technology was the elimination during the late 1950s of the Fleet Air Gunnery Unit (FAGU), which emphasised ACM and gun skills. Possessing no BVR capability, F-8 pilots knew that they had to drive to the heart of the enemy's rear to obtain a good gun or heat-seeker kill.

But the Navy's failure to abide by time-tested ACM tactics was only half the story. There was a serious hardware problem as well. Simply put,

In standard fighter configuration, the F-4 carried four AIM-7E Sparrow III missiles on stations 3, 4, 6 and 7, and two AIM-9D Sidewinders (one apiece) on stations 2 and 8. Strike configured Navy F-4s carried their air-to-ground ordnance, plus two AIM-7Es on stations 3 and 7. It was the employment of all this weaponry that concerned senior naval aviators as *Rolling Thunder* ground on, and they in turn created Topgun to ensure greater success for Phantom II crews 'hassling' with VPAF MiG-17s and MiG-21s. This photograph was taken in December 1964 by the CO of VF-96, Cdr Bill Fraser. Specially cleaned up for the camera, F-4B BuNo 150638 is seen in BARCAP/TARCAP (and eventually MiGCAP) configuration. Aside from the jet's eight missile load-out, note its ubiquitous centreline 600 US-gal 'fixture' tank (*via Robert F Dorr*)

the missiles provided to the Navy and Air Force crews – the same ones that were touted as the 'end-all' to close-in dogfighting – were not living up to their advertised use. Regularly, missiles would not launch, or failed to track, and even when they did track, there were still numerous occasions when they failed to explode or simply missed the target altogether.

Prior to the Vietnam War, the AIM-7 Sparrow had been held out as the world's premier BVR missile. The weapon had shown both in pre-delivery testing and in-fleet training exercises that it could down enemy aircraft at long-range before the target even knew F-4s were in the area. While this was a fine concept when being launched over test ranges in the Nevada or California deserts, or the Pacific missile ranges, the Sparrow failed miserably in an environment governed by restrictive ROE that required visual identification before launch.

And with the small size of the MiG-17 and MiG-21, abiding by these ROEs meant that the bandit was now within the Sparrow's minimum range, and essentially useless unless the crew could extend and re-acquire.

Moreover, ROEs aside, the AIM-7 was simply conceptually ahead of its engineering time. For various reasons, Sparrows had a very high failure rate (overall 63 per cent), and even when launched within envelope, suffered from guidance problems (29 per cent missed). The missile was complex to operate, and took five seconds between lock-on and launch, which was totally unsuitable for the fast-moving dogfight environment.

To further complicate matters, the AIM-7's symbology was geared towards a straight and level flying target such as a Soviet bomber, rather than a manoeuvring VPAF fighter. Moreover, it left huge white smoke plumes, making its presence well known to its intended foe.

The heat-seeking AIM-9B Sidewinder proved equally problematic. While experiencing a somewhat better kill ratio than the Sparrow, the AIM-9 nevertheless suffered a 56 per cent failure rate, and missed approximately 28 per cent of its targets. Actual combat also exposed the Sidewinder's exceptionally small firing envelope, which shrunk dramatically if either the target or the host aircraft manoeuvred!

The AIM-9 was also distracted by clouds and ground-clutter, and crews often misunderstood the missile's firing envelope, taking its 'tone' as an indicator that the missile was ready to fire, rather than an indication that it had sensed a heat source. Even with good tone, the Sidewinder had to be launched within its envelope – some 28 per cent of AIM-9B firings were out of envelope. Fortunately, this figure dropped some to 13 per cent with the introduction of the greatly improved AIM-9D.

There were other problems as well. The F-4 itself had many limitations built into its design, as John Nash remembers;

'The radar was unreliable. The F-4 cockpit was not configured or designed to function in the high-g ACM environment. We (VF-121/Topgun) supplied ACM cockpit optimisation recommendations in 1968-69 which helped considerably, but "too little-too late" mods didn't make it until the war was over.'

ANSWERS TO QUESTIONS

It is interesting to note that the Navy and the Air Force, when faced with essentially the same dilemma, came to drastically different conclusions as to the root cause of the F-4's lack-lustre performance in *Rolling Thunder's* air-to-air engagements. The Air Force ignored the possibility that it had a training problem, and instead focused its efforts during the bombing halt on reviving its technology. It introduced the F-4E, with its highly-accurate radar-guided M61 internal cannon and APX-80 IFF interrogator, and also sought the development of an AIM-9B replacement in the form of the AIM-9E and an improved 'dogfight' Sparrow, the AIM-7E-2. This, of course, ignores the Air Force's efforts to develop the AIM-4 Falcon, which proved a total disaster.

By coincidence, one of the five kills credited to the flawed Falcon missile was scored by US Marine Corps pilot Capt Doyle D Baker. On exchange with the USAF, flying F-4Ds with the 13th TFS/432nd TRW out of Ubon, in Thailand, he and WSO, 1Lt John D Ryan, 'bagged' a MiG-17 in 66-7709/OC on 17 December 1967.

Despite drastically upgrading the hardware, the USAF made no co-ordinated efforts to revitalise aircrew training, or to re-evaluate its tactics. Indeed, Air Force F-4 training continued to de-emphasise air-to-air combat, and actually decreased the number of ACM training sorties in favour of air-to-ground sorties.

The Navy, on the other hand, quickly realised that its F-4 crews had been neglected in respect to the amount of ACM training they had received. Part of this realisation came from the recognition of the outstanding performance of F-8 pilots during the *Rolling Thunder* years.

Despite the obvious differences between the aircraft and how they could best fight MiGs, the more significant difference was the quality and quantity of ACM training. While the Navy did introduce some technological improvements such as the F-4J (with AN/APG-59 pulse-Doppler radar) the AIM-9D (and later -9G) and the 'dogfight' Sparrow, the primary focus was on the F-4 crews' lack of any advanced ACM training.

Certainly, there were efforts to boost the jet's abilities as a close-in fighter, and VF-121 took significant steps towards that end by increasing the number of ACM training hops, as well as adding dissimilar ACM hops against F-8s from fellow Miramar-based fleet training unit VF-124.

FORMATION

The Navy Fighter Weapons School (NFWS) formed as a department within VF-121, the West Coast F-4 Replacement Air Group, or RAG, in September 1968 under the direction of Lt Cdr Dan Pederson. The purpose of the department was to serve as a graduate-level course for ACM, and to teach these advanced crews how to return to their squadrons and impart the new knowledge to their cohorts.

Crews coming to the school were expected to already be familiar with basic ACM, and were to have 'a working knowledge of fighter tactics'. According to John Nash, 'Topgun (as the NFWS was soon dubbed) was nothing more than an extended course of the RAG tactics syllabus – a post-graduate course that allowed and demanded that students eat and sleep ACM, and associated air superiority considerations. Topgun used the best and most combat experienced F-4 "drivers" and RIOs that were available, and taught the students to think, plan and execute ACM'.

Earlier that year, in March, the Navy 'brass' in Washington had requested Capt Frank Ault, former CO of the *Coral Sea* and a veteran of several deployments to Vietnam, to form a committee to study the

US Marine Corps Capt Doyle Baker downed a MiG-17 on 17 December 1967 while flying an F-4D on exchange duty with the USAF's 13th TFS/432nd TRW (*via Peter Mersky*)

deficiencies in fighter weapons systems, and in particular the Sparrow. Ault surrounded himself with a capable staff, and left no stone unturned in his quest for answers. 'I was given *carte blanche* to pick anybody I wanted to assist, and to conduct the study in any manner I saw fit'. Ault has described how he approached this selection;

'I looked for people who were recognised by their peers/contemporaries as the most knowledgeable in their respective area of expertise. This resulted in a team of two officers and three civilians – each a self-starter, deeply experienced in their field, capable of independent thought, and with the courage of their convictions. All shared the common characteristics of listeners, not talkers.

'Compartmentalising the "womb to the tomb" study effort permitted me to focus narrowly on each of the five subject areas, and identify the specific credentials required in each case. I wasn't looking for "men for all seasons", but rather "men looking for reasons".'

One of these men was Merle Gorder, a former F-8 tactics instructor at the East Coast F-8 RAG. Ault was told to find a way to increase combat kills by no less than three-fold over that which had already been experienced in Vietnam.

His group started by reviewing all of the prior reports and analysis of air-to-air systems. 'A first order of business', Ault explained in his 1989 article in *Tailhook* magazine, 'was to review what the Navy already had on file'. This included a review of *Sparrow Shoot*, *Combat Sage* and *Red Baron*, as well as other systems-related reports. Ault also conducted field examinations of manufacturing processes, carrier handling and maintaining procedures of the various missiles, and crew weapons employment.

Finally, on 1 January 1969, Capt Ault released his formal written report, totalling 480 pages in length, officially titled the *Air-to-Air Missile System Capability Review*, but later dubbed the 'Ault Report'. In all, the document cited 232 recommendations, one of which championed the establishment of a graduate-level fighter weapons course taught by experts in the field of ACM.

Although many commentators have stated so, Topgun was not created directly from the Ault Report. Indeed, when the findings of the Ault committee were released, work was already underway at VF-121 to develop the Topgun course. However, according to Capt Ault the report played a substantial role in its future.

As previously mentioned, the Ault Report embodied 232 recommendations. Only one of these was the establishment of a fighter weapons school. Precedent for this had been established by the FAGU at NAF El Centro, in California, which had been disestablished some years earlier.

The majority of the meetings of the study group were held at the Naval Missile Center at NAS Point Mugu, again in California. These meetings were usually well attended by members of the West Coast fighter community, and their advice and assistance was always available, and they were always ready to implement work-in-progress recommendations, which, in many cases were their own.

In late 1968 it was decided by Op-05 (pushed by Merle Gorder) to establish an NFWS as a department within VF-121. The latter unit, motivated by people like Pederson and Ruliffson, had already made some modest starts with air-to-air combat training, and the first *official* class

commenced on 3 March 1969. An independent NFWS was not officially commissioned as a command separate from VF-121 until 7 July, 1972.

None of this would have happened without the following;

(1) a report clearly spelling out the need for such training.

(2) participation in the preparation of that report by people who recognised the need for increased ACM training, endorsed the recommendations (which were frequently their own) and were in line to be involved with their implementation.

(3) people who were willing to stick their necks out to get on with it.

(4) low visibility, but effective, support (especially monetary) from Washington.

The report reinforced what the Topgun founders had been preaching. New and improved ACM tactics *must* be taught to the F-4 community.

Also taking place at about the same time, and perhaps equally revealing, were two secret projects called *Have Drill* and *Have Doughnut*, which tested a MiG-17 and MiG-21 'acquired' from the Israelis. Both aircraft were obtained following defections, the MiG-17 hailing from Syria and the MiG-21 from Iraq. The jets were extensively flown by US Navy and Air Force pilots in an attempt to determine first hand the capabilities of the MiGs, and to decipher means to defeat them by using superior tactics.

Following his tour at VF-121 and Topgun, John Nash worked with Project *Have Idea* at VX-4;

'There is no better way to learn to fight MiGs than to fight MiGs. The *Drill* and *Doughnut* projects were quick, and only allowed a limited number of pilots to "see and fight" the MiGs. The projects did allow us to find ways to beat a superior turning fighter. Tactics were written as gospel, and we all trained like we would fight FINALLY! The ringer was that the projects used the best pilots (Navy and Marine), and the MiGs were never flown as effectively in combat as they were in *Drill* or *Doughnut*.

'Flying the MiGs revealed several of their feature characteristics. Both the MiG-17 and MiG-21 were great fighter aircraft. They could out turn any fighter or tactical jet that the Navy had during that period. The MiG-21 could go faster and pull more gs than anything we owned. However, it had zip for radar, zip for missiles, zip for rear visibility (although the F-4 was worse), was a single-piloted aircraft and bled energy like a mother.

'It was hard to see, and if it had been flown by equals to the Navy pilot in Vietnam, it would have been responsible for dozens of kills. The way the US conducted – or ignored – the air war, the MiG-21, in company with the MiG-17, should have wreaked havoc on US Air Forces, rather than just posing a nuisance to our war. The MiG-17 could turn forever,

A 'plain jane' F-4B from VF-121 fires off a Sparrow III over the Pacific in May 1966. The West Coast F-4 Replacement Air Group (RAG) unit which trained new pilots and Radar Intercept Officers (RIOs) trained for Pacific fleet units, VF-121 supplied instructors and aircraft for the first Topgun courses run at Miramar in 1969 (*via The Boeing Company*)

but its speed and energy bleed rates were poor. It was a single-piloted aircraft, with no radar and poor weapons and weapons range.'

As the Ault Report began filtering throughout naval aviation, and particularly the fighter community, the initial instructor cadre was formed under Lt Cdr Pederson's leadership. All of the instructors were experienced crew members, many with Vietnam tours already under their belt. A typical example was Jim Ruliffson, who had completed one combat tour already, and was in the tactics section of VF-121. His speciality with the school was missiles, particularly the Sparrow III. Ruliffson was a superb pilot, and very strong in ACM.

Mel Holmes was also a veteran of a Vietnam deployment, and was regarded as one of the best F-4 pilots in the Navy. Darrell Gary and Jim Laing (a MiG killer with VF-114 in April 1967) were exceptional RIOs, as was Steve Smith, and all had seen action from either the *Kitty Hawk* or the *Enterprise*. These RIOs worked to prepare the school's radar syllabus.

John Nash rounded out the original group, and brought to the school his air-to-ground experience. A superb pilot, he had completed two Vietnam cruises. Pilot Jerry Sawatzky and Intelligence Officer Chuck Hildebrand also joined just before the March classes began. Sawatzky was also rated by his peers as an outstanding pilot.

SCHOOL STARTS

3 March 1969 marked the start of the first course at the NFWS, now informally called Topgun. The course lasted four weeks, and consisted of 75 classroom hours and 25 aircrew sorties. Courses were taught in aerial combat manoeuvring procedures, air-to-air gunnery, air-to-ground delivery, electronic warfare and fighter performance, with briefings on enemy aircraft and weapons.

Three weeks were devoted to air-to-air tactics and one week to air-to-ground tactics. The latter was later dropped, as the air-to-air portion was too complex to be limited to a three-week course. As an indication of its complexity, the course – later to be known as the Power Projection Course – was extended to five weeks.

Students for the NFWS were selected by their squadrons, and were supposed to represent the finest the fleet had to offer. The students, together with two aircraft and two maintenance crews, came to Topgun for the one-month course, and were intended to return to their squadron to impart their knowledge and assume the role of tactics co-ordinators. Topgun was not intended to make the students stars, while leaving their squadronmates behind.

Students for the first class were selected from VF-142 and VF-143, as these units had just completed a Vietnam deployment. This class included Ron Stoops, Jim Nelson, Jerry Beaulier, Cliff Martin, John Padgett, Jack Hawver, Ed Scudder and Bob Cloyes. The first class graduated in April and the crews

Reflecting the classified nature of its subject matter, much of the photography of the early stages of the *Have Drill* Project is decidely 'vague' in quality. Sadly, this is true of these shots of Vice Adm Tom Connelly, who is seen before, during and after a flight in the ex-Syrian MiG-17F (*US Navy*)

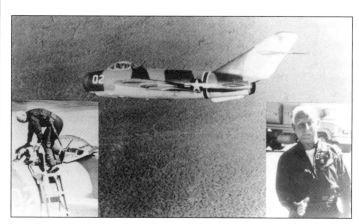

immediately returned to the fleet, ready to share their finely-honed ACM tactics with their fellow pilots. As Jim Ruliffson describes;

'Who got sent to Topgun was the prerogative of the fleet squadron CO. Through message traffic, we and our chain-of-command superiors (VF-121 CO and Commander Fighter Wing Pacific) encouraged the squadron COs to pick one-cruise "polished nuggets – both pilots and RIOs" – and, ideally, assign him/them to be the squadron Training Officer upon their return so that the unit could benefit from his/their experience for the rest of that turnaround training, and the subsequent cruise.

'This worked pretty well. It was also generally true, but left unsaid, that the selectees were to be aircrew who were staying in the Navy. By late 1971 every F-4 squadron deploying had at least one crew – sometimes more – that had been through the course. And by then some of us instructors were also rolling back into the fleet.'

When the school started, it had no equipment of its own, and had to 'acquire' its own trailer at NAS Miramar. John Nash commented, 'The problem was simple. We had no extra money, no place to have a Topgun, no aircraft and no syllabus'. These 'asset' problems were in addition to the fact that the instructors were also flying an incredible schedule with VF-121, Topgun's parent command.

Jim Ruliffson explained that conflicts were minimised as much as possible by scheduling the RAG tactics classes around the incoming Topgun classes. 'Once the RAG students passed through the tactics phase, they headed to the boat for CQs (Carrier Qualifications), which meant that we had time to focus on our Topgun commitments.'

To solve the aircraft dilemma, two-seat TA-4 Skyhawks were borrowed from neighbouring VA-126 (the West Coast instrument flying training RAG) and used by the instructors to simulate communist jets. The TA-4s and later A-4Es simulated the subsonic MiG-17, while the F-8, T-38 Talon and later F-5E Tiger II simulated the MiG-21.

The syllabus was created by the instructors and finalised just as the first class was beginning. Yet, it was recognised that the syllabus would have to evolve. Nash noted, 'The enemy and target for the day/war will dictate the tactics development required'. Moreover, it was understood that there would be some deficiencies in the course work as the instructors honed their skills. 'We began to respond to our "students" inputs and their performance after the first class graduated', Nash explained. 'We tried to fill the holes we saw in the results versus the desired results'.

As the course developed, instructors and students were allowed short flights against the *Have Drill/Doughnut* MiGs. Topgun instructors initially flew the MiGs, followed later by 2v2 instructor/student hops. VX-4 pilots Lt Cdr Foster Teague and Lts Ron McKeown and Mike Welch were 'excellent tacticians in their own right, and quick to exploit any mistakes in the F-4. The common mistakes were trying to turn with the adversary, "arcing" as one tried to separate from the adversary, and lack of precise F-4-to-F-4 team work'.

Topgun was anointed temporary detachment status and became an official detachment on 1 January 1972. This meant that the school could now have its own requisitions, and was no longer dependent on VF-121. On 21 July that same year, Topgun became a separate command, under the leadership of Cdr Roger Box.

Ronald 'Mugs' McKeown, shown here in his Admiral's dress blues, was an important player in discovering the limits of the Phantom II against the MiGs and, while at VX-4, worked closely with the *Have Drill* and *Have Doughnut* projects, evaluating 'captured' MiG-17s and a MiG-21. Putting all this experience to good use once he had returned to the fleet, McKeown downed two MiG-17s on 23 May 1972 while flying with VF-161 (*US Navy*)

PROVING THE POINT

T he bombing halt of November 1968 gave both sides time to reorganise their forces and re-evaluate their tactics, thereby setting the stage for the second segment of the Vietnam air war. The North Vietnamese, despite their assurances to President Johnson that they would seriously pursue peace talks, simply used the time to reinforce their air defences and brace for what they knew would be a renewed US air operation. The VPAF acquired more MiGs and expanded its air defence and GCI network south to Vinh.

The US Navy also used the time wisely, as detailed in the previous chapter, re-examining in detail its air-to-air tactics via Topgun, and deploying a new generation of electronic devices and weaponry to counter the Soviet-built SAMs and radars. This effort left many in the fleet anxiously awaiting the validation of their efforts. But that could only come through a resumed battle 'up North', which had yet to materialise.

The air war in early 1970 consisted of operations over South Vietnam and *Blue Tree* missions for the *Yankee Station* carriers. Any offensive actions against North Vietnam were prohibited – especially any attack on the MiG bases. Indeed, MiG encounters were authorised only as a self-defence measure. However, on 28 January, in a break from prior practice, a 921st Fighter Regiment MiG-21 flown by Vu Ngoc Dinh ventured into southern Laos and shot down an Air Force HH-53B helicopter of the 40th Aerospace Rescue and Recovery Squadron that was attempting to rescue the crew from a downed F-105G. All six crewmen were killed.

In March, in an effort to deter further such attacks, the Navy began experimenting with keeping its BARCAPs low, under the Vietnamese radar, and trying to pull the MiGs down the 'panhandle' to a position where they could be intercepted. On the 27th this tactic worked, for two F-4Js from VF-143 (embarked on the *Constellation*) were despatched to

CVW-14's VF-143 conducted its first *WestPac* with the F-4J between 11 August 1969 and 8 May 1970. During the cruise the unit was restricted primarily to flying bombing sorties against targets in Laos (VF-143 suffered the sole Phantom II loss of the deployment during just such a mission on 22 November 1969) and South Vietnam, and escorting RA-5Cs on *Blue Tree* photo-recce missions of North Vietnam. However, in a break from the norm, two F-4Js from VF-143 came close to downing a pair of MiG-21s on 27 March. Indeed, two Sparrow missiles were fired, but both rounds failed to find their targets. This immaculately presented Phantom II was photographed on the ramp at Miramar several weeks after VF-143 had returned home (*via Brad Elward*)

intercept two MiGs. The crews were given clearance to fire and one of the Phantom IIs launched two Sparrows, but missed.

The next day VF-142 enjoyed greater success.

BEAULIER AND BARKLEY'S MiG

The sole MiG kill claimed by US Air Forces in Vietnam between August 1968 and January 1972 fell to Lts Jerome E Beaulier and Steven J Barkley of VF-142 on 28 March 1970. In the following first-hand account, RIO Barkley describes the engagement, and his relationship with his pilot;

'Both Jerry and I were formerly enlisted (Barkley had seen brief service in the USAF), so we found ourselves several years older than most of the first-tour people. That didn't make much difference, except that our sense of humour was at a higher level. Not to say that we were always on the "up and up" in the cockpit. Beaulier and I often joke about several "divorces" during sorties, but we could never stay mad at each other ("divorced") for an entire flight.

'Being a bit older and perhaps more focused on quality and survival, our missions tended to be fairly well planned and "by our book". By this, I mean we had a set of procedures, checks and counter-checks in which we (privately) took a great deal of pride – look-out doctrine (never miss a bogie), radar search doctrine (never miss a target), equipment checks, navigation and airmanship.

'We spent a great deal of time together apart from flying, and I suppose we discussed every aspect of our various missions. We wanted to have a plan. For example, we discussed whether it was prudent to drop our tanks at the slightest provocation. Our external tanks, given the length of our missions, were necessary. Our concern was why drop the tanks if we probably won't engage? At that point in the war MiGs were almost never sighted, much less a crew would get within Sparrow range of a bandit.

'We concluded that it was more prudent to keep the tanks until the first turn of the engagement. With that kind of drag it wouldn't be tough to be below proper jettison speed for the tanks. The problem was, of course, to remain aware of your speed.

'Beaulier was a recent graduate of Topgun. His class was the first one at the school which spawned the likes of Tom Cruise! He attended Topgun while it was still in the middle hangar of Hangar One at Miramar. That was early in the genesis of Topgun, and the philosophy at the time was a mix of simply making good pilots better, and to provide Fleet units with people prepared with a recent infusion of tactics to be training officers.

'Although the squadrons more or less supported the idea of Topgun, it wasn't apparent at the time that they were ready to embrace everything that the returning warriors had to say. For example, Beaulier was awarded "NATOPS (Naval Air Training and Operating Procedures Standardisation Program) Officer" duties on his return from the course. So much for immediate assignment to Training Officer! But he had frequent opportunities to hold forth in the ready room, so some of what was absorbed at Topgun made its way to a mix of willing ears. So, in a way, Topgun was working even then, but not as some would suggest.

'It took a few years for Topgun to evolve a compelling mission statement, and even then it was a matter of personality and personal ability to make a difference at squadron level (silk purses and sow ears!).

'Certainly it was clear to everyone that speed was life in the McDonnell Phantom. The need for speed was never greater than it was for an engaged Phantom, and management of energy was paramount. That message made it from Topgun and VF-121 instructors to the squadron loud and clear, and the Crusader pilots were always willing to emphasise that point to the F-4 crews.

'My class at VF-121 was the first F-4J class for the RAG. Our class enjoyed distinctions – flights in the F-4A (really!), the F-4B and the newly-introduced F-4J. Our first flights were in the "lead nose" F-4J – without a radar. More importantly, however, our class was the first to enjoy a period of intense tactics training. Before our class, believe it or not, replacement pilots and RIOs would fly ACM now and then, but never more than a couple of flights in a row. ACM flights happened whenever "things came together". It wasn't thought prudent to pack all those flights together and get some focus on what it was all about.

'We were given three aircraft and four instructors, and enjoyed a three-week period of ACM-only flights, interspersed with periods of classroom discussion and ACM "homework" such as mathematically describing manoeuvring "eggs" of various "g", and graphic illustrations of comparative manoeuvring by the F-4 and MiG variants. Who knows if it worked, but it did make a lot more sense than occasional ACM flights accomplishing who knows what? Thereafter, the RAG followed this approach, except the "middle hangar" at Miramar was out – Topgun grabbed it after our class finished.

'By March 1970 Jerry Beaulier and I were well into the routine of a *WestPac* cruise aboard the USS *Constellation*. The ship would sortie out of Subic Bay to Vietnam for about 30 days, followed by five or six days in the Philippines, Hong Kong or Japan. We had 15 crews flying 20 to 22 sorties a day. This translated into one or two sorties a day each, plus standing a "spare" for one sortie. The spare was meant to ensure the squadron launched the requisite number of aircraft (usually two) for each mission.

'A spare aircrew briefed, manned the aircraft, started engines and then watched their buddies launch on a terrific mission. Spare aircrews were launched when one of the main aircraft went "down". This only happened when the mission was either boring (such as BARCAP, approximately 10,000 miles from the nearest threat!), or when it was a moonless night and bad weather.

'Combine a couple of missions with a spare, plus one or two five-minute Alert spells, and you have a full day. Our flying "period" was

Future 'MiG killers' Lts Jerry Beaulier and Steve Barkley received expert tuition flying Phantom IIs with West Coast RAG, VF-121. In fact, they almost certainly logged cockpit time in this nondescript F-4J, photographed on the transient ramp at Edwards AFB during a base open house on 18 May 1969. Beaulier was participating in the very first Topgun course, run by VF-121 instructors, at the time, while Barkley was being taught by the self-same naval aviators to be a fleet-qualified RIO (*via Brad Elward*)

typically 12 hours, but Alert 5s were manned 24 hours a day. This meant that your time for Alert always came in the middle of what would appear to be prime sleeping time.

'Our sorties were mainly into Laos and South Vietnam for bombing missions – a lot of BARCAPs and occasionally a *Blue Tree* (RA-5C escort) into North Vietnam. *Blue Trees* were relatively short and invariably a non-event, as we would sweep through the North at very high airspeeds, spending only a few short minutes overland.

'There was never any defence by the North Vietnamese, apart from an occasional "paint" by a fire-control radar. We never saw a missile fired. Sorties into Laos and South Vietnam were more eventful, as they were usually flown at night, and flak (usually 37 mm) was forthcoming, especially in Laos near the North Vietnamese border. It could be easily seen at night, and there was enough to be interesting, but don't for a minute think about "30 minutes over Tokyo or Berlin". I wasn't in that war, but I'm sure our sorties were pastoral by comparison. Occasionally someone would be hit or shot down, so you didn't want to duel with what you saw.

'We were about two or three weeks into a line period when a USAF rescue helicopter was shot down in Laos by a MiG-21 staging out of the southernmost airfield in North Vietnam. This was quite unexpected, as the North Vietnamese hadn't done anything like this in some time. We were a couple of years into the "no bombing" strategy, so encounters such as these were very rare. They were probably enjoying the lack of attention, and we found it interesting that they should seemingly thumb their noses at us in this manner.

'On 27 March a two-aircraft section from our sister-squadron, VF-143 "Pukin' Dogs", was vectored towards two MiGs. Both F-4Js dumped all tanks, and one aircraft shot a couple of missiles to no avail. I'm not sure that anyone even saw an aircraft, but they were in radar range. That got everyone pumped up. "Now we were in a real shooting war", we thought. That the encounter was the first in over a year, and that the probability of another was very unlikely, was not to be thought about.

'Incidentally, the encounter left the ship short of drop tanks. One section of jets dropped tanks and the ship was short. Good thing it wasn't a real war! We despatched a couple of F-4Js to Cubi to pick up some more. That night Beau and I revisited our plan for tanks, and decided to go with our conviction to drop tanks in a fight when we got slow.

'That night too I was up late writing the flight schedule for 28 March. As Schedule Officer, I was responsible for assigning flights to everyone, including Alerts. My job was to make sure everyone got a fair share at the good flights, that pilots kept night-proficient and Alerts were evenly distributed.

'The Skipper usually reviewed the flight schedule each night. His big deal was that pilots were absolutely even in everything – he didn't keep much track of the RIOs. This meant that a few of us fire-breathing RIOs were a little more even than others.

'The schedule was posted for the 28th, and there we were standing Alert 5 during a midday launch. It didn't help that "scuttlebutt" had it that the ship would be making a fighter sweep over the North during that launch. So, Beaulier and I were destined to sit on the deck and watch our buddies launch into glory. And it was all my fault!

'We manned up for the Alert 5 (in BuNo 155875/NK 201, callsign *Dakota 201*) while the rest of our buddies were manning their aircraft for the scheduled launch. We didn't always start the aircraft at the change of Alert crews, but Beaulier decided he wanted to start up and await the launch with engines running. The Plane Captain cranked the "huffer" (external starter), and we started up and began pre-flight checks.

'Meanwhile, our CO (Cdr Ruel Gardner) and his RIO (Ed Scudder), were spotted on the waist cat and were having trouble getting started. At this point I recall hearing indications on the radio that something was up. We had switched to the CAP frequency and were hearing chatter that led us to believe that, impossibly, the scuttlebutt was right. MiGs were airborne and were being tracked! We quickly switched back to the launch frequency and scanned the deck.

'Gardner and Scudder hadn't started yet, and the rest were beginning preflight checks. Things looked reasonable for our launch, as we were started and ready to go. The next thing we heard over the flightdeck loudspeaker was, "Launch the Alert 5".

'Our attention went up several notches. Gardner was on the catapult, but something wasn't right. The flightdeck crew immediately moved the aircraft off the waist catapult and signalled us to begin to taxy to catapult three on the waist. With the precision borne of a thousand launches, our aircraft was quickly moved into position and made ready for an immediate launch. The nose kicked up and the Catapult Officer gave Beaulier the signal for full power, then afterburners. Everything looked good, and Beaulier gave me an assurance that he was signalling for a launch.

'With a snappy salute from the Cat Officer, the aircraft moved from zero to 140 kts in less than two seconds and we were airborne. We left the ship with two wing tanks, a centreline tank, full internal fuel plus two Sparrows and three AIM-9Ds.

'After the usual VFR departure from *Constellation*, we began an outward track toward *Red Crown* which, on that day, was the USS *Horne*, about 50 miles north-west of the carrier. As other aircraft were being launched, we were instructed to circle as they caught up and radar status was checked. Our radar was fine, and the missiles were okay except for the Number 1 Sidewinder, which was approximately 30 mils off centreline.

'Two F-4Js showed up, crewed by Cdr Paul Speer (the Commander Air Group, or CAG for short) with Lt(jg) John Carter, and Lt Cdr Paul Hakanson with Lt(jg) Dave Van Asdlen. Dave reported his radar was

In an ironic twist of fate, Beaulier and Barkley used *Dakota 201* to down their MiG on 28 March 1970, this machine being assigned to VF-142 CO Cdr Ruel Gardner. The head 'Ghostrider' had in turn been left behind on the deck of CVA-64 when his Alert 5 jet 'broke' prior to launch. Chained down over one of the waist catapults, and ready to launch within five minutes of receiving the word to go, Gardner must have realised it was not going to be his day when his inoperable F-4J was towed out the way so that Beaulier and Barkley could take off in his place . . . in his jet! *Dakota 201* was photographed at Miramar in the late summer of 1970 – note the 'MiG killer' marking near the base of the splitter plate (*via Brad Elward*)

down, and John said his was okay. Hakanson and Van Asdlen were instructed to maintain an orbit in reserve. We joined CAG's aircraft to form the section, which was immediately given a vector: "Vector 273 for bandits at 43 miles".

'CAG Speer (whose fighter experience went back to Korea and three F-8 Crusader tours of Vietnam, and included a MiG-17 kill whilst CO of VF-211 on 19 May 1967) took the lead and we began to close on the coast. Our controller (Petty Officer White) kept us appraised of what was going on: "Bandits at 25 miles, you're cleared to fire. 21 miles, and they've dropped their tanks". It's worth wondering how he knew this, but it would be a pretty good guess to conclude that someone was monitoring their frequency. Either that, or White had some really good binoculars!

'All aircraft were accelerating, and the closure speed was probably greater than 1000 (nautical) mph, so information was useless almost immediately, but White was really doing his stuff. He sounded cool, calm and organised. I was desperately looking for a radar contact as we crossed the beach – then the radar died! I fought it for five miles and then gave up. This was no place for Built-In Tests! I was really disappointed – the perfect set-up for a head-on shot, and no radar! I went heads-up as we were about to go into a fight, and the radar problem could be sorted out later.

'By this time our section was really "hauling the mail". We were in the neighbourhood of 550 kts, and had moved down to about 12,000 ft as White had estimated the MiGs' altitude at about 20,000-22,000 ft. CAG was north of us about a mile, and we were stepped down 2000-3000 ft from him. We still had our tanks, since significant fuel remained, plus we were being "cheap" about our tanks.

'Beaulier got first sight of the MiGs (and so took over the lead in the engagement) as they "flew" out of the canopy bow at one o'clock. He called the sightings and a turn into the MiGs at two o'clock and 22,000 ft, beginning a right-hand climbing turn into the bandits, who apparently didn't see us. Someone in our aircraft commented, "They don't see us!" Neither Beaulier nor myself will admit to making that call, but somebody did and, as you might expect, that's all it took for both MiGs to see us and begin aggressive manoeuvring.

'The fight began with our nose on the MiGs as they crossed in front of us, left to right. CAG was "sucked" (behind us) and trailing us about two miles back. The MiGs turned right into us and began a vertical manoeuvre down into us as they split into singles from the "fighting wing" formation they were maintaining. We turned right into the nearest MiG and kept a visual on the second aircraft, beginning our turn at about 18,000 ft and pulling 5g as we chased the lead MiG through a 360-degree turn.

'The F-4 rapidly lost energy through one of these manoeuvres, especially with the three tanks that we were still dragging. As we struggled through the 90 degrees of turn, our airspeed was 400 kts, and appropriate for you know what! So Beaulier's trusty RIO called "Tanks" when the speed was right, and off went the wing tanks as planned. We kept the centreline tank, as we were still transferring fuel. I've often wondered what the MiGs thought when they saw a jet calmly jettison tanks in the middle of a life or death fight. Did they think we were organised, or just nuts?

'Anyway, we were now fighting for airspeed to keep up with the MiGs, who were now joining up as a fighting wing again (can you believe it?). As

CHAPTER SEVEN

they joined up, somehow they were head-on with CAG Speer, who was out of phase with us and the MiGs, and coming from the opposite direction! The lead MiG launched an "Atoll" at CAG. Remember, this was not CAG's first real fight, but it was certainly John Carter's baptism of fire, and John was focused.

'He saw the "Atoll" launch and called CAG's attention to it, probably in a near-falsetto voice. CAG saw the launch (a big puff of smoke) and the missile leave the MiG. His response to Carter's frantic call was, "No chance". He never varied his course one degree, and the missile passed harmlessly. That's experience!

'The MiGs then split up again, one going left and the other right. We followed the right-turning one and kept a visual on the second MiG, who passed from right to left at our six o'clock as we turned right, chasing the lead aircraft. Beaulier was onto him, and my responsibility was to track the remainder of the fight. I followed the second MiG through our six, and then it turned west and disappeared, with CAG in close pursuit.

'They chased it nearly to Hanoi and then turned back – Cdr Speer was a little late in noticing that the MiG had lit afterburner and dived for home. Alone over enemy territory, and overcast, he heard several SAM warnings and broke off the engagement. Carter, who thought he had a good radar, could never get contact with the MiG. After they were "feet wet" and tanking, he discovered that the radar had an effective range of one mile! What a great radar we had in the F-4J!

'It was later suggested that Speer might have been able to get the MiG because controllers aboard the *Constellation* had been told that the jet was about to run out of gas. This message, however, was not relayed to CAG for fear that it might be intercepted and compromise the fact that we were monitoring voice communications between the MiGs and their controllers.

Dakota 201 accelerates down waist cat four in full afterburner at the start of yet another sortie during 'Connie's' 1969-70 *WestPac*. Written off when it suffered an in-flight engine fire on 26 April 1973, Beaulier and Barkley's 'MiG killer' served exclusively with VF-142 during its four-year career with the Navy (*via Peter Davies*)

'Beaulier and I were lagging our descending MiG about 40 degrees when he apparently lost sight of us and reversed his course. Jerry quickly corrected his turn and put our Phantom at the MiG's dead six o'clock, with Sidewinder selected. Of course, the first Sidewinder to come up was the one with 30 mils offset from centreline. He had checked this earlier and anticipated the correction, which he made.

'With the Sidewinder furiously buzzing, we fired the first missile at the MiG's dead six o'clock at approximately half a mile. It hit the MiG's tailpipe and exploded. With the second Sidewinder now howling, I suggested maybe a second shot might be in order, so we shot it and there was another explosion on the MiG, which was now engulfed in a fireball from the leading edge of the wing backwards. The nose and canopy were visible in front of the fireball. We pulled up at the MiG's four o'clock and took a look as the doomed aircraft descended into the cloud below us. We never saw an ejection.

'One point I always make to younger fighter crews is that looking at a stricken aeroplane is possibly the worst thing you can do, as well as the most difficult to ignore. The first kill only happens once, and it's nearly impossible not to want to sneak a peek. My point is that unless someone has given absolute assurance that there is only one bandit airborne (an unlikely assurance), your self-congratulatory stare at your own handiwork is just asking for it. We weren't that smart, so we looked and looked some more. Then it was time to get out of town, and where was CAG?

'We decided we weren't going to circle Thanh Hoa looking for him, so I gave Beaulier a vector and we hauled ass. Almost immediately we were feet wet and were vectored to a tanker for refuelling – the same KA-3B that CAG and Carter eventually joined.

'Beaulier and I were jubilant about our recent good fortune, and looking forward to getting back to the ship to begin the fun of telling what happened. We, of course, felt that heroes such as ourselves would get the King's treatment, with a red carpet extending 50 miles behind the ship. That wasn't the case, however.

F-4J BuNo 155885 served alongside *Dakota 201* for much of its time with VF-142. Near-identically marked, the still factory-fresh fighter was seen at Miramar on 2 August 1969 – the jet had only been delivered to the navy by McDonnell Douglas the previous April. VF-142 commenced its fifth wartime *WestPac* nine days after this photograph was taken (*via Brad Elward*)

'*Constellation* was still fighting a war, and our MiG didn't warrant any change in the flight schedules. We were told to "delta" for an hour and ten minutes until the next scheduled recovery. Can you imagine the effrontery? Telling two red-blooded heroes to just wait? Of course we waited, and recovered, with Beaulier taking credit for an underlined three wire trap – best you can get! And it was the best day we ever had.

'The F-4J, with all its foibles, was a great machine which, although not as nimble as the MiG-21, could be properly fought, as many MiG drivers learned to their misfortune. The aircraft has now gone, but Beaulier and I can proudly remember the day we grabbed the brass ring over Thanh Hoa in the Phantom.'

There was little air activity in the North as 1970 came to a close, although US troop withdrawals continued. *Blue Tree* missions were still being flown as well, drawing occasional fire from North Vietnamese troops and air defences. On 3 November, fearing that the North Vietnamese were attempting to expand their intricate SAM network into Laos, air force strikes were launched against SAM sites being constructed near the Mu Gia and Ban Karai passes, which led to the Ho Chi Minh Trail.

Undoubtedly the highlight of the year for the air war was the 28 March encounter, which went a long way towards proving that Topgun had worked.

CONCLUSIONS OF WAR

The *Rolling Thunder* campaign will long stand as a major event in the annals of military aviation history. Even though it was primarily a bombing effort aimed at reducing the North's will to fight, and its ability to support the communist insurgency forces in the South, the war saw a significant amount of air-to-air combat as VPAF MiGs sought to disrupt American strike packages.

If anything, the war taught the US that its air warfare policy and equipment needed to be upgraded and improved, and that missile technology of the period was not the 'end-all' to aerial dogfighting as had been promised. The Phantom II, though a phenomenal interceptor, had to be re-evaluated as a close-in fighter, relying on the short-ranged Sidewinder instead of the long-range Sparrow III – and it needed an internal gun. Phantom II crews, likewise, had to relearn air combat tactics, which was something only the F-8 community seemed to appreciate at the start of the 1960s.

While statistics can often be misleading, no true coverage of the 1965 to 1970 aerial battles can be complete without at least presenting them for discussion. From the Navy's standpoint, F-4 units were officially credited with 12 VPAF MiGs, one Communist Chinese MiG and two VPAF An-2 cargo aircraft during *Rolling Thunder* and into 1970 – a further two MiG kills have since been recognised. In return, five (and possibly as many as seven) Phantom IIs were lost – four (or six) to the VPAF and one to the Communist Chinese.

Computing the official figures, Navy Phantom IIs tallied a 3.25-to-1 kill ratio versus VPAF MiGs and, if the 9 April 1965 engagement with the Chinese is included, that overall ratio becomes 2.8-to-1. Adding in the two An-2s modifies this number further to 3.2-to-1. As one can see, regardless of the numbers used to form the ratio, the results were not encouraging, nor were they in line with historical figures experienced in World War 2 or in Korea.

The F-8 community faired somewhat better, officially downing 18 VPAF MiGs while losing only three F-8s, thus yielding a kill ratio for 1965 to 1970 of 6-to-1. Combining these figures for all Navy fighter aircraft (excluding the PRF·and An-2 engagements) yields a ratio of 4.43-to-1. During the same period Air Force F-4s claimed 59 MiGs at the cost of 15 Phantom IIs for a ratio of 3.93-to-1. Adding the F-105 engagements changes this to 2.02-to-1 (87 MiGs downed versus 43 USAF fighters destroyed). As with the Navy numbers, those accumulated by the USAF fell below historical figures.

In John Nash's words, '*Rolling Thunder* was another phase in Vietnam which was hardly discernible from the others. The combat was serious AAA, SAMs and lots of bombing for the F-4s. *Everybody* got some exposure to real, "no-joke, look-them-in-the-eye combat". That experience has a lasting effect on the individual and to a lesser extent on naval aviation'.

Indeed, Nash's words can be seen by the number of pilots that went on to make the Navy their career post-war, and moved into prominent positions as captains and admirals. Topgun legends Pederson, Ruliffson, Nash and Holmes all went on to command their own squadrons and became Navy captains, while MiG-killers Hickey and Davis eventually attained admiral rank.

It was these men who saw combat, and the consequence of bureaucratic short-sightedness at first hand, who formed the mentality of today's naval aviation.

Just how much these lessons – and the US military's ability to learn from them and implement the new doctrines – impacted the Cold War during the late 1960s and 1970s may never fully be appreciated. But this much can be said. Virtually all of the equipment and most of the tactics employed by the VPAF were of Soviet and Communist Chinese origin.

Aside from the fighters themselves, the complex GCI system (described by many as the most sophisticated in the world until that faced by the US and Coalition allies over Iraq in 1991 during Operation *Desert Storm*) was also based on Soviet design, and was often controlled by Soviet 'advisors'.

Even in a limited sense, with their proverbial hands tied, US Navy aircraft performed well against the GCI network, be it the MiGs, SAMs or radar-guided AAA. All of these systems were of the type that US forces, and those of its NATO allies, would face in the event of a major war in Europe. The Soviets must have realised that their systems and tactics were faulty, if not of limited value against the Americans and the western nations.

Had US Air Forces, or the military for that matter, been permitted to run the campaign as they saw fit, rather than constrained by political necessity, it is likely that the MiGs would have played a much less significant role in the overall war, as tactics would have been modified and the fighter bases actively attacked from day one.

Many aircrews lost their lives or were captured during *Rolling Thunder*, a number of whom had fallen victim unnecessarily to VPAF MiGs.

APPENDICES

APPENDIX A

US NAVY F-4 PHANTOM II MiG KILLERS 1965-70

Date	Squadron	BuNo	Crew	Carrier/Air Wing	Aircraft	Weapon
9 April 1965	VF-96	151403	T Murphy R Fegan	Ranger/CVW-9	MiG-17	AIM-7
17 June 1965	VF-21	151488	L Page J C Smith	Midway/CVW-2	MiG-17	AIM-7
17 June 1965	VF-21	152217	J Batson R Doremus	Midway/CVW-2	MiG-17*	AIM-7
6 Oct 1965	VF-151	150634	D MacIntyre A Johnson	Coral Sea/CVW-15	MiG-17	AIM-7
13 July 1966	VF-161	151500	W McGuigan R Fowler	Constellation/CVW-15	MiG-17	AIM-9
24 April 1967	VF-114	153000	C Southwick J Laing	Kitty Hawk/CVW-11	MiG-17	AIM-9
24 April 1967	VF-114	153037	H Wisely G Anderson	Kitty Hawk/CVW-11	MiG-17	AIM-9
10 Aug 1967	VF-142	152247	G Freeborn R Elliot	Constellation/CVW-14	MiG-21	AIM-9
10 Aug 1967	VF-142	150431	R Davis G Elie	Constellation/CVW-14	MiG-21	AIM-9
26 Oct 1967	VF-143	149411	R Hickey J Morris	Constellation/CVW-14	MiG-21	AIM-7
30 Oct 1967	VF-142	150629	E Lund J Borst	Constellation/CVW-14	MiG-17	AIM-7
9 May 1968	VF-96	153036	J Heffernan F Schumacher	Enterprise/CVW-9	MiG-21**	AIM-7
10 July 1968	VF-33	155553	R Cash J Kain	America/CVW-6	MiG-21	AIM-9
28 Mar 1970	VF-142	155875	J Beaulier S Barkley	Constellation/CVW-14	MiG-21	AIM-9

* Some years later, a second MiG-17 kill was also credited to the crew following this action
** Never officially credited by the Navy or Air Force

APPENDIX B

US NAVY FIGHTERS VERSUS THE VPAF 1965-70

Year	F-4 losses to MiGs	F-4 MiG kills	F-8 losses to MiGs	F-8 MiG kills	Navy losses
1965	1*	4***	0	0	1*
1966	0	1	3	4	4
1967	2	6	0	9	5
1968	2**	2****	0	5	3
1969	-	-	-	-	-
1970	0	1	0	0	0
TOTALS	**4 + 1***	**13***/**** **	**3**	**18**	**12 + 1***

* VF-96 F-4B downed by Chinese MiG-17
** A third F-4 destroyed may have been downed by his wingman
*** A third kill for VF-21 was credited some years after the war
**** VF-96's kill for this year was never officially recognised

APPENDIX C

F-4 VIETNAM COMBAT CRUISES BY SQUADRON 1964-70

Squadron	Variant	Cruise	Modex	Carrier	Squadron	Variant	Cruise	Modex	Carrier
VF-11	F-4B	6 Jun 67 to 14 Sep 67	AA 1xx	*Forrestal*	**VF-114** (cont.)	F-4J	6 Nov 70 to 17 Jul 71	NH 2xx	*Kitty Hawk*
VF-14	F-4B	21 Jun 66 to 21 Feb 67	AB 1xx	*Roosevelt*	**VF-142**	F-4B	5 May 64 to 1 Feb 65	NK 2xx	*Constellation*
VF-21	F-4B	6 Mar 65 to 23 Nov 65	NE 1xx	*Midway*		F-4B	10 Dec 65 to 25 Aug 66	NK 2xx	*Ranger*
	F-4B	29 Jul 66 to 23 Feb 67	NE 1xx	*Coral Sea*		F-4B	29 Apr 67 to 4 Dec 67	NK 2xx	*Constellation*
	F-4B	4 Nov 67 to 25 May 68	NE 1xx	*Ranger*		F-4B	29 May 68 to 31 Jan 69	NK 2xx	*Constellation*
	F-4J	26 Oct 68 to 17 May 69	NE 1xx	*Ranger*		F-4J	11 Aug 69 to 8 May 70	NK 2xx	*Constellation*
	F-4J	14 Oct 69 to 1 Jun 70	NE 1xx	*Ranger*	**VF-143**	F-4B	5 May 64 to 1 Feb 65	NK 3xx	*Constellation*
	F-4J	27 Oct 70 to 17 Jun 71	NE 1xx	*Ranger*		F-4B	10 Dec 65 to 25 Aug 66	NK 3xx	*Ranger*
VF-32	F-4B	21 Jun 66 to 21 Feb 67	AB 2xx	*Roosevelt*		F-4B	29 Apr 67 to 4 Dec 67	NK 3xx	*Constellation*
VF-33	F-4J	10 Apr 68 to 16 Dec 68	AE 2xx	*America*		F-4B	29 May 68 to 31 Jan 69	NK 3xx	*Constellation*
VF-41	F-4B	10 May 65 to 13 Dec 65	AG 1xx	*Independence*		F-4J	11 Aug 69 to 8 May 70	NK 3xx	*Constellation*
VF-74	F-4B	6 Jun 67 to 14 Sep 67	AA 2xx	*Forrestal*	**VF-151**	F-4B	7 Dec 64 to 1 Nov 65	NL 1xx	*Coral Sea*
VF-84	F-4B	10 May 65 to 13 Dec 65	AG-2xx	*Independence*		F-4B	12 May 66 to 3 Dec 66	NL 1xx	*Constellation*
VF-92	F-4B	5 Aug 64 to 6 May 65	NG 2xx	*Ranger*		F-4B	26 Jul 67 to 6 Apr 68	NL 1xx	*Coral Sea*
	F-4B	26 Oct 65 to 21 Jun 66	NG 2xx	*Enterprise*		F-4B	7 Sep 68 to 18 Apr 69	NL 1xx	*Coral Sea*
	F-4B	19 Nov 66 to 6 Jul 67	NG 2xx	*Enterprise*		F-4B	23 Sep 69 to 1 Jul 70	NL 1xx	*Coral Sea*
	F-4B	3 Jan 68 to 18 Jul 68	NG 2xx	*Enterprise*	**VF-154**	F-4B	29 Jul 66 to 23 Feb 67	NE 4xx	*Coral Sea*
	F-4J	6 Jan 69 to 2 Jul 69	NG 2xx	*Enterprise*		F-4B	4 Nov 67 to 25 May 68	NE 1xx	*Ranger*
	F-4J	10 Apr 70 to 21 Dec 70	NG 2xx	*America*		F-4J	26 Oct 68 to 17 May 69	NE 2xx	*Ranger*
VF-96	F-4B	5 Aug 64 to 6 May 65	NG 6xx	*Ranger*		F-4J	14 Oct 69 to 1 Jun 70	NE 2xx	*Ranger*
	F-4B	26 Oct 65 to 21 Jun 66	NG 6xx	*Enterprise*		F-4J	27 Oct 70 to 17 Jun 71	NE 2xx	*Ranger*
	F-4B	19 Nov 66 to 6 Jul 67	NG 6xx	*Enterprise*	**VF-161**	F-4B	12 May 66 to 3 Dec 66	NL 2xx	*Constellation*
	F-4B	3 Jan 68 to 18 Jul 68	NG 6xx	*Enterprise*		F-4B	26 Jul 67 to 6 Apr 68	NL 2xx	*Coral Sea*
	F-4J	6 Jan 69 to 2 Jul 69	NG 1xx	*Enterprise*		F-4B	7 Sept 68 to 18 Apr 69	NL 2xx	*Coral Sea*
	F-4J	10 Apr 70 to 21 Dec 70	NG 1xx	*America*		F-4B	23 Sep 69 to 1 Jul 70	NL 2xx	*Coral Sea*
VF-102	F-4J	10 Apr 68 to 16 Dec 68	AE 1xx	*America*	**VF-213**	F-4B/G	19 Oct 65 to 13 Jun 66	NH 1xx	*Kitty Hawk*
VF-114	F-4B	19 Oct 65 to 13 Jun 66	NH 4xx	*Kitty Hawk*		F-4B	5 Nov 66 to 20 Jun 67	NH 1xx	*Kitty Hawk*
	F-4B	5 Nov 66 to 20 Jun 67	NH 2xx	*Kitty Hawk*		F-4B	18 Nov 67 to 28 Jun 68	NH 1xx	*Kitty Hawk*
	F-4B	18 Nov 67 to 28 Jun 68	NH 2xx	*Kitty Hawk*		F-4B	30 Dec 68 to 4 Sep 69	NH 1xx	*Kitty Hawk*
	F-4B	30 Dec 68 to 4 Sep 69	NH 2xx	*Kitty Hawk*		F-4J	6 Nov 70 to 17 Jul 71	NH 1xx	*Kitty Hawk*

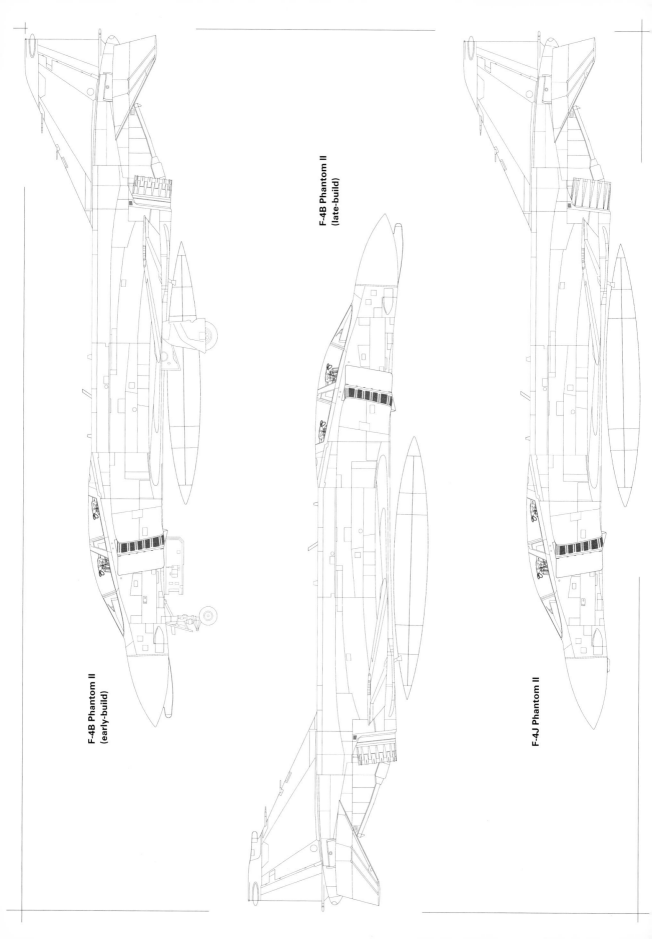

F-4B Phantom II
(early-build)

F-4B Phantom II
(late-build)

F-4J Phantom II

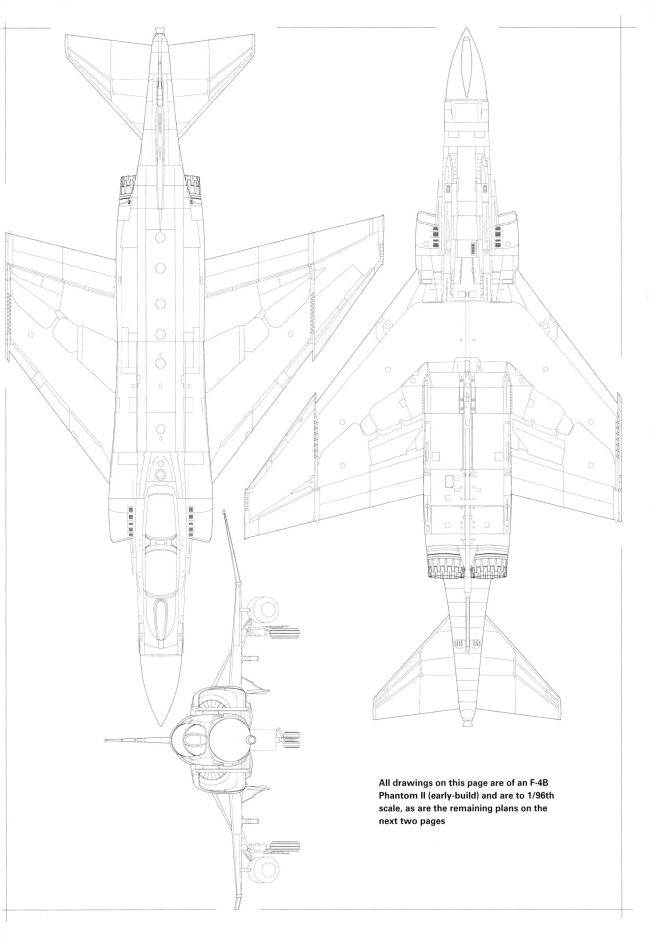

All drawings on this page are of an F-4B
Phantom II (early-build) and are to 1/96th
scale, as are the remaining plans on the
next two pages

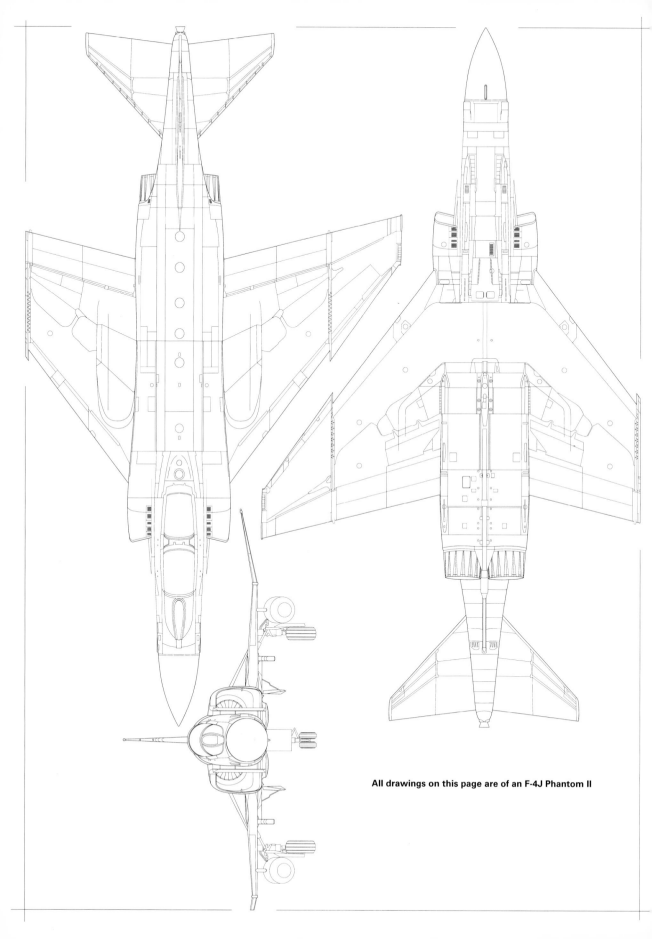

All drawings on this page are of an F-4J Phantom II

COLOUR PLATES

1

F-4B BuNo 151403/NG 602 of Lt(jg) Terrence M Murphy and Ens Ronald J Fegan, VF-96, USS *Ranger*, 9 April 1965

This Phantom II was accepted by the Navy at McDonnell's St Louis, Missouri, plant on 11 September 1963 and transferred to VF-21 at NAS Miramar exactly one week later. A participant in the unit's first *WestPac* with the F-4B (from 8 November 1963 to 31 May 1964), BuNo 151403 spent six months on deployment with CVW-2 aboard the *Midway*. Passed on to VF-96 on 9 June 1964, the fighter remained with the 'Fighting Falcons' until lost in action during an engagement with communist Chinese MiG-17s over Hainan Island on 9 April 1965. BuNo 151403 had completed just 430 flight hours.

2

F-4B BuNo 152219/NE 102 of Lt Jack E D Batson and Lt Cdr Robert B Doremus, VF-21, USS *Midway*, 17 June 1965

Accepted by the Navy on 19 January 1965, this aircraft was assigned to Miramar-based fleet squadron VF-21, and accompanied the unit on its *WestPac* deployment aboard the *Midway*, commencing on 6 March 1965. The highlight of BuNo 152219's 144 days on the line was its 'MiG killing' sortie of 17 June. Although VF-21 and CVA-41 returned home in November, BuNo 152219 remained in-theatre when it was transferred to MCAS Iwakuni, Japan, for use by VMFA-513 (with whom it served for just three days) and then VMFA-323. In turn passed on to VF-96 (and given the modex NG 603) on 8 June 1966, the jet was lost on 12 February 1967 when its pilot became disorientated during air intercept and ACM training whilst on a CAP mission from *Enterprise*, then on *Yankee Station*. *Showtime 603's* crew, Lt Cdr Martin J 'Marty' Sullivan and Lt(jg) Paul V Carlson, were conducting mock combat with squadron CO, Cdr Sheldon O 'Lefty' Schwartz and Lt Cdr Dean E Nordell over the South China Sea at the time of the accident – neither Sullivan or Carlson survived the crash. BuNo 152219 had amassed 876 flight hours.

3

F-4B BuNo 151488/NE 101 of Cdr Louis Page and Lt John C Smith, VF-21, USS *Midway*, 17 June 1965

Accepted by the Navy on 2 July 1964, and passed on to VF-213 two weeks later, this jet was in turn transferred to Pacific Fleet RAG VF-121 on 26 August. Sent to NAS Atsugi, Japan, on 17 March 1965, BuNo 151488 was take on strength by VMFA-542. Its aircraft history card indicates that the fighter stayed with this unit until 14 October, although published reports state that it was used by VF-21 to down the Navy's first VPAF MiG of the war on 17 June. Sticking with the history card,

BuNo 151488 was passed on to VMFA-513 at Iwakuni in mid-October 1965, and from there returned to Miramar in early January 1966 for service with VF-21. Participating in the unit's second wartime *WestPac* (on the *Coral Sea*) in 1966-67, the fighter saw further flying with the Marines between February and April 1967 from MCAS El Toro, California. Following this brief stint with VMFA-122, BuNo 151488 returned to Miramar, and VF-21, for three months, and then joined VF-161 in time for the squadron's 1967-68 *WestPac* aboard the *Coral Sea*. On 17 November the aircraft was lost near Hanoi while en route to a flak suppression mission when its crew, Cdr W D McGrath and Lt R G Emrich, either stalled the Phantom II and spun out of control or were caught in a heavy AAA barrage while taking SAM evasive manoeuvres below 6000 ft. Both men were killed in the subsequent crash. BuNo 151488 had amassed 1161 flight hours.

4

F-4B BuNo 150634/NE 107 of Lt Cdr Dan MacIntyre and Lt(jg) Alan Johnson, VF-151, USS *Coral Sea*, 6 October 1965

One of 27 F-4Bs initially issued to the USAF to equip its first Phantom II unit (the 4453rd Combat Crew Training Wing) in 1962, this aircraft served with the Air Force as 62-12174 until returned to the Navy once sufficient F-4Cs had been delivered. Following its successful MiG engagement of 6 October 1965, BuNo 150634 saw further action at the very end of VF-41's sole Vietnam cruise, aboard the *Independence*, in November-December 1965. Passed on to VF-92 early the following year, it remained in-theatre with the unit aboard the *Enterprise* until CVN-65 returned home in June. Two months later BuNo 150634 was transferred to VF-121. The 12th of 228 B-models upgraded to F-4N specification by the Naval Air Rework Facility (NARF) at NAS North Island, California, between 1972-76, this aircraft served with VF-151 as NF 207 from 1973. The unit was part of CVW-5, forward-deployed to NAS Atsugi, in Japan, and assigned to the *Midway*. When VF-151, and sister-squadron VF-161, transitioned to F-4Js in early 1977, BuNo 150634 was duly retired to the Military Aircraft Storage and Disposition Center (MASDC) at Davis-Monthan AFB, in Arizona, on 8 July 1977. It had completed 3370 flight hours. The veteran jet remained in Arizona until 22 June 1983, when it was moved by road to Indian Springs Air Force Auxiliary Field, Nevada, to see out its final days as a range target.

5

F-4B BuNo 151500/NL 216 of Lt William M McGuigan and Lt(jg) Robert M Fowler, VF-161, USS *Constellation*, 13 July 1966

Starting its naval career with VF-21 on 4 September 1964, and participating in the first weeks of the unit's 1965 *WestPac* aboard the *Midway*, this Phantom II was transferred to VF-151, via NAS Cubi Point, in the Philippines, in late May. BuNo 151500 was subsequently passed on to sister-squadron VF-161 on 5 May 1966, and departed with CVW-15 on 'Connie's' second Vietnam War *WestPac* exactly one week later. Remaining in-theatre when CVA-64 returned to California in November, the jet spent four months at NAS Atsugi undergoing routine maintenance before being issued to VMFA-314 in May 1967. Flying from Da Nang and then Chu Lai, the Phantom II was transferred to VMFA-115 on 19 December and was eventually lost to AAA on the night of 23 May 1968 during an air support mission over South Vietnam. Both crewmen managed to successfully eject, and were quickly rescued by a US Army helicopter. BuNo 151500 had completed 908 flight hours.

6

F-4B BuNo 153019/NH 110 of Lt David McCrea and Ens David Nichols, VF-213, USS *Kitty Hawk*, 20 December 1966

Accepted by the Navy at McDonnell's St Louis plant on 5 May 1966, this aircraft was issued new to VF-213 on 29 July and embarked with the unit on the *Kitty Hawk* on 5 November for the 'Black Lions'' second (of six) *WestPacs*. It went on to complete a further two combat cruises with CVW-11/CVA 63 prior to its transfer to VF-121 on 29 December 1969. Remaining with the RAG until 17 March 1971, BuNo 153019 then joined VF-111 and participated in its fourth *WestPac*, aboard the *Coral Sea* – a fifth combat cruise followed in 1973. Transitioning to the F-4N in mid-1974, VF-111 duly passed BuNo 153019 on to VMFA-531 at MCAS El Toro, California, in October. The veteran jet was sent to the NARF at NAS North Island in March 1975, where it remained in cocooned storage until converted into an N-model as part of Project *Beeline* between June and September 1976 – it was the 198th F-4B to be upgraded. The newly-configured fighter was issued to reserve-manned VF-201 at NAS Dallas on 23 May 1977, and it continued to serve with the Texas-based unit until transferred to VF-171 at NAS Key West, Florida, on 10 February 1984. Stricken from the inventory two weeks later, having completed 3811 flight hours, BuNo 153019 has guarded the gate at the Florida naval air station since October 1984. It is the sole survivor of the 16 Navy F-4s to have claimed a victory during the *Rolling Thunder* campaign.

Although the fighter's An-2 kill was credited to Lt David McCrea and Ens David Nichols, it could so easily have fallen to VF-213's John Nash, then a young first tour lieutenant;

'We flew out sorties every day, and at nights there was always Alert 5 (two F-4Bs with crews strapped in, ready for take-off at five minutes' notice). On my first cruise the longest period of sleep I had was four-and-a-half hours. You could fly two or three times a day and, with the limited numbers of pilots we had, you'd have an Alert 5.

This was two hours in the cockpit, in flight gear, on the catapult. I went up one night to relieve a guy called Dave McCrea. Our stateroom was close to the forward wardroom, so I said to my RIO, "Let's stop and get a coffee and a couple of doughnuts". We spent about ten minutes there, and then we went to the aeroplane sitting on the cat. I beat on the side of the Phantom, woke up McCrea, and said "OK, come on down now".

'No sooner had I said that when the Air Boss came up on the speaker and said "Launch the Alert 5". In those days we had a contest to see who could get the most night traps (we were young and didn't know any better). Anyway, I said "Come on down", and he gave me the finger and said "The heck with you, I'm going to take off". So they got the aeroplane started, and the Air Boss came on the horn again and said, "Your bogie is at 350 degrees at 25, and you're cleared to fire". At that point I realised I had made a big mistake with the coffee and doughnuts.

'McCrea and Nichols launched from the carrier (at 1815 hrs) with VF-114's Wisely and Jordan, and despite marginal visibility, they soon locked on to the two bogies. As there were no other US aircraft in the area, the slow-moving plots were assumed to be hostile. They turned out to be two An-2s flying in and out of the clouds calibrating the surface-to-air radar off Than Hoa. Possibly, they were trying to drag out the alert guys too. Both aircraft were destroyed with single AIM-7Es.'

7

F-4B BuNo 153022/NH 215 of Lt H Dennis Wisely and Lt(jg) David L Jordan, VF-114, USS *Kitty Hawk*, 20 December 1966

Delivered new to VF-121 directly from the St Louis plant on 15 June 1966, this aircraft was transferred to VF-114 on 30 September 1966 and completed CVW-11's 1967-68 *WestPac*. It was passed on to VF-96 on 15 November 1967, and participated in the 'Fighting Falcons'' 1968 *WestPac* on the *Enterprise*. Transferred to Chu Lai-based VMFA-314 on 1 July 1968, following the end of CVW-9's last period on *Yankee Station* during the cruise, BuNo 153022 was written off on 11 June 1970 whilst still serving with 'Black Knights'. The fighter had been badly damaged in action on 20 May 1970 when AAA struck the port engine bay door, splitting it open. Collateral or subsequent damage was severe enough to cause the Phantom II to be stricken instead of being repaired. It had completed 1652 flight hours.

8

F-4B BuNo 153000/NH 210 of Lt Charles E Southwick and Ens James W Laing, VF-114, USS *Kitty Hawk*, 24 April 1967

Struck by flak early into its MiGCAP mission in support of a strike on Kep, BuNo 153000 nevertheless survived long enough to allow its crew to down a MiG-17 with a well-aimed Sidewinder. Minutes later Lt Southwick found that he could not transfer fuel from the jet's wing tank due to flak damage, leaving the crew with little option but to eject. Delivered to the Navy in May 1966, BuNo 153000 had enjoyed a brief spell with VF-121 prior to arriving at VF-114 on 6 July 1966. It had completed 548 flying hours by the time it was lost. This particular aircraft was one of the first F-4Bs in the fleet to be retrofitted with fin tip AN/APR-30 RHAW antennae. It lacks the under-radome antenna, however.

9
F-4B BuNo 153037/NH 200 of Lt H Dennis Wisely and Lt(jg) Gareth L Anderson, VF-114, USS *Kitty Hawk*, 24 April 1967

'Denny' Wisely used this jet to become the Navy's top scorer for the *Rolling Thunder* years of the Vietnam War. Like many B-model Phantom IIs assigned to Pacific Fleet squadrons, BuNo 153037 initially served with VF-121 following its delivery to the Navy on 20 July 1966. Transferred to VF-114, via NAS Atsugi, on 8 April 1967 as an attrition replacement for BuNo 152990 (which had been lost in an operational accident 48 hours earlier), BuNo 153037 participated in the final two months of CVW-11's second combat cruise. This deployment was a hard one for the 'Aardvarks', as the unit lost four F-4s in combat and three in operational accidents, resulting in three crewman being killed and four captured. The aircraft then briefly returned to VF-121, in October 1967, before being passed on to the VF-92 in December of that same year. BuNo 153037 participated in the unit's *WestPac* with CVW-9, aboard the *Enterprise*, from January to July 1968, although it did not return to Miramar with the 'Silver Kings' at the end of the six-month cruise. Instead, it was transferred to Marine-manned VMFA-314 at Chu Lai, and it remained with this unit until written off on 16 May 1969 when its pilot over-rotated at too low a speed on take-off from NAS Cubi Point. The aircraft stalled and crashed, although the crew ejected safely. BuNo 153037 had completed 1187 flight hours prior to its destruction.

10
F-4B BuNo 152247/NK 202 flown by Lt Guy H Freeborn and Lt(jg) Robert J Elliot, VF-142, USS *Constellation*, 10 August 1967

This aircraft lasted just 11 days after shooting down a MiG-21 on 10 August 1967, the jet being struck in the starboard wing by 85 mm gunfire during a flak suppression mission near the Chap Khe highway bridge. Its crew, Cdr R H McGlohn and Lt(jg) J M McIlrath, successfully ejected and were recovered by a Navy helicopter. Three A-6As from fellow CVW-14 squadron VA-196 were also lost on this day – one to a SAM over North Vietnam and two to communist Chinese MiGs. Returning to BuNo 152247, this aircraft had been accepted by the Navy at St Louis on 20 April 1965, and issued to VF-142 48 hours later. Participating in CVW-14's 1965-66 *WestPac* aboard the *Ranger*, the fighter was well into its second combat deployment when it was lost on 21 August 1967. BuNo 152247 had amassed 1128 flight hours (much of this over Vietnam) by the time of its demise.

11
F-4B BuNo 150431/NK 210 of Lt Cdr Robert C Davis and Lt Cdr Gayle O Elie, VF-142, USS *Constellation*, 10 August 1967

Issued to the Navy on 12 October 1962, this Phantom II arrived at Miramar for service with VF-121 five days later. It remained with the RAG until 5 June 1963, and then joined VF-193, again at Miramar, just as the unit transitioned from the F-3B Demon to the F-4B – the unit was re-designated VF-142 the following month. BuNo 150431 spent the remainder of its life with VF-142, completing three *WestPacs* up until it was lost on 27 April 1968 whilst on a training flight from CVA-64 during CVW-14's pre-deployment cruise. It had clocked up 1905 flight hours.

12
F-4B BuNo 149411/NK 311 of Lt(jg) Robert P Hickey and Lt(jg) Jeremy G Morris, VF-143, USS *Constellation*, 26 October 1967

Accepted as an F4H-1 on 1 February 1962, this early-build Phantom II initially served with VF-121, before spending short spells with VF-143, VF-21, VF-121 again, VF-114, VF-96, a third spell at VF-121, and VF-154, with whom it completed its first *WestPac* in 1966. There is some contention as to whether the fighter was serving with VF-143 at the time of the unit's MiG kill in 1967, for according to its official service history BuNo 149411 was undergoing Standard Depot Level Maintenance (SDLM) at NARF North Island from January 1967 through to March 1968! These same records note that the jet returned to VF-121 following its overhaul, and then transferred to VF-96 on 28 April 1968 as an attrition replacement for BuNo 150463 (lost in an operational accident on 5 April). Joining the unit halfway through its *WestPac* aboard the *Enterprise*, it was passed on to VMFA-314 (like BuNo 153037, which served with sister-squadron VF-92 during the same deployment) on 1 July 1968. The aircraft flew with the Marines from Chu Lai until written off on 20 December 1968, having completed 1602 flight hours.

13
F-4B BuNo 150629/NK 203 of Lt Cdr Eugene P Lund and Lt(jg) James R Borst, VF-142, USS *Constellation*, 30 October 1967

Although ordered as a 'vanilla' F-4B, this aircraft was one of 12 converted to F-4G specification on the McDonnell production line. Fitted initially with an AN/ASW-13 datalink (later replaced with the improved AN/ASW-21) which, amongst other things, allowed for hands-off landings on carriers that boasted AN/APS-10 radar and AN/USC-2 datalink, this Phantom II was issued to VF-96 in the summer of 1963. Transferred to VF-213 early the following year (when these aircraft were officially redesignated F-4Gs), it completed one *WestPac* with the unit aboard the *Kitty Hawk* in 1965-66. The datalink equipment was removed from the 11 surviving F-4Gs (one was lost in combat to AAA on 28 April 1966) upon their return to the US in mid-1966, and they were in turn redesignated F-4Bs. Transferred to VF-121 in December 1966, BuNo 150639 was in turn briefly used by Air Development Squadron Four (VX-4) at NAS Point Mugu, in California, in June 1967. Returned to the RAG by the end of the month, it was transferred to VF-142 as a replacement for F-4B BuNo 149498/NK 205, which was lost to a SAM on 23 August. Joining the unit halfway through its *WestPac*, aboard the *Constellation*, BuNo 150629 was lost just minutes after claiming a MiG-17 on 30 October. The crew had launched an AIM-7E at a second VPAF fighter, only to see the round prematurely explode less than 200 ft in front of them, sending debris shooting down the jet's starboard engine intake. Coaxing the Phantom II back out to sea, the crew safely ejected near their ship and were rescued.

14

F-4B BuNo 153036/NG 602 of Capt John P Heffernan USAF and Lt(jg) Frank A Schumacher, VF-96, USS *Enterprise*, 9 May 1968
This long-lived Phantom II was accepted by the Navy at St Louis on 16 June 1966 and issued to VF-121 on 21 July. Used by the training unit until 13 December 1967, it then joined VF-96 and embarked with the unit on the *Enterprise* the following month for CVW-9's fourth Vietnam *WestPac*. The aircraft scored an unconfirmed MiG kill with a USAF exchange pilot in the front seat and a Navy RIO in the back on 9 May 1968. It was transferred to VMFA-323 at NAS Cubi Point on 1 July 1968, who in turn passed it on to VMFA-115 at Chu Lai on 3 October. The Phantom II enjoyed a long spell in-theatre with the 'Silver Eagles', remaining forward-deployed with the unit until late 1975. In that time it flew from Cubi Point (again), Da Nang, Naha, on Okinawa, Iwakuni and finally Cubi Point once again. VMFA-115 then transitioned to the F-4J, and BuNo 153036 was in turn sent back to the NARF at North Island for upgrading to F-4N specification. The 191st airframe to be converted as part of Project *Beeline*, the aircraft was in rework from 29 December 1975 to 4 March 1977. Issued to reserve-manned VMFA-321 at NAF Andrews, Maryland, on 6 March, the veteran 'MiG killer' was finally written off in a landing accident at MCAS Yuma, Arizona, on 21 January 1981. BuNo 153036 had deployed with the unit to the Marine Corps air station for live bombing training, and after pulling out following its attack run, the jet developed chronic hydraulic and fuel leaks from its port engine. As the pilot fought to land the crippled fighter back at Yuma, its port wing dropped and the F-4 drifted left of the runway centreline, forcing the crew to eject. By the time of its demise, BuNo 153036 had amassed 4263 flight hours.

15

F-4J BuNo 155553/AE 212 of Lts Roy Cash and Joseph E Kain, VF-33, USS *America*, 10 July 1968
Issued new to VF-33 at NAS Oceana, Virginia, in

early 1968 when the unit transitioned from the F-4B to the F-4J, this aircraft served exclusively with the 'Tarsiers' during its five-year career with the fleet. The fighter participated in VF-33's sole *WestPac* (between April and December 1968), aboard the *America*, and subsequently completed two Mediterranean deployments with CVW-6, embarked on the *Independence*. BuNo 155553 was lost in a training accident on 1 December 1972, having completed 1526 flight hours.

16

F-4J BuNo 155875/NK 201 of Lts Jerome E Beaulier and Steven J Barkley, VF-142, USS *Constellation*, 28 March 1970
Accepted by the Navy at McDonnell Douglas's St Louis plant on 10 April 1969, this aircraft joined VF-142 four days later as one of twelve J-models issued to the unit at Miramar as replacements for their combat-weary F-4Bs. On 28 March 1970 it downed a MiG-21 using an AIM-9D. The aircraft continued in service with the 'Ghostriders', completing a second *WestPac* with the unit, aboard the *Enterprise*, in 1971-72. Indeed, it was coming towards the end of its third *WestPac*, again with CVN-65, when an in-flight fire broke out and destroyed the aircraft on 26 April 1973. It had completed 1540 flight hours by that stage, most of which were in combat.

Back cover

F-4D 66-7709/OC of Capt Doyle Baker USMC and Capt John D 'Jack' Ryan USAF, 13th TFS/432nd TRW, Udorn, 17 December 1967
The first of two USMC pilots to claim MiGs whilst flying F-4s on exchange tours with the USAF, Doyle Baker was on his 30th mission over North Vietnam when he claimed a MiG-17 in Route Pak IVA on 17 December 1967. Having previously completed a Vietnam tour with VMFA-513 in 1965, he returned to the 'Corps in July 1968 with 226 combat missions to his credit. Posted to VT-21 at NAS Kingsville, in Texas, as an instructor, Baker related details of his kill to the naval air station's newspaper, *The Flying K*, in October1968;

'It was one of those beautiful days when the visibility was unrestricted. The targets for more than 40 strike aircraft were located in the Hanoi complex, and our four-aeroplane division was assigned as fighter cover for the strike aeroplanes. We were approaching the target when the division leader broke away to identify an approaching aircraft, leaving me leading the second section. Shortly after the leader identified the bogie as a friendly F-105, I spotted a low-flying MiG-17 approaching the flight from the opposite direction. We jettisoned our external fuel tanks and rolled in on the MiG-17 from about 10,000 ft. The MiG spotted our two Phantoms and started a tight turn into the formation.

'I set up my centreline gun pod and opened fire with short bursts of the 20 mm ammunition as soon as the MiG passed in front of the gunsight. I was losing altitude too fast, so I climbed back up to 10,000 ft for a second pass. The MiG kept flying as low as it could, then tuned into us when we started back down again. After the fourth pass, I ran out of ammunition.

'Since I had used all of the 20 mm, I set the switches to fire the AIM-4 heat-seeking air-to-air Falcon missile. The MiG appeared to be heading home, so I climbed back up for an altitude advantage. Still climbing, I ignited the afterburners on the Phantom, rolled the aeroplane and pulled downward, increasing the speed to keep the MiG in sight.

'The forces of acceleration were so great I could hardly see anything, let alone a MiG. The Phantoms were pulling over 11gs, and just 5 or 6 can cause a pilot to black out. My rear seat pilot, Capt Jack Ryan, read off the altitudes as we went through them. Finally, at 500 ft, visibility returned to normal. Travelling at well over 600 kts, with the MiG in sight, missile locked, I fired.

'The Falcon worked perfectly, going directly into the tailpipe and exploding. We broke to the right, overtaking the flaming MiG. The MiG pilot ejected, and enemy gunners immediately began firing. We climbed out of range without being hit.'

There is some confusion as to exactly which F-4D Capt Baker used to down his MiG-17 on 17 December 1967, most published sources stating that it was the aircraft depicted here (66-7709). However, recent research carried out specially for this volume at Maxwell AFB by USAF Historical Research Agency archivist Archie DiFante casts doubt on 66-7709's 'MiG killing' credentials. According to its aircraft history cards, this particular jet was assigned to the 4th TFW at Seymour-Johnson AFB, North Carolina, when Baker claimed his MiG kill. It also spent time on detachment at Kunsan AFB, Korea, in February 1968, but according to its paperwork, the fighter did not serve in South-East Asia at any time. Transferred to the Air Force Reserve in the late 1970s, 66-7709 was handed over (along with 23 other D-models) to the Republic of Korea Air Force in early 1988, and is still reportedly in frontline service as this volume went to press.

Research carried out by Archie DiFante shows that F-4D 66-8719 could have been Doyle Baker's 'MiG killing' mount, as this machine flew with the 432nd TRW at Udorn in 1967. Another long-lived example, this particular aircraft last served with the reserve-manned 457th TFS/301st TFW at Carswell AFB in the late 1980s, as did 66-7709. Indeed, there are published photographs showing both aircraft sat side-by-side on the Carswell ramp in May 1984, and 66-7709 proudly bears a red MiG kill star on its port splitter plate! 66-8719 was then sent to AMARC at Davis-Monthan AFB in January 1989, and according to an 'unofficial source', it was transported to Avon Park, in Florida, in August 1998 to end its days as a range target.

The Authors were unable to contact Doyle Baker to confirm the identity of his 'MiG killing' F-4D Phantom II.

COLOUR SECTION

1
VF-21's *Sundown 111* participated in the unit's 'MiG killing' *WestPac* on CVA-41 in 1965. Note aircraft's unusual configuration of a solitary AIM-7 on the port shoulder pylon and two AIM-9s on the starboard hardpoint (*via B Elward*)

2
Seen in the final weeks of VF-21's 1965 *WestPac*, BuNo 151482 flies over South Vietnamese jungle armed with a full load of 12 Korean War-vintage M117 750-lb bombs (*via Peter Mersky*)

3
The flightdeck of *Coral Sea* is arranged in orderly fashion for the vessel's portcall to Hawaii in January 1965. Within weeks the vessel would be participating *Flaming Dart I* strikes (*Don Willis*)

4
Switchbox 104 has just recovered back aboard CVA-43 following a routine BARCAP (*Don Willis*)

5
A section of bombless F-4Bs from VF-161 'hit the tanker' after attacking their target in North Vietnam in late 1966 (*via Peter Davies*)

6
This trio of F-4Bs from VF-96 are all armed with Zuni rocket pods and AIM-9Bs (*via Peter Davies*)

7
The 'MiG killing' F-4B of Lt Charles Southwick and Ens James Laing in late 1966 (*via Brad Elward*)

8
An An-2 'killer' BuNo 153019 enjoyed a long fleet career, including *WestPacs* with VF-111 in 1971 and 1973 (*via Angelo Romano*)

9
VF-102's AE 112 (BuNo 155540) was lost to AAA on 25 July 1968. Pilot Lt C C Parish was killed and RIO Lt R S Fant captured (*via Brad Elward*)

10
This VF-33 F-4B took part in the 1966 Paris airshow, its assigned pilot being future 'MiG killer' Gene Tucker, who bagged a MiG-21 in August 1972 whilst serving with VF-103 (*via Peter Davies*)

11 and 12
VF-33's 'MiG killer' is seen with varying styles of fuselage and tail decoration at later stages in its career with the unit. BuNo 155553 served exclusively with the 'Tarsiers' until lost in a training accident on 1 December 1972 (*both via A Romano*)

13
BuNo 155875 claimed the only MiG kill between July 1968 and January 1972 (*via A Romano*)

PHANTOMS OVER VIETNAM

PART 2

PHANTOMS OVER VIETNAM

PART 2

RISING TENSIONS

By the first weeks of 1972, American aircraft had been conducting 'reprisal' raids against targets in North Vietnam – called 'protective reactive' strikes – for a number of months. These missions usually followed North Vietnamese attempts to attack US aeroplanes flying *Blue Tree* reconnaissance sorties. These reprisal raids were the first strike missions to be flown against North Vietnam since the end of the *Rolling Thunder* campaign in October 1968.

Under the Rules of Engagement (ROE) then in place, if a reconnaissance aircraft was fired on, the crews were prohibited from calling back to the carrier for strikes to hit the offending AAA or SAM site. However, if the strike aeroplanes were actually flying with the recce package when it came under fire, they could execute 'protective reaction strikes'.

While at first these 'strikes' were defensive in nature, being aimed at the air defence batteries that fired on the American aircraft, they soon became larger operations against specific targets such as fuel storage facilities and MiG bases, complete with strike, flak suppression and CAP sections.

Although the MiGs had not been active in the latter months of 1971, some did stage out of Kep, Phuc Yen, Yen Bai and Quan Lang, using heavy Ground Control Intercept (GCI) radar control. Communist pilots would occasionally try to lure US air forces into anti-aircraft artillery (AAA) and surface-to-air missile (SAM) traps by flying low through site fields-of-fire (which would be the case on 10 May 1972).

On 19 January 1972, two F-4Js on MiGCAP engaged VPAF jets for the first time since March 1970. The Phantom IIs were from VF-96, and they had launched in support of a 19-aeroplane Alpha strike sortied by Carrier Air Wing Nine (CVW-9) from USS *Constellation* (CVA-64). The F-4s were crewed by Lt Randall H 'Duke' Cunningham and Lt(jg) William 'Willie' P Driscoll (in BuNo 157267, call sign 'Showtime 112') and Lts Brian 'Bulldog' Grant and Jerry Sullivan.

The strike was a protective reaction sortie in retaliation for the downing of a CVW-9 A-6A Intruder (from VA-165) by a SAM on 30 December 1971. This aircraft was participating in a five-day aerial campaign called Operation *Proud Deep Alpha*, which was intended to destroy the stockpiles of weapons and supplies that North Vietnam was assembling near the Demilitarized Zone. VF-111, flying off the USS *Coral Sea* (CVA-43), had also lost an F-4B to a SAM that same day.

In the early afternoon of 19 January 1972, Lt Randall 'Duke' Cunningham and Lt(jg) William 'Willie' Driscoll of VF-96 downed a MiG-21 with an AIM-9 missile. This was the first aerial kill claimed by an American aircraft in 22 months, and to prove that it was no fluke, Cunningham and Driscoll went on to down a further four MiGs over the next four months to become the only Navy aces of the Vietnam war. This photograph was taken at NAS Miramar on 5 October 1972, three months after the completion of VF-96's penultimate wartime *WestPac*. Note the five MiG-17 silhouettes, in red, painted on the crews' 'bone domes', and the red VPAF kill markings on the splitter plate behind Cunningham's right leg (*via Peter Mersky*)

Returning to 19 January, *Constellation's* Alpha strike was tasked with attacking caves suspected of housing MiGs, as well as three SAM sites. All were located in the Quan Lang area.

According to 'Duke' Cunningham, the strike force was briefed to expect SAMs en route to the target area, and a long egress had been planned to bypass this threat. 'We were told that we would encounter AAA, SAMs and MiGs in the target area. Two MiG-21s were known to be operating out of Quan Lang field and six were based at Bai Thuong, about 60 miles to the north.'

The entire strike force departed the ship (only the F-4s refuelled immediately after take-off) and ingressed to a point 45 nautical miles south-west of Quan Lang (designated as Point Alpha). To help conceal their intent, the package flew over northern South Vietnam, turned north and flew up into Laos until opposite Quan Lang, then flew back east to the target. To conserve fuel, maximum range cruise profiles of 20,000-22,000 ft altitude and 310 knots were flown.

A flight of three Shrike anti-radiation missile-equipped A-7E Corsair IIs (dubbed 'Iron Hand') and two F-4 flak suppression aircraft led the force, followed by the main package of A-6A and A-7E attack jets trailing to the left and right, respectively. A solitary RA-5C Vigilante photo-recce aircraft and its F-4 escort flew above and behind the Alpha package, while the MiGCAP (Cunningham/Driscoll and Grant/Sullivan) trailed the recce jet. Finally, an A-3 ECM/tanker and KA-6 tanker remained behind the formation in support.

The photo Vigilante drew fire upon reaching Point Alpha, so the A-7 'Iron Hand' and F-4 flak suppression aircraft turned right and started their run into the target, while the remainder of the force continued on course toward a point 30 nautical miles south-east of Quan Lang (called Point Bravo). There, the two strike divisions and the MiGCAP turned in an easterly direction towards the target, while the RA-5 and its escort continued on course north. The two tankers then established an orbit.

According to aircrews participating in this mission, the intent was to confuse the enemy as much as possible by having the aircraft converge on the target from several different angles.

As the strike divisions turned towards Point Bravo, Cunningham and Driscoll, and their wing (Grant and Sullivan, on their left, line-abreast, about one nautical mile away) started a slow, descending turn to approach the target slightly north of the strike track. Cunningham later said that he intended to pass just north of the airfield and establish an orbit point about 20 nautical miles north-east of Quan Lang, between the target area and the MiG base at Bai Thuong. His idea was to position the MiGCAP to intercept any jets launching from Bai Thuong, but at about 15 nautical

Although of indifferent quality, this rare photograph more than qualifies for inclusion in this volume by dint of the fact that it shows 'Randy' Cunningham and 'Willie' Driscoll at the controls of 'Showtime 112', which was their 'MiG-killing' jet of 19 January. Indeed, this shot was taken just days prior to them claiming their MiG-21 (*via Peter Mersky*)

miles west of Quan Lang, he started picking up height-finder and AAA radar on his Radar-Homing and Warning (RHAW) gear, and he could see the southern group taking heavy 23 and 37 mm groundfire. According to Cunningham, this route had been a mistake, as they were smack in the middle of two SAM sites.

The lead VF-96 jet was at 17,000 ft, flying at 500 knots north-west of the field, when Cunningham received positive SAM-launch indications, and he saw a missile rising from the northern site. 'The missile was coming right up under Grant's belly – he couldn't see it. I called, "Break left", but he didn't break hard enough, so I called for a harder break'. The missile passed about ten feet from Grant's canopy and detonated high at 20,000-25,000 ft. Cunningham later suggested that the missile must have been defective because the proximity fuse warhead fitted to the SA-2 was effective up to a distance of 350 ft.

He then received further RHAW warnings that the southern SAM site (at his 'two o'clock') had him locked-up. Cunningham reversed to the right and saw a SAM launch. 'I could see a little white glow and the dust flying'. Still at about 17,000 ft, he and his wingman broke right and down. 'This one kept tracking – I wasn't defeating it. So, I rolled inverted, waited until the missile was within half a mile of us, then pulled hard into a split-S type manoeuvre. I put the stick in my lap and pulled about 9G'. The missile sailed harmlessly by and exploded about 1000 ft high.

Cunningham recovered and headed north-west at a height of 10,000 ft and 300 knots. He immediately saw another SAM launched at him from the northern site. 'The F-4 can pull only about 3-4G at 300 knots, so I engaged "burner". I still had the tank, so I unloaded. I was hanging in the straps. I rolled into the missile, and as it approached me, I buried the stick in my lap'. The SAM detonated in the immediate vicinity of the Phantom II, flipping it from about a 135-degree nose low, left bank to about a 45-degree right bank, nose high, but remarkably caused no damage.

While trying to regain altitude, Cunningham looked down and saw what he believed to be two A-7s at his 'one o'clock', three nautical miles away, heading north through a canyon at a height of 500 ft. 'As I was looking around for more SAMs, although I wasn't having any RHAW indications, it dawned on me that those two birds were in afterburner, and the A-7 doesn't have a 'burner! I looked back at them and started my nose down, still in 'burner'.

Indeed, Cunningham's 'A-7s' were actually two silver MiG-21s. The fighter on the left was flying at about 500 ft, while the second MiG was abeam to the right in a fighting wing, stepped up a further 300-500 ft above his leader. Cunningham made the call, 'Bandits! Blue Bandits! North of the field!' Descending rapidly to about 200 ft, he accelerated to 500 knots and closed on the lead MiG from behind.

'I thought about punching off my centreline tank, but at that airspeed in the F-4 we were having problems with it hitting the stabilator – at that altitude I didn't want any control problems. I told my RIO (Radar Intercept Officer, Lt(jg) Driscoll) that the pipper was on him – he hit the boresight switch and called "Locked-on, 50 knots closing – shoot, shoot, shoot your Sparrow". I reached over and hit the "heat" switch. It didn't make my RIO very happy, but from the tail aspect I was much more confident with the Sidewinder than I was with the Sparrow.'

Cunningham and Driscoll's five kills were claimed using these two machines, 'Showtime 112' (BuNo 157267) and 'Showtime 100' (BuNo 155800). Both jets had served with VF-96 for some time prior to them 'bagging' five of the eight MiGs credited to the unit in 1972, BuNo 157267 joining from VF-121 on 2 February 1971 and BuNo 155800 arriving fresh from McDonnell Douglas's St Louis plant on 19 October 1968. This photograph was taken soon after the squadron commenced operations from *Yankee Station* in November 1971 (*via Angelo Romano*)

Cunningham (now at 300 ft, and speeding over the jungle at 500 knots) launched one AIM-9G at the lead MiG from 'six o'clock' at a distance of about two miles, calling 'Fox Two!' He said that neither MiG appeared to have seen him until his missile launched, at which point the lead MiG broke hard to the right. He believes that the second MiG must have called a 'break', because his victim couldn't have seen the Sidewinder. From a 'six o'clock', tailpipe position at the time of missile launch, the next thing Cunningham saw was a plan view of the lead MiG 'really hauling, still in afterburner'. The AIM-9 missed and impacted the ground. 'They must have been H or J-model MiGs', Cunningham later explained, 'as the MiG-21 just can't turn that fast without hydraulically-boosted controls'.

Expecting the MiG to continue its turn into him, Cunningham pulled up into a high speed 'yo-yo' and made a 'baby barrel roll' to the left to maintain position. 'I expected the big cross-turn – they were trying to bring me right down between them. Instead, his wingman just left him – he pushed over and ran.'

After Cunningham's first weapon missed its mark, the lead MiG reversed its turn and continued towards Bai Thuong. 'A lot of my BQM (drone) training went through my mind as I engaged that MiG – my overtake, altitude and airspeed. And when he reversed, it was just like I'd called for the BQM to reverse', Cunningham remembers.

The MiG's reversal repositioned it directly in front of 'Showtime 112', and from less than a mile away, Cunningham triggered a second AIM-9, which went directly up the jet's tailpipe. The aft section of the MiG appeared to come off, the nose tucked down violently, and the aircraft hit the ground, tumbling head-over-tail – no 'chute was seen. As Cunningham quickly turned right to avoid ingesting debris, he saw the second MiG at '12 o'clock', about two-and-half nautical miles away, fleeing the area.

The MiG had pushed over in an acceleration manoeuvre and was heading north-west, starting to pull away. Cunningham was now at 450 knots, still in afterburner, and carrying his centreline tank as he started pursuit. He chased the second MiG for about 30 nautical miles, with the communist jet slightly increasing the separation distance. The MiG pilot then started to climb, and Cunningham began to close on him. 'I was going to chase him right to Bai Thuong but my RIO asked me for our (fuel) state. I said, "Willie, don't bother me know. I'm chasing a MiG", and he replied, "No shit. I want your state RIGHT NOW!" I glanced at it and was astounded to see that we were down to 6500 lbs – when using the afterburner, fuel just went like that. We now barely had enough to exit through the SAMs to a tanker'.

By this time Cunningham and Driscoll (who were flying at tree-top height) were taking ground fire from both sides, and could see tracers

'Showtime 112' traps back aboard the *Constellation* at the end of its historic 'MiG killing' mission on the afternoon of 19 January 1972. And despite the adrenaline coursing through 'Randy' Cunningham's body after he had downed the Navy's first MiG in almost two years, he still looks set to snag a three-wire on landing! After service with VF-96, BuNo 157267 briefly rejoined Pacific Fleet Replacement Air Group (RAG) squadron VF-121, before moving to VF-114 on 19 December 1972. It remained with the 'Aardvarks' until 28 April 1975, completing a further two *WestPac* deployments (aboard *Kitty Hawk*) in this period. Serving with VF-121 for the last time between May 1975 and May 1976, BuNo 157267 then joined VF-21. It remained in the frontline with the 'Freelancers' until September 1977 (and completed a solitary *WestPac* aboard the *Ranger*), when the jet was transferred to MCAS Kaneohe Bay-based VMFA-232. BuNo 157267 was flown by this unit in Hawaii and Japan (MCAS Iwakuni) until issued to fellow Kaneohe Bay resident VMFA-235 in March 1979. Sent to the Naval Air Rework Facility (NARF) at NAS North Island, San Diego, in October of that same year, the fighter emerged from its overhaul on 15 July 1980 as an F-4S. BuNo 157267 was then sent to VMFA-122 at MCAS Beaufort, South Carolina, where it remained until retired to the Military Aircraft Storage and Disposition Center (MASDC) at Davis-Monthan AFB, Arizona, on 13 December 1984 – the F-4 had completed some 4354 flight hours by this time (*via P Mersky*)

passing over their canopy. However, they had a full system lock-on, and Cunningham felt compelled to try a desperation shot. Moreover, he knew that he was not going to catch the MiG for an AIM-9 shot. With his F-4 just 200 ft above the ground, he triggered off an AIM-7E-2 at the MiG, which was at 400 ft some three nautical miles away, and opening, in front of the Phantom II. The Sparrow failed to launch, however, and it was later discovered that there was a shorted cable that prevented the ejector cartridge from firing. Cunningham, with his wing still flying cover, then made a left climbing turn to 20,000 ft, egressed and headed for the tanker.

The RA-5 pilot had seen the lead MiG crash and attempted to photograph the scene, but was forced to abort because of SAMs. A total of 18 SA-2s were launched at the force but none inflicted any damage.

'Duke' Cunningham and 'Willie' Driscoll received a warm welcome once they got back to CVA-64. 'There was real elation among the 5000 people on the "Connie". It was the first kill in almost two years, and we had quite a welcoming committee. In fact, one of the enlisted men knocked the Admiral over to jump up on the aeroplane and grab my arm to say "Mr Cunningham, we got our MiG today, didn't we?!"'

According to the *Red Baron* intelligence report written up by the Navy after this engagement, 'the most significant comment we can make regarding this event is that the crews were well prepared mentally. They knew how to effectively employ their weapons and had the ability to manoeuvre their aircraft to the desired position. It is significant that they felt they had "been there before" because of their training with the ACM'.

Furthermore, Cunningham's backseater, 'Willie' Driscoll, had insisted on a fuel check during the engagement, which probably saved them from walking home.

Following this action, air activity slowed down for the next two months, although *Blue Tree* protective reaction strikes continued, permitting the Americans to stage the largest ongoing 'unofficial' campaign against North Vietnam since the cessation of *Rolling Thunder* in October 1968.

'SUNDOWNER' SUCCESS

The next Navy Phantom II MiG kill occurred during the afternoon of 6 March 1972, when a pair of F-4Bs from VF-111 'Sundowners' successfully manoeuvred a MiG-17 into a 'sandwich' for a kill.

The two jets from the *Coral Sea* had launched as a FORCAP (Force CAP) section in support of a photo-reconnaissance mission to Quan Lang airfield. FORCAP referred to fighters that were directed to a spot north of the carriers to intercept any MiGs that may attempt to attack the vessel. However, if a reconnaissance jet saw any 'bogies', the FORCAPs were cleared to intercept the enemy aircraft as they returned north.

Lt James 'Yosemite' Stillinger (a former F-8 Crusader pilot with a prior combat tour, and a recent Topgun graduate) and Lt(jg) Rick Olin crewed the lead Phantom II, while Lt Garry L Weigand and Lt(jg) William C Freckleton flew as their wing (in F-4B BuNo 153019, call-sign 'Old Nick 201').

Interestingly, Weigand and Freckleton had originally been scheduled to fly as wing for Lt Cdr Jim Ruliffson and his 'nugget' RIO, Lt(jg) Clark van Nostrand. Ruliffson (call-sign 'Cobra') was one of the founding members of Topgun, and he was well respected in the fleet for his tactical expertise. Indeed, his ability as a Phantom II pilot was legendary. But as the F-4s were holding on the catapults, Ruliffson's jet sprung a hydraulics leak and had to be scratched. 'He was livid', Bill Freckleton recalled.

Moustache-toting Stillinger and Olin, who were waiting on hot-fuel standby, were then moved onto the starboard catapult and assumed section lead. Both F-4s were experiencing radar problems (Olin had only pulse search and Bill Freckleton's radar was absolutely dead), which ruled out the employment of Sparrows should MiGs being engaged.

As with the 19 January photo-mission to Quan Lang, the crews conducting the reconnaissance flight on 6 March planned to use the 'back door' route into Laos, before flying back towards the target.

Quan Lang was one of many MiG airfields that had been extensively reinforced during the bombing halt following *Rolling Thunder*. When that campaign ended in October 1968, Quan Lang was home to some 150 MiGs, mostly MiG-17s. By 1972, the base had grown to accommodate some 260 fighters, 95 of which were MiG-21s and 30 Chinese-built MiG-19s. These jets were being regularly sortied by the VPAF to harass B-52 missions to Laos, and to provide cover for the build-up of supplies for the coming offensive against South Vietnam.

After launch, Stillinger and Weigand were vectored into the area by the *Red Crown* controller, who on this day was Senior Chief Radarman Larry Nowell aboard the cruiser USS *Chicago* (CG-11). The senior chief would

VF-111's sole F-4 'MiG killer' basks in the sun at NAS Miramar in August 1972. Note the MiG-17 silhouette on the jet's splitter plate. Accepted by the Navy at St Louis on 5 May 1966, this aircraft remained with McDonnell for research and development work until 29 July, when it was issued to VF-213. BuNo 153019 embarked with the unit on *Kitty Hawk* on 5 November for the 'Black Lions'' second (of six) *WestPacs*. It went on to complete a further two combat cruises with CVW-11/CVA-63 prior to its transfer to VF-121 on 29 December 1969. Remaining with the RAG until 17 March 1971, BuNo 153019 then joined VF-111 and participated in its fourth *WestPac*, aboard the *Coral Sea*. The jet completed a fifth combat cruise, again with VF-111, in 1973. Transitioning to the F-4N in mid-1974, the 'Sundowners' duly passed BuNo 153019 on to VMFA-531 at MCAS El Toro, California, in October. The jet was sent to NARF North Island in March 1975, where it remained in cocooned storage until converted into an N-model as part of Project *Beeline* between June and September 1976 – it was the 198th F-4B to be upgraded. BuNo 153019 was issued to reserve-manned VF-201 at NAS Dallas on 23 May 1977, and it continued to serve with the Texas-based unit until transferred to VF-171 at NAS Key West, Florida, on 10 February 1984. Stricken from the inventory two weeks later, BuNo 153019 has guarded the gate at the Florida naval air station since October 1984. It is the sole survivor of the 16 Navy F-4s to have claimed a kill during *Rolling Thunder* (*via Brad Elward*)

Four of the five key players involved in securing VF-111's MiG-17 kill (on the afternoon of 6 March 1972) pose for the ship's photographer in *Coral Sea's* hangar deck the day after the mission. They are, from left to right, Lt(jg) William 'Farkle' Freckleton ('Old Nick 201's' RIO), Senior Chief Radarman Larry Nowell (the 'ace' *Red Crown* fighter controller from the cruiser *Chicago*), Lt Garry 'Greyhound' Weigand (the pilot of 'Old Nick 201') and Lt James 'Yosemite' Stillinger (section leader on the 'MiG killing' mission) (*via Angelo Romano*)

'Old Nick 204' (BuNo 150466) and 'Screaming Eagle 113' (BuNo 149457) drop their standard low-drag Mk 82 500-lb bombs through broken cloud whilst flying over North Vietnam at medium level in March 1972. Note how the aircrafts' Triple Ejector Racks (TERs) are secured to the underside of the twin Sidewinder mounting. This photograph was taken just 48 hours after Garry Weigand and Bill Freckleton had destroyed their MiG-17. Three months later, on 11 June, 'Screaming Eagle 113' got in on the action when its crew downed CVW-15's fifth, and final, MiG of the air wing's highly eventful 1971-72 *WestPac* deployment (*via Aerospace Publishing*)

subsequently be involved in no less than 13 successful MiG-killing sorties, and was awarded a Distinguished Service Medal on 17 August 1972 for his efforts, becoming only the second Navy enlisted man so honoured.

Once in communication with the VF-111 crews, Nowell directed them to establish an orbit on-station above Brandon Bay. As soon as they arrived, they heard the photo jet call 'Bandits! Bandits! Two Blue Bandits!', indicating MiG-21s, then, 'More! Red bandits! Red bandits! Two, no I think I see three Red Bandits!', indicating the presence of the more nimble MiG-17s. At this point, the MiGCAP, which had been orbiting in Laos (two F-4Bs from VF-111's sister unit, VF-51, crewed by squadron CO Cdr Foster S 'Tooter' Teague and RIO Lt Ralph M Howell, and Ops Officer Lt Cdr Jerry B 'Devil' Houston and RIO Lt Kevin T Moore), entered the fray to protect the Vigilante.

It is worth noting that the Navy came close to scoring two kills that day, for the F-4s flown by Teague and Houston engaged four MiG-17s, and Teague managed to launch a Sidewinder against one of the communist jets. The AIM-9 exploded close enough to damage the MiG, but in the ensuing battle Teague lost track of it and a kill could not be confirmed. Teague and Howell launched a second Sidewinder against another MiG, but it had been launched too close to arm and failed to detonate. The section eventually evaded the remaining jets, who outnumbered the VF-51 crews, and returned safely to their carrier.

Stillinger and Weigand listened to the engagement until vectored north-west at 15,000 ft by *Red Crown*, switching to strike frequency 'Miramar Tower' on 315.6 UHF,

and assuming combat spread formation with Weigand on Stillinger's starboard wing. Their station was 50 miles north of Quan Lang, where they could intercept the MiGs fleeing to their bases. However, no sooner had the Phantom IIs arrived on station when they received another call from *Red Crown* telling them that they had 'bogies' in their area.

The initial vector positioned a 'bogey' at 326 degrees and 14 nautical miles, about 80 degrees to their right. *Red Crown* called the bogey at eight and then six nautical miles, but no radar or visual contact could be acquired. *Red Crown* then called 'Merge plot', which meant that the VF-111 jets were almost on top of the MiGs, yet neither crew saw them. 'No Joy! No Joy!', hollered Stillinger.

Senior Chief Nowell came back with 'Look low, look low, three miles'. Lt Wiegand remembers, 'We rolled up into a left bank, looked down, and there was the MiG! It looked as though he had just pulled his nose up to come after us'. The Phantom II pilots had visually sighted a MiG-17, low, at 'ten o'clock', and at a height of approximately 500-1000 ft. 'Tally ho!' Stillinger called, followed a couple of seconds later by Weigand's, 'Roger, Tally ho on one MiG-17!' The section was in a starboard turn at about 3000 ft, descending and picking up airspeed, when the silver MiG was sighted.

Bill Freckleton later praised Senior Chief Nowell's reading of the situation on his radar scope. 'If he hadn't told us to look down exactly when he said to, we would have continued our starboard turn and the MiG would have come around behind our section and bagged one or both of us'. Such a timely intervention would mark out Senior Chief Nowell as the fighter crews' favourite controller – crews would soon call him by name during radio communications with *Red Crown*. Nowell summed up his role in one sentence. 'My job is to draw the pilot a continuous mental picture of where he is in relation to the overall tactical situation'.

Freckleton continued, 'We knew it was going to be pretty much an energy fight since the MiG could easily out-turn the F-4. We had to use our speed and energy to climb, dive, extend and pitch back, as opposed to laying on a 6G turn that would not get us inside the MiG's turn radius'.

Stillinger directed Weigand to go to trail. 'I'm engaging, go to cover', he radiocd. Pitching over the top, Stillinger fell in trail on the MiG from a barrel-roll manoeuvre. As he was descending in a starboard turn, a little outside of the MiG's turn radius, the VPAF jet suddenly reversed left and pulled up hard into him. After the engagement, Stillinger later recalled, 'I don't know if he saw us or if his GCI said there was somebody behind him, but he turned'. Stillinger followed the MiG through several reversals, looking at its 'six o'clock' area, but he could not get his nose on it.

The MiG manoeuvred fairly level, with turns from 15-20 degrees nose high to 15-20 degrees nose low, while Stillinger continued to work in the vertical. Each time the F-4 pilot came off high and started his nose down toward the MiG, it would reverse its turn, positioning Stillinger on the inside. This forced Stillinger to repeatedly barrel-roll or high-speed 'yo-yo' away from the MiG to regain his position.

Stillinger continued manoeuvring until, as he related, 'I decided, "To hell with maintaining energy". I decided to pull the aeroplane around the corner and shoot him. I was outside his plane of turn, looking up at him, and I could see his tailpipe. I had a very good tone'. However, as Stillinger

107

Devoid of all external stores, VF-111's 'CAG bird' closes on CVA-43's steel deck during CARQUALs (carrier qualification) in the spring of 1972. CVW-15 had two CAGs for its 1971-72 *WestPac*, its original CO, Cdr Thomas E Dunlop, being killed over North Vietnam in an A-7E on 6 April 1972. He was replaced by Cdr Roger E 'Blinky' Sheets, who led CVW-15 for the remaining three months of its deployment (*via Peter E Davies*)

pulled the trigger at a range of 4500-6000 ft, the MiG rolled into him and pulled extremely hard.

Stillinger recalls, 'That was the first time he (the MiG pilot) really turned his aeroplane to its maximum. At least that turn was much tighter than anything he showed me before'. His AIM-9 made one small twist as it tried to turn back to the target, but then went ballistic. 'I don't think it ever had a good chance', Stillinger continued, 'once the MiG pilot rolled his aeroplane and pulled extremely hard. He blanked out my view of the tailpipe, and I didn't have a tone on my next missile'.

Stillinger again tried to roll away and come back down, but the MiG-17 generated 'quite a bit of angle-off in that one turn'. Deciding that there was no way that he could get another shot better than the one he had taken, Stillinger radioed Weigand, 'I can't stay behind him. I'm going to unload and run. Do you have me in sight?' Weigand and Freckleton replied in the affirmative, having pulled above the engagement to a 'cover' position for Stillinger. Now perched to take over the fight, Weigand told his leader, 'I am rolling in on the MiG'.

Once Stillinger established that Weigand and Freckleton had the engaged MiG in sight and were positioned for an attack, he manoeuvred his Phantom II into a pure-pursuit attack. He put his nose on the MiG and lit the afterburners coming downhill. 'As I went by him' Stillinger said, 'I went ahead and relaxed the G and rolled away a little bit, almost wings-level, passed 500 ft behind him, then rolled back and pulled so I was sure I could see him. This was where his slow roll-rate was pretty obvious. I went by and he lazily rolled the aeroplane around toward me, and it made for his own lateral separation. It took him so long to roll into

Although US naval vessels are 'dry', which precluded the traditional toasting of aerial success with a suitably alcoholic libation, one of the ship's galley staff could always be relied upon to rustle up a suitably decorated cake in short order! Photographed in the 'Sundowners'' ready room, the four crewmen involved in the 6 March MiG-17 kill prepare to hand out the cake to all and sundry. They are, from left to right, Lt(jg) William 'Farkle' Freckleton ('Old Nick 201's' RIO), Lt Garry 'Greyhound' Weigand (the pilot of 'Old Nick 201'), Lt James 'Yosemite' Stillinger (section leader on the 'MiG killing' mission) and Lt(jg) Rick Olin (Stillinger's RIO) (*via Brad Elward*)

a tracking position that I think he was outside gun range because I never saw him fire at me.'

Now on the defensive, Stillinger called Weigand in from overhead while he continued to extend. Keeping the MiG at his right 'four o'clock' low, Stillinger began to 'drag him out'. The MiG pilot lit his afterburner and drove towards Stillinger's 'six o'clock' in an effort to close for a missile shot, but did not enter a lead-pursuit track. According to Freckleton, Weigand kept his 'eyes padlocked' on the MiG while he swivelled his head, watching their 'six'. With the radar out, Freckleton had little to do in the back seat but post watch for bandits. Garry Weigand, on the other hand, was busy earning his flying pay.

'I rolled up over the top of the MiG, then continued around in a left-hand roll, coming out below and behind the MiG. I figured that he was preoccupied with Jim, and had not seen me. He pulled hard into Jim, who was now running straight out. Then, just as I put my nose on him, he straightened up and pulled hard into me! I figured he had now seen me, and was going to come around and start fighting with me. But I pushed down, trying to get into his "blind six", and then he reversed back onto the flight lead, who was now directly in front of him – he hadn't seen me after all!

'When I had first rolled in on him I had a lot of excess airspeed, and had started to overshoot. To correct this, I went to idle and put the speed brakes out. As the MiG pilot reversed onto the lead, he lit his 'burner and got his speed up pretty good. I got the speed brakes in and went to military. The MiG was fairly close to Jim, but his reverse had cost him some position, and Jim had picked up a lot of energy when he unloaded. We were down to 500 ft and Jim was pushing 600 knots. Jim was opening on him pretty fast. The MiG must have thought he had a chance at a gunshot though, and that's why he lit his 'burner and continued to jockey for position.'

Seconds later, Stillinger called to Weigand 'Okay, the MiG is now back at my right "four o'clock". Shoot him, shoot him. We're holding him off'. As Stillinger said, 'Shoot him', Weigand moved directly behind the MiG and fired an AIM-9D. 'Garry and I were "dead six" (to the MiG), a half-mile away at 500 knots when we shot', Freckleton remembers. The missile went directly up the MiG's tailpipe and exploded. Both F-4B crews saw several large pieces of the MiG's tail come off as it continued straight ahead for a while and then started to pitch over.

Freckleton continues. 'We entered a starboard turn to avoid the flying debris. I didn't see the impact because it was "dead 12 o'clock", but I got a good eyeful of the debris flying past on our port side. The MiG crashed into the ground and erupted in a huge fireball. The pilot was killed'.

But the crew had little time to bask in the glory of their success, for moments later *Red Crown* called 'MiGs!' Weigand again. 'By this time the North Vietnamese Air Defence Controller had vectored four MiG-21s onto us. They were only about 15 miles away, and closing fast. We were low on fuel and couldn't afford another engagement, so we lit the 'burners and exited North Vietnam, supersonic at 1200 ft, outdistancing the MiG-21s. Once in the relative safety of our own naval forces, we refuelled and returned to the *Coral Sea*'.

Garry Weigand and Bill Freckleton's kill earned them both a Silver Star, and it marked the second victory for the *Coral Sea* (VF-151 had

Weigand and Freckleton are literally mobbed on the deck of the *Coral Sea* in front of 'Old Nick 201' just minutes after shutting down and getting out of the jet on the afternoon of 6 March 1972. Note the proliferation of gear attached to the pilot's upper torso harness (*via Angelo Romano*)

claimed a MiG-17 on 6 October 1965) and the second for their Phantom II, BuNo 153019. On 20 December 1966, while flying with VF-213, it had downed a VPAF An-2.

INVASION

On 30 March 1972, the long predicted North Vietnamese invasion of South Vietnam commenced. Thirteen of the North Vietnamese Army's fourteen divisions were involved in a three-pronged assault dubbed the 'Easter Offensive' or 'Spring Invasion'. NVA troops and armour stormed across the DMZ into the Central Highlands, and across the Cambodian border towards Saigon.

Immediately, President Richard Nixon ordered strikes against the invaders, and urgently despatched more aircraft to the region. Only two carriers were on *Yankee Station* at the time, but soon there would be six, establishing a record for the entire war.

Operation *Freedom Train* began on 5 April, as more air power poured into the region. These strikes were the first large-scale attacks to be flown above the 20th Parallel since 1968, and Navy aeroplanes completed a total of 680 sorties during the first week of April. This marked a significant change from the *Rolling Thunder* campaign, where many lucrative targets were declared off limits by American politicians.

During April, Task Force 77 had swelled in size to include five carriers – *Constellation* (CVA-64), *Kitty Hawk* (CVA-63), *Hancock* (CVA-19), *Coral Sea* (CVA-43) and *Saratoga* (CV-60). And this massing of American air power would lead to the first Navy air-to-air loss of 1972 on 27 April (see *Osprey Combat Aircraft 29 - MiG-21 Units of the Vietnam War* for a full description of the action). F-4B BuNo 153025 of VF-51's Lt Al Molinare and RIO Lt Cdr J B Souder was brought down by an R-3S (K-13 Atoll) missile fired by Hoang Quoc Dung, who was flying a silver MiG-21PFM of the 921st 'Sao Do' Fighter Regiment.

REVENGE FOR VF-51

On 6 May a section of two F-4Bs from VF-51 were assigned as TARCAP for a 19-aeroplane Alpha strike on the airfield at Bai Thuong, situated 25 miles west of Thanh Hoa. Lead (F-4B BuNo 150456, call sign 'Screaming Eagle 100') was flown by Lt Cdr Jerry 'Devil' Houston and his RIO Lt Kevin Moore, with Chuck Schroeder and Rick Webb as their wing.

Expectations were high of meeting MiGs, for intelligence from the evening prior had indicated that there were 14 enemy aircraft at Bai Thuong, and that the runway was in good shape. The plan of attack called for the strike force to approach the target from the south and split into two groups, with the TARCAP coming in with the higher, slower bombers (A-6As with Rockeye munitions) in the second group.

Once through the throng of well-wishers, Weigand and Freckleton descended one level below the flight deck to VF-111's ready room, where this photograph was taken. RIO Freckleton remembers, 'We had been surrounded by an entire flightdeck of men who swarmed up to congratulate us. We made our way to the VF-111 ready room, where the ship's photographer told us he wanted one more shot. He said "Smile, and give the victory sign". One of us complied. The other was giving the peace sign!' (*William C Freckleton via Peter E Davies*)

On 6 May 1972 it was the turn of
VF-111's sister-squadron VF-51 to
celebrate an aerial kill, when
squadron Operations Officer Lt Cdr
Jerry 'Devil' Houston (second from
left) and Lt Kevin Moore (extreme
left) 'bagged' a MiG-17 near Bai
Thuong airfield. Flying wing for the
crew were Lt Cdr Chuck Schroeder
(second from right) and Lt Rick
Webb (extreme right). Schroeder
was VF-51's Maintenance Officer,
and he was in charge of keeping the
unit's F-4s airworthy, as Jerry
Houston explains;

'It was exciting news when VF-51
found out it was receiving F-4Bs in
place of its F-8s. What we didn't
know was that our F-4s would be
coming from USMC rejects. The jets
we were assigned had been
preserved in whatever state they
had been in a couple of years earlier
when the Corps had declared them
unairworthy. Maintenance *Tiger
Teams* from all the F-4 squadrons at
Miramar were assigned the job of
going to MCAS El Toro and
performing overdue scheduled
maintenance, and getting those
hulks capable of flying to Miramar.
Chuck Schroeder succeeded in the
Herculean undertaking of getting
those over-the-hill rustbuckets
ready for deployment, despite
competing against my back-
breaking training schedule.'

Here, RIO Webb is describing how
he would have fought the MiGs that
they had encountered earlier in the
day, much to the amusement of his
squadronmates (*Jerry Houston*)

As the strike force went 'feet-dry', *Red Crown* called '"Screaming Eagles", heads up' – a pre-arranged signal meaning that the MiGs had gone to strip alert, and that airborne activity was imminent. Almost immediately, the first group of A-6As began giving numerous calls of MiGs in the area. According to the Intruder crews, some of the MiGs were doing 'touch-and-goes' on the Bai Thuong runway, while others circled overhead. The latter jets scattered when the strike aircraft appeared, indicating that the MiGs were possibly being flown by rookie pilots.

As the F-4s continued inbound with the second wave of A-6As, the fighter crews monitored UHF strike transmissions. Apparently, a dark-camouflaged MiG-17 was attacking three Intruders from the first group who were egressing in front of Houston's flight. Moore quickly spotted the Intruders and the communist jet, calling 'Tally Ho. There's your A-6s . . . one . . . two . . . three . . . and here's your MiG!' Houston peered out of the cockpit until he could see them too. 'I looked out to my "two o'clock" and spotted the MiG. He was painted black, grey and white in a normal terrain-type camouflage. It was a MiG-17, and it was very easy to recognise, although I wasn't close enough to spot any national markings'.

Houston manoeuvred for position using a 6G, descending 180-degree starboard turn, jettisoning his centreline tank in the process. 'It was a clean pickle', he remembers, 'except for one bent Sparrow that we found out about later. I felt comfortable "pickling" it (the centreline tank) under any speed conditions with G on the aircraft, and was not concerned with it coming back and hitting the aeroplane'.

Schroeder had been holding a combat-spread formation on Houston's left side at the time the flight began the right descending turn. During the manoeuvre, the trailing Phantom II was forced to cross over, and ended up about 3000 ft away at Houston's 'five o'clock' at roll-out. He at once came under attack from a second MiG-17. Moore saw the second MiG about 3000 ft behind Schroeder and called twice for him to break, but without response. 'Kevin called the MiG, but in our particular aeroplane, which was old and had a history of radio problems, the Sidewinder tone was also transmitted, effectively blocking the rest of the transmission', Houston explained.

With the MiG now closing, Moore made two more 'break' calls, but there was still no acknowledgement. As Schroeder later recalled, 'I didn't hear anything. The Sidewinder tone was on, and every time we pulled G the radio would go to about half strength'. Houston again. 'Chuck didn't know about the MiG behind him until the bright red 37 mm "golf balls" began whistling by his canopy!' He immediately began a left defensive turn, with the MiG following.

Houston had been oblivious to all this, for he was busy chasing his camouflaged MiG. 'I had the blinders on, concentrating on our MiG'. Directly in front of the enemy jet was a solitary A-6A, shooting across North Vietnam at 450-475 knots at an altitude of just 100 ft. Houston quickly moved behind the MiG-17, closing at nearly 600 knots and placing himself within Sidewinder missile range. He had a solid lock-on tone.

Unknown to Houston or Moore, the A-6A that was now coming under fire from the VPAF jet was being flown by CVW-15's CAG (Commander Air Group), Cdr Roger 'Blinky' Sheets, a former fighter pilot. Flying an S-turn, Sheets had managed to position his Intruder between the MiG and the two other VMA(AW)-224 A-6As that the VF-51 crew had spotted when they first arrived on the scene. This selfless manoeuvre had seen the CAG drag the MiG onto his jet, and away from his flightmates.

With the A-6 travelling at such a high subsonic speed, Houston and Moore knew that the MiG-17 was flying too fast for its flight controls to function properly. 'At that particular speed the MiG-17 pilot had a problem. He didn't have control authority to do very much, since he lacked the power-assist on his controls. In fact, the controls got so stiff that it was actually possible to bend the stick without getting control response', recounts 'Devil' Houston.

Apparently Sheets knew this too, which was why he continued to lead the MiG. He hoped that the F-4 crew would trigger a missile, at which time the CAG would break away, knowing that the MiG could not break with him.

While Houston was now in a prime position for a missile launch on the MiG, he also ran the risk of hitting the A-6A. He called repeatedly for the Intruders to 'break right' to enable him to shoot, but only two of them appeared to follow his break call. Houston describes his thoughts at this moment. 'We were behind the MiG for a long time with good tone and we couldn't, or wouldn't, shoot because he was directly behind the A-6. Although we had our pipper on the MiG and were getting good tone, we couldn't be sure that the tone wasn't being produced by the A-6 as well, and we couldn't get the bomber pilot to break. Here was the opportunity we had waited all our lives for and it was going to worms because the A-6 wouldn't break!'

Houston wondered if it was his radio which was giving him trouble, preventing his 'Break' calls from

Another kill, another cake. All four crewmen from VF-51 are joined in their ready room by other participants in the 6 May mission, namely Marine Corps Capt Charlie Carr (CAG's Bombardier/Navigator on 6 May, and assigned to VMA(AW)-224 – front row, extreme left), CAG Cdr Roger 'Blinky' Sheets (described by 'Devil' Houston as a 'Don Knotts look-a-like, with more guts than a slaughterhouse' – front row, second from left) and Capt Bill Harris, captain of the *Coral Sea* (back row, right) (*Jerry Houston*)

being received by the A-6 crew. His F-4B was an ex-Marine Corps jet that had had its UHF radio modified to carry the AIM-9 tone when in use. 'The Marines had modified their radios to transmit the Sidewinder growl over the UHF radio when the transmit button was pressed. The transmitted tone overrode all other UHF transmissions, and effectively put us without communications during the most important couple of minutes in my airborne career. I didn't know that Sheets couldn't hear my frantic calls to "Break and get the hell out of there". All he heard was the transmitted Sidewinder tone', remembers Houston.

Having reached minimum Sidewinder launch range, Houston squeezed the trigger from 'dead six o'clock', about 3000 ft behind the MiG. 'The AIM-9G came off and went straight down, then straight up! And as we flew through the hump-backed smoke trail of the Sidewinder, it straightened out and headed for the MiG. CAG Sheets saw the missile come off the rail and broke, having played the role of ultimate decoy to the end! The MiG couldn't break, and the Sidewinder flew up his tailpipe, blowing his tail off. We were so low that the explosion of the missile was followed immediately – just bam! bam! – by the explosion the MiG made as it impacted the karst ridge'.

From after action reports, it appears that the MiG pilot had given such complete attention to shooting down the A-6A that he was never aware of Houston's presence.

MORE MiG KILLS

But the day had not ended for the American carrier aircrews. The attack against Bai Thuong airfield by CVW-15 had been a major success, and the call immediately went out for a follow-up strike. *Coral Sea's* bombers had cratered the runway, and it appeared that the MiG-17s were trapped on the ground. *Kitty Hawk's* CVW-11 responded by cancelling cyclic ops and immediately readying a number of aircraft for an Alpha strike. The rush to launch the strike caused some problems, with a number of jets being sent aloft without first being properly reconfigured, while others, such as the VF-114 'Aardvarks' jet of Lt Cdr Pete 'Viper' Pettigrew (F-4J BuNo 157245, call sign 'Linfield 201') received less than a full complement of missiles – instead of the traditional four Sparrows and four

Houston and Moore were flying VF-51's CAG jet when they claimed their MiG, this aircraft boasting a multi-coloured rendition of the unit's famous 'Screaming Eagle' motif. Dubbed the 'supersonic can opener' by rival fighter crews, this scheme was possibly the most flamboyant worn by any F-4 unit. Jerry Houston remembers;

'This scheme came about following a competition within VF-51 to design a squadron paint scheme. The Miramar wags said all the design lacked were mud flaps and a long racoon tail on some aerial!'

This photograph was taken prior to the unit deploying in November 1971 (*via Peter E Davies*)

Capt Harris congratulates Houston and Moore on the flightdeck on 6 May 1972. 'Devil' claims that he 'kept his sunglasses on to hide tears of joy' (*Jerry Houston*)

VF-114 also got in on the 'MiG killing' act on 6 May 1972 when a pair of MiG-21s were destroyed by this quartet of 'Aardvarks', (from left to right), Lt Bob Hughes, Lt(jg) Joe Cruz, Lt(jg) Mike McCabe and Lt Cdr Pete 'Viper' Pettigrew (*via Angelo Romano*)

Sidewinders, Pettigrew's aircraft received just two of each.

Two F-4Js from VF-114 were hastily scheduled to launch as one of two fighter sections assigned to separate stations to cover the evening Alpha strike against Bai Thuong. The western section, designated for MiGCAP, was on station north of Bai Thuong, while the eastern section, designated for BARCAP, was stationed 'feet-wet' off the coast of Thanh Hoa. At the start of the operation, Lt Robert G Hughes and RIO Lt(jg) Adolph J Cruz were flying MiGCAP (in F-4J BuNo 157249, call sign 'Linfield 206') with the squadron XO, Cdr John Pitson, while Lt Cdr Pete Pettigrew and RIO Lt(jg) Michael J McCabe were part of the BARCAP.

When Pitson experienced a radar failure during rendezvous, he switched with Pettigrew and McCabe, and they assumed lead of the western station. TARCAP for the strike was provided by the 'Aardvark's' sister squadron, VF-213 'Black Lions'.

Crossing the beach over the 'hourglass' rivers north-east of Thanh Hoa, Pettigrew and Hughes were flying at about 10,000 ft and 420 knots on the way to their station when they received a vector from *Red Crown*, aboard the *Chicago*. The section remained in military power and descended to about 8000 ft in combat-spread formation, heading 250 degrees. At about ten nautical miles 'feet dry', they picked up a strobe (contact) on their RHAW (Radar Homing And Warning) system emanating from behind them.

Lt Cdr Pettigrew later recalled, 'The whole squadron had been briefed that in order to protect our "six", we would cross-turn, which is not a very good offensive manoeuvre, but is an exceptionally good defensive one. We made one cross-turn because of the AI (air intercept) strobe, then returned to our original course and picked up the same AI strobe. We were heading back in the direction of "feet-wet" by this time, and realised that the strobe was triggered from the ground, so we cross-turned again and went back on our original vector.'

But this manoeuvring did not end their problems. *Red Crown* then called a 'bogey', and directed them south, only for the Phantom IIs to intercept elements of their own strike package. Vectoring back onto their original course, the crew were relieved to hear the voice of a new controller on the radio – Senior Chief Larry Nowell, the famed *Red Crown* 'ace' aboard the *Chicago*.

The Phantom II crews continued down towards Bai Thuong, where they picked up the TARCAP which was apparently the target of their original vector. About this time *Red Crown* came up and said, 'I have a new contact. Come starboard 010 degrees. Contact is 010 for 30 miles'.

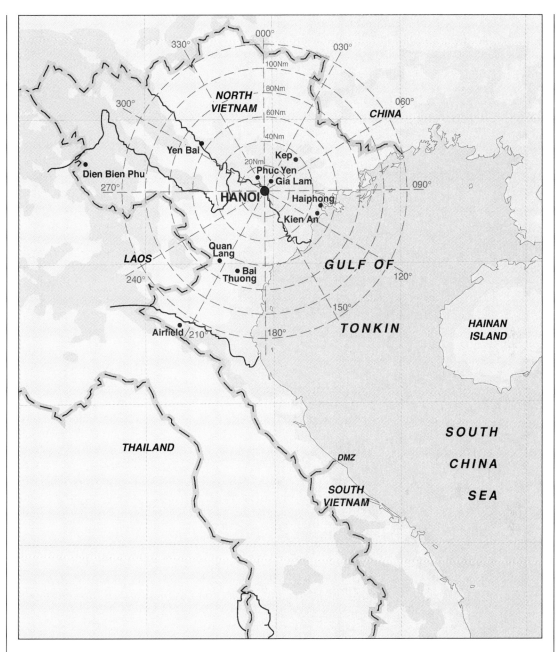

McCabe was working in the pulse-Doppler mode at this time, and called, 'Contact 330 at 25'. He locked-up the return and called a 900-knot closing velocity before the radar broke lock when the MiG went to beam.

At about 15 nautical miles Lt Hughes reacquired the contact and secured another radar lock-up. Pettigrew immediately called his wingman. 'I'll go shooter. You've got the VID (visual identification)', then slid back slightly off the port side of 'Linfield 206', with a separation distance of about one nautical mile.

The section went into minimum afterburner at 12 nautical miles and continued to close on the bandits. McCabe made first contact, and described the situation;

Red Crown fighter controllers used a *Bullseye* brevity code during the *Linebacker I* and *II* operations to provide guidance for aircrews – *Bullseye* represented Hanoi. A MiG sighting near Kep, for example, would be conveyed as, '*Bullseye*, 45 for 40', meaning that the MiG was at 060 degrees from Hanoi, and 40 nautical miles out

'We were proceeding along the ridge about 30-35 miles north of Thanh Hoa (210 degrees at 40 nautical miles from *Bullseye* – the codename for Hanoi, which was used as a reference point for broadcast reports on the position of NVAF fighters) when I picked the MiGs up at "ten o'clock" about four miles away, 4000 ft low. We were at 7000 ft, about 3000 feet above the karst. The first section was at about "10-11 o'clock". There were four MiGs in a kind of "box-four" formation, and the wingmen were flying a tactical wing position known as "welded wing". MiGs' one and two were so close that they generated a single "paint" on the radar. My aircraft commander called a turn into them for positive identification, and from that point on we were in the engagement.'

As the MiGs approached, passing underneath the Phantom IIs, they emerged from out of the sun. It appeared that they had still not seen the F-4s. 'Through most of it', McCabe continues, 'I kept track of the first section, which eventually made it all the way around to our "one o'clock", just one mile away, but they never did get into any kind of firing position. Their noses were always 70-90 degrees off'.

Pettigrew added, 'We had visually acquired all four enemy jets, and from the time we first spotted them, we never lost sight of any of them throughout the engagement. It was now about 1830 hrs, and we were low, looking into the sun to see them. When the sun goes down and you're looking into a haze, sometimes an aeroplane will show up very well at long range because it's much darker than any of the surrounding haze. This is how they appeared – very, very dark shaped aeroplanes, which stood out very well'.

Pettigrew and Hughes then turned into the jets of the second section, which were performing a shallow left turn. According to Pettigrew, who described the initial attack, 'They didn't have much airspeed, so we immediately had about 90 degrees off on them. You might almost call it a hat stern conversion – quite a bit hotter than you would want to run. However, they didn't seem to be turning very hard. In fact, the first section continued back to almost our "7-8 o'clock" before they really started turning, which gave them so much distance behind us that they never got back into the fight again. Since Hughes was outside of my turn, which put him in a better position as a shooter, I said, "You're engaged, I'm free – go get him".'

Hughes pressed the attack, picking the fourth MiG, which was in the outside rear position flying as wing for the section leader. Rolling in from a high angle-off (which he estimated as 'about 45 degrees'), Hughes

Handed over to the Navy at St Louis on 24 September 1969, BuNo 157245, was issued new to VF-114 on 24 September 1969. The fighter would serve with the unit for no less than six years, and by the time it left the 'Aardvarks' in December 1975, the jet had completed four *WestPacs* (two of which were combat tours) and downed a MiG-21 on 6 May 1972. When VF-114 commenced it conversion onto the F-14 in January 1976, BuNo 157245 was transferred to VF-51. Its time with the 'Screaming Eagles' lasted just a matter of months, for in May it was sent to NARF North Island for heavy maintenance. The fighter returned to service exactly one year later, when it was flown to Kaneohe Bay to join VMFA-212. Transferred to fellow-Kaneohe residents VMFA-232 on 13 October 1977, the jet remained with this unit until September 1979. BuNo 157245 then returned to Miramar to serve with VF-121, and it stayed at 'Fightertown USA' until flown to nearby NARF North Island on 30 September 1980 to commence its upgrade to F-4S specification. Emerging from rework in June of the following year, the Phantom II was issued to VF-103, and it served with the Oceana-based unit until December 1982. BuNo 157245 participated in the unit's solitary Mediterranean cruise with the F-4S aboard *Forrestal* in 1982. Transferred to VMFA-251 at Beaufort, the jet served with the Marines until 29 August 1985, when it was flown to Davis-Monthan AFB for storage. It had completed 4582 flight hours by the time of its arrival. Stricken from the Navy's inventory on 9 August 1995, this aircraft is still resident within AMARC today (*via Angelo Romano*)

thought that the trailing MiG was 'kind of outside the envelope, but I had this good tone'. Hughes report of the action continues;

'I said, "Jesus, MiG-21, good tone – maybe I'll never see this again", so I pulled the trigger. The Sidewinder came off and went out to the right, underneath my nose. I thought I'd wasted a round, but about that time you could tell it was pulling itself back in, and it ripped off part of the MiG's tail. It didn't appear to me that he ever saw me, or knew that I was coming.'

When Hughes fired, he was about 45 degree angle-off, flying at 480 knots some 3000 ft above the ground. The MiG was just 1.6 nautical miles away.

After downing his target, Hughes was only a few degrees off position for a successful attack on the next MiG. Closing rapidly, he slid his throttles into idle to prevent further closure inside the 6000-ft range he now had. 'The MiG started to pull harder', Hughes said. 'I was looking right up his tailpipe from a distance of about a mile. I got a tone and pulled the trigger. However, by the time the Sidewinder came off the rail after pulling the trigger I'd lost the tone. I tried it again, got another tone, pulled it again, and the same thing happened once more! I was really pissed by this time. I had wasted two good 'Winders, and I didn't know if it was my fault or if the guy was really "warping my cone"'.

Both rounds missed. 'The first went off to the right', Hughes explained, 'and the other went ballistic to the inside of the turn'. Apparently the MiG was not in afterburner for either of the missile shots.

Obtaining yet another good tone, Hughes squeezed off his last AIM-9 and watched as it shredded off pieces of the MiG's tail when it detonated.

Having literally just stepped out of his jet and onto the flightdeck of CVA-63, Lt Bob Hughes is warmly greeted by the carrier's CO. Having survived his combat tour, Bob Hughes would later perish on 31 January 1979 in a mid-air collision between a TA-4J (BuNo 154288) of VF-126 and an F-4J (BuNo 153878) of VF-121. Serving as an adversary pilot with VF-126, Hughes was leading two Skyhawks in a two-v-two free-flight manoeuvring evolution at 25,000 ft off the California coast, near San Diego. The lead Phantom II was being chased in a turn by Hughes in his TA-4J at 25,000 ft when the pilot of F-4J BuNo 153858 attempted to come to the aid of his leader by allegedly performing an out-of-order 'blind lead turn' into his adversary – a manoeuvre that was strictly prohibited during ACM training. The end result of this turn was that the VF-121 jet collided with the pursuing Skyhawk, rendering the F-4J uncontrollable and forcing the crew to eject. Both men were quickly recovered with minor injuries. Neither the TA-4J or its two crewmen (Hughes's passenger was VF-121 RIO Tom Rippinger, who was catching a bonus hop) were found, however, despite a detailed search of the surrounding waters (via Peter Mersky)

At almost the same time he saw another missile go directly up the MiG-21's tailpipe, blowing the aircraft to pieces.

Pettigrew, meanwhile, had seen Hughes' down the first MiG, and then saw him go for its leader. He recalls telling his RIO, 'That SOB isn't going to get the next one too', and then pulling into hard 8G turn just as the communist pilot broke to the inside of Hughes's F-4. As Pettigrew broke and headed for the MiG, Hughes fired his second and third missiles. Continuing its hard turn, the MiG-21 was rapidly dissipating energy, while both Phantom IIs were closing at about 480 knots. Pettigrew again;

'I got back on the inside of the turn a little bit aft of Hughes at a height of 800 ft. We were both within ten degrees of the MiG's tail, and I looked up and pulled my nose up onto the MiG. By this time, he was at a height of about 4000 ft, and I got a tone and went to "arm". I was pulling to the inside of the turn, and just as I was about to fire, I saw another missile come off Hughes's aeroplane. I think I fired about the same time that his missile came off the rail. We had about a one-second difference in the missiles.

'We were really close inside by now. I figured I was down to about 2500 ft, with about ten degrees off, when I fired. I pitched the nose up and rolled right because I was overshooting badly. Continuing to roll right, I pulled back on the stick a little bit and saw the missile go all the way up the MiG's tailpipe, before reversing roll to the left.

'Hughes's missile hit first, knocking pieces off the stabilator, and about a second later mine hit and the aeroplane disintegrated. There wasn't anything left of it. I pulled the nose of my jet up higher because I was starting to run into the debris of the MiG, and as I flew some 200 ft wide of the point of impact, the pilot's 'chute opened just off my left wing – we almost ran into him.'

The entire engagement had lasted for little more than a minute. It was simply a 360-degree turning fight, which had taken place in the horizontal plane. Both VF-114 crews had the advantage throughout the engagement, and the MiGs made no attempt to turn in the vertical.

The lead section of MiG-21s, meanwhile, had now turned around and were two miles in-trail, but they were unable to close. *Red Crown* advised

Mission almost over, an F-4J from VF-114 powers its way towards a three-wire trap aboard *Kitty Hawk* during May 1972. One of the Navy's most successful fighter units in terms of aerial victories, VF-114 was credited with two MiG-17s, two MiG-21s and an An-2 destroyed during the Vietnam conflict. Its highest scoring pilot was Lt 'Denny' Wisely, who claimed a MiG-17 and the solitary An-2 during his tour with the 'Aardvarks' in 1966-67. At that stage in the war, the unit's F-4Bs were a little more subtly marked, lacking the diagonal fuselage stripe. Not overly impressed with the latter adornment, Wisely told the Editor that 'the big orange stripe made the aircraft look like a Coast Guard cutter'! (*via Peter Mersky*)

Pettigrew and Hughes about them, calling 'Four miles behind you. They are no threat, get the hell out 120 degrees'. Both F-4 pilots unloaded down into the karst and adopt a tight spread-formation. They also continued to jink until the SAM threat had passed. When the Phantom IIs were about halfway out, *Red Crown* finally called and said, 'Okay, they've turned away – no threat'.

After rendezvousing with their tanker, Pettigrew and Hughes returned to the carrier. The former describes their return as follows;

'We came back to the ship and asked them for a low pass. There was a big thunder storm right off the bow of the ship on the left hand side. We came on down, and of course neither of us could fly worth a damn by this time because we were shaking so much. We came in for a victory pass with the hooks down, "fogged over", looking up at the ship, and there is an A-6 with his gear down on the right hand side, a helo coming right across, and a guy rolling into the groove, all above us! So we closed our eyes, went through that, picked our noses up, and went into our victory roll and right into a thunder storm. That was the worst part of the whole engagement, trying to do the victory pass!'

In reviewing the incident, Pete Pettigrew later commented, 'We were talking the whole time. It's not very difficult after you've done it so many times before. I thought I'd seen this type of fight fought before against A-4s. A lot of things become instinctive. Hughes and I had never flown together before, yet we had no problem at all communicating. I think we knew exactly what each of us was thinking, or all four people knew exactly what the others were thinking the whole time. I think it's primarily because of the training'.

Mike McCabe added, 'All the way through this engagement my helmet was slid down over my eyes. When I turned around and we pulled 8G, my mask came right off my face and they (the MiGs) were at "seven o'clock". I had to take both my hands and put the mask up to talk!'

Bob Hughes remembered, 'There was no question about the fact that Pettigrew was on my wing the whole time. He crossed a couple of times to keep inside of the turn or abeam of me, and called out his position, so I knew exactly where he was the whole time we were going in. That was really nice knowing you have the support to go ahead and attack with somebody there to watch out for you'.

According to the *Red Baron* authors, both Pettigrew and Hughes 'demonstrated a high degree of mutual support and co-ordination during this engagement. They were able to take advantage of the element of surprise, achieve two quick kills, and separate from the area without being seriously threatened by any of the MiGs. Good radio procedures enabled them to effectively press home their attack'.

DOUBLE KILL

VPAF jets were next encountered just 48 hours after VF-114's successful engagement on 6 May, and the resulting action led to the Navy being able to boast its first double-MiG killing crew of the war.

On the 8th, VF-96 was tasked with providing part of the MiGCAP support for 'Fresh Bath Alpha' – a major multi-carrier Alpha strike against a large truck-park area near Son Tay, some 25 nautical miles west of Hanoi. This mission was to be a combined Navy/Air Force effort. The

target area contained an estimated 400 trucks, being used for both freight staging and driver training. The total attacking force consisted of 50 strike aircraft, plus large supporting forces.

Being a joint Navy/Air Force operation, several MiGCAPs were airborne. The Navy was providing CAP for its own forces, while the Air Force undertook MiGCAP coverage around the airfield at Yen Bai and north of Hanoi. 19 January 'MiG-killers' Lt Randy Cunningham and Lt (jg) Willie Driscoll crewed one of two CAP F-4Js put up by VF-96 – their jet was, in fact, 'Showtime 112', which they had employed so effectively to claim their first kill almost four months earlier.

Heading for the target, Cunningham and his usual wingman, Lt Brian 'Bulldog' Grant (along with RIO Lt Jerry Sullivan), positioned themselves about ten minutes ahead of their strike force to help clear the skies of MiGs. They entered North Vietnam as a section at the mouth of the Red River Valley Delta, 160 degrees and 75 nautical miles from Hanoi. As they went 'feet-dry', two SAMs were launched at them from north of the 'hourglass' rivers, but both missiles failed to guide and appeared to have been merely fired in their direction. More SA-2s were then launched, and 85 mm AAA also began to appear at their height, forcing Cunningham to lead his wingman down behind a nearby karst ridge in search of cover.

Proceeding towards the target area, he and Grant received a message from *Red Crown* informing them of bandits some 50 nautical miles away. However, the fighter controller quickly called again and told the section to 'skip it'. Apparently they had dropped below the hills and had broken radar contact. By now the two F-4s were 20 miles up the Red River from their assigned station, and the crews were getting nervous with the 'hide-and-seek' tactics of the MiGs. At this point they turned around and headed back south.

As they returned to their CAP station, Cunningham and Grant received another *Red Crown* vector onto four 'unknown' bandits at 340 degrees, some 20 nautical miles from their position – the direction of Yen Bai, which was then under attack by Air Force fighter-bombers. The VF-96 crews were following this vector towards the bandits when Cunningham realised that he was no longer receiving *Red Crown*. Sud-

denly, Grant hollered, '"Duke", in place port. Go!' Remembering a similar situation from a few weeks back where, VF-51's Al Molinare and J B Souder had been surprised by a MiG from behind in this very area, he instantly complied and banked sharply left, before engaging afterburner and pitching up into the vertical.

The section was now flying at about 450 knots at an altitude of 4000 ft (about 2000 ft above the cloud layer), with Cunningham pulling to the inside of the turn in an attempt to restore the section's combat-spread position. As he passed through Grant's 'six', he called that his tail was clear. About ten seconds later, however, Cunningham noticed a MiG-17 coming up through the cloud layer in afterburner.

'Randy' Cunningham and 'Willie' Driscoll enjoy a brew (or perhaps something stronger, courtesy of the ship's doctor!) in the VF-96 ready room after downing their second MiG on the morning of 8 May 1972 (*via Angelo Romano*)

The jet closed rapidly on Grant, who did not see the threat, and began firing his 37 mm cannon at a range of about 2000 ft. 'He had popped up through the clouds and was right behind Brian and shooting!', Cunningham remembers. 'He must have been last in his class in gunnery, however, because I wasn't pulling that many Gs, yet the MiG's tracers were falling short. I called Brian and said, "You've got a MiG-17 on your tail and he's shooting! Get rid of your centreline tank, unload and outrun him'.

The two F-4 pilots immediately jettisoned their centreline tanks and Grant rolled and pulled slightly out of the path of the MiG's rounds. The communist pilot reversed and tried to get back onto Grant's tail, but the latter also reversed slightly, unloaded and kept opening the gap.

'I was really impressed', Cunningham recalled, 'by the slow roll rate that the MiG-17 has. It looks like a butterfly because it goes so slow. The MiG was probably doing between 350 and 400 knots, and it must take a gorilla in there to turn the aeroplane, because Grant would roll and the MiG would roll, super slow. Rather than have him reverse, come back, and look, I told Grant to roll and not reverse, just unload. You could see the MiG roll and pull, but he still would never pull lead. His nose was almost directly on Grant and the "BBs" (cannon rounds) were falling short. Two rolls and Grant was able to push out quite a bit beyond the MiG'.

Because Grant did not have to pull a lot of G, Cunningham was able to position his F-4 on the MiG, and he reduced his angle-off to about 40 degrees. However, as Grant completed his second roll, the VPAF fighter launched an Atoll, which took both crews by surprise. 'They briefed us that the MiG-17s didn't have Atolls', explained Cunningham, 'so it scared the hell out of me'. He screamed, 'Atoll! Break port!' He continued, 'I called another break turn. The missile guided and it started coming around the corner, but then it went to the outside and went ballistic. Right then I shot a missile that was on the edge of the envelope. It was about 35 degrees off, and I knew that the MiG could see me, but I thought he was going to shoot another Atoll, and I wanted to give him something to think about, even if it didn't hit him'.

As soon as Cunningham fired his first missile, the MiG broke into it. While the AIM-9 detonated immediately under its target, it apparently did no damage, leaving the MiG to renew his attack on Grant. Just as the Sidewinder had left 'Showtime 112', Cunningham heard Driscoll say, '"Duke"! Look up!' The pilot saw two MiG-17s pass directly over his canopy, about 200 ft above him, one on each side. 'I told Willie to keep an eye on them, for I figured that we had lots of time to get a shot at the first MiG before these two got turned around. I was about to get my first lesson in the turning ability of the MiG-17! They actually turned inside of each other and started down after us!' Cunningham later recounted.

As this action unfolded, one of the MiGs fired an Atoll, which passed behind 'Showtime 112' but did not detonate. Cunningham continued to press his attack as Grant disengaged from the first MiG. Reducing the angle-off to about 20 degrees from the tail of the communist jet, Cunningham squeezed off another missile.

'It looked like he (the MiG) was trying to roll the opposite way', Cunningham recalled. 'I squeezed the trigger as he rolled and the missile hit him, but it only knocked a little piece off his tail. I almost started to squeeze the trigger again when I saw a flame shoot out. He was already in 'burner, but a big flame shot out and he went into a shallow turn and crashed right into the side of a peak. There was very little structural damage to the aeroplane, but he never tried to eject'.

When Cunningham fired, Grant was about 1.5 nautical miles ahead of him, and he had two MiGs about 3000 ft behind him, blazing away with their guns. Cunningham called to Grant to 'pitch up and go vertical' to a high-perch position in order to drag the MiGs to the inside of Grant's turn so that Cunningham could get them off of his tail. But the

Rearmed and refuelled, seven Phantom IIs from VF-92 and VF-96 prepare to launch from the *Constellation* on 9 May 1972. The following day, all of these aircraft were heavily involved in the largest aerial battle of the Vietnam War. Nearest to the camera is F-4J BuNo 155769, which was used by Lts Michael Connelly and Thomas Blonski to down two MiG-17s. Alongside it is 'Silver Kite 207' (BuNo 155560), which was damaged beyond repair when struck by 85 mm flak shells. It was coaxed back to the 'Connie' on one engine by pilot Rod Dilworth. 'Showtime 110' was crewed by Lts Brian Grant and Jerry Sullivan, who occupied the wing position for 'Randy' Cunningham and 'Willie' Driscoll as the latter pair set about downing three MiGs. 'Silver Kite 212' (BuNo 155797) was shot down by the same 85 mm flak that gravely damaged 'Silver Kite 207'. Its pilot, squadron XO Cdr Harry Blackburn, was killed either during or soon after capture, and his RIO, Lt Steve Rudloff, made a PoW. Chained down to the right of 'Silver Kite 212' is 'Showtime 112' (BuNo 157267), which had of course been used by Cunningham and Driscoll to claim MiG kills on 19 January and 8 May. To its right is 'Silver Kite 210' (BuNo 155813), crewed by Lts Austin Hawkins and Charles Tinker during the morning engagement that saw Lt Curt Dosé and Lt James McDevitt claim a MiG-21 in 'Silver Kite 211' (BuNo 157269). The latter jet is the final Phantom II visible in this historic photograph (*via Angelo Romano*)

MiGs were closing. Cunningham told Driscoll, 'I'm going to use the disengagement manoeuvre. I can't drag them to the inside anymore – they're getting too close'.

As he rolled left and came down, Cunningham momentarily lost sight of the MiGs. He told Driscoll to watch the MiGs. 'Okay, one's at "five" and one's at "seven", "five" and "seven", and they're closing', the RIO replied. But Cunningham could still not visually locate the MiGs, so he reversed, pulled his nose through and finally picked up a MiG just as it fired an Atoll. He broke hard into the missile and it shot past his 'six o'clock'.

Cunningham and Driscoll now had two MiGs closing on them, one to their left and one to their right, and tracers were passing over their canopy. They were trapped. If they rolled right, the MiG on their right fired, and if they rolled left, the other MiG shot at them.

'Never break into a MiG-17', Cunningham remembered. 'I couldn't disengage. I used every ounce of strength I had and kicked the rudder (essentially performing a "snap-roll") and got the nose down almost into a defensive spiral or a high-G, nose-low barrel roll. I pulled and pegged the G-meter. I pulled panels off the top of the aeroplane, off the top of the wing and from the underside. The jet was declared down by the maintenance department when I got back to the carrier because both flaps were broken. I pulled 12G on the aeroplane. You know what the MiG-17 pilot did? He rolled to the inside and rendezvoused on me! I had nothing left, so I radioed Brian. "Two, get in here. I'm in deep trouble". I was scared'.

The MiG-17 was still on the inside of Cunningham's turn, pulling lead, with his nose bristling with muzzle flashes. Just above the top of the cloud deck, Cunningham pushed over into the undercast and immediately reversed as hard as he could, unloaded, and selected afterburner. Accelerating to 500 knots, he pitched up into the sun, thinking that it would mask his afterburner from any VPAF heat-seeking missiles. Moreover, he knew the MiG-17s could not follow him at that speed.

As two MiGs came out of the clouds after Cunningham, Grant rolled in on them from his 'seven o'clock' position overhead. The communist fighters saw Grant in pursuit and immediately disengaged, heading back down into the clouds. Both Cunningham and Grant made a couple of cross-turns searching for the MiGs, then egressed the area.

The weather cleared as the crews headed towards the beach, and they noted numerous trucks in the area. Cunningham's account continued, 'I had tried many times to get a Sidewinder tone on a truck and couldn't do it, so I flew down right along a big highway, and I don't know if the guy had bad plugs, or needed a tune-up, or what, but I got a beautiful Sidewinder tone on a big truck and shot the damned thing. I rolled in there almost supersonic, got the tone and pressed it down low, which was a dumb thing to do. It blew the devil out of the truck and really nailed it. I pitched up, rolled and took a look at my target, and the thing was flaming'.

After the engagement, Cunningham told the *Red Baron* investigators, 'It's the one thing you should get across to everybody. The MiG-17 disengagement manoeuvre, as they did it in *Have Drill*, really works. I guarantee it. In two or three unloadings, it works. Once the MiG-17s have their angle of bank established, the damned things will turn like an SOB'.

FROM *FREEDOM TRAIN* TO *LINEBACKER*

On 10 May 1972 Operation *Linebacker* officially commenced. Essentially an outgrowth of *Freedom Train*, the air campaign had originally, albeit briefly, been christened *Rolling Thunder*, but was soon renamed – some say to reflect President Nixon's love of football.

On this first day of *Linebacker*, the Navy refocused its attention from targets in South Vietnam, where the bulk of the ground fighting was taking place, to the coastal regions from Haiphong north to the Chinese border. In all, 173 Navy attack sorties were flown in this area on the 10th, including strikes on targets in and around the Hanoi/Haiphong area.

By this stage of the campaign, the massive US air strikes had stopped the North Vietnamese advance into South Vietnam, allowing bombing missions to be switched to disrupting and destroying the NVA's supply and logistics systems, hence the start of *Linebacker*.

10 May was clearly the most intense air-to-air combat day of the entire Vietnam War. On that day, the *Constellation* was readying three major Alpha strikes against port and storage facilities in Hon Gay, north of Haiphong. The first would be launched in the morning, with the second scheduled for midday and the third for late afternoon.

A section of two F-4Js from VF-92 (VF-96's sister-squadron on CVA-64) was providing TARCAP support for the morning Alpha force, which included four other F-4Js as flak suppressors, two A-7Es in the anti-SAM *Iron Hand* role, nine A-7Es and five A-6As as the strikers and five EKA-3B ECM/tankers. The force's targets were the Haiphong Kien An airfield and nearby AAA batteries.

Each TARCAP Phantom II was armed with four AIM-7E-2 and four AIM-9Gs apiece, with a single 600-gallon centreline tank completing the array of external stores. BuNo 157269 (call sign 'Silver Kite 211') was crewed by Topgun graduate Lt Curt 'Dozo' Dosé and RIO Lt Cdr

A spotless F-4J from VF-92 cruises over broken cloud during a training mission over the South China Sea in early 1972. This photograph was taken by future MiG killer Lt Curt Dosé. Note the crown motif stencilled onto 'Silver Kite 206's' splitter plate (*Curt Dosé via Peter E Davies*)

James 'Routeslip' McDevitt, with Lts Austin Hawkins and Charles J Tinker flying lead.

The initial strike was rather uneventful for the CAP crews, for although they had heard numerous MiG calls on *Guard* (emergency VHF channel monitored as a secondary frequency by all air and ground stations in the area) during ingress, neither Hawkins or Dosé could make out a visual or radar contact. However, as the strike force was leaving the area, the F-4 section again heard *Red Crown* say, 'Bandits, north-east at 35 nautical miles'. Responding to the call, the section turned into a northerly heading and made a radar search, but failed to establish contact with the reported bandits.

Looking for MiGs, Hawkins and Dosé headed toward Kep airfield, where they expected to find some enemy activity. They were flying at 6000 ft and 600 knots when they sighted the field from a distance of about eight nautical miles and manoeuvred onto a northerly heading. Dosé was in combat-spread to the left of Hawkins. Approaching the airfield, both pilots saw two MiG-19s in revetments at one end of the runway and two MiG-21s holding short at the other.

As Dosé flew over the site, he wondered how they were going to strike at the MiGs on the ground, for neither F-4 had a gun, and the Sidewinders would need more heat to track stationary targets. Suddenly, McDevitt called out, 'MiGs rolling!' He had spotted two more MiG-21s taking off!

Responsible for stirring up a veritable hornet's nest over Kep airfield on the morning of 10 May 1972, this quartet of 'Silver Kites' were lucky to return to the 'Connie' alive. And Lt Curt 'Dozo' Dosé (extreme right) and Lt Cdr James 'Routeslip' McDevitt (second from right) also managed to 'bag' a MiG-21 before hastily departing the area. Flying lead on this mission were Lts Austin 'Hawk' Hawkins (left) and Charles J Tinker (second from left). Hawkins had planned to probe Kep following the completion of the fighters' TARCAP support for CVW-9's Alpha strike on targets in Hon Gay. He was nearing the end of his tour, and had yet to successfully encounter any MiGs. His bold plan was unauthorised, and strictly forbidden, and he informed only his RIO, Charles Tinker, of his intentions. 'He told me there were MiGs at Kep airfield, and once our attack guys were on their way out we were going to take a look at Kep', Tinker remembers. The RIO had to promise Hawkins not to tell anyone of his plan! Tinker continues, 'Once we got back to the boat, everyone was excited about Curt's MiG kill, but "Hawk" was in deep shit for leaving the strike to go trolling. The "elephants" were still deciding our fate when we manned up for the strike on Hai Duong. We were punished by tying us to an *Iron Hand* A-7 as escort. "Hawk" was told, "If you don't come back with him, don't come back at all!"' (*via Peter Mersky*)

Lt 'Hawk' Hawkins pre-flights his F-4J, which is already secured to one of CVA-64's waist catapults (*via Angelo Romano*)

Curt Dosé and Jim McDevitt pose for the camera prior to strapping into their Phantom II and manning the alert (*Curt Dosé via Peter E Davies*)

Dosé recalled this moment. 'Sure enough, there were two MiG-21s on a section take-off, about a third of the way down the runway, accelerating towards us fast. I called for the tactical lead and said, "Come port and down". Hawkins called for afterburner, which I think I had already done, or did simultaneously, and we came slicing down in an in-place turn back along the runway at about 1000 ft. We were straddling the runway, with me on the right and Hawkins on the left.

'By this time the MiGs were airborne. They were two miles off the end of the runway when we first started coming down, and I could see they were in afterburner and were climbing pretty much straight ahead.'

As Hawkins and Dosé closed to about 1.5 nautical miles, the MiG-21s simultaneously jettisoned their centreline tanks, apparently responding to a radio call, then started pulling to port in a gentle climbing turn. The tanks hit the ground and exploded in a fireball. Both MiGs were still low – about 100 ft above the deck – when Hawkins called out, 'You take the one on the right (MiG 1), and I'll take the one on the left (MiG 2)'.

Dosé continues his account. 'I had a tone before I even looked. I did check the null while I was still closing to make sure that I had the Sidewinder on him (the MiG). There was no doubt about it. It was a beautiful tone, and we squeezed off the first Sidewinder and watched it. The missile guided very nicely, but it seemed like it took forever to come off the aeroplane, and it took forever to get there. It finally detonated immediately behind the MiG.

'I thought I had him, but he kept flying, so I immediately fired a second Sidewinder at the same MiG (MiG 1). They were in a sort of "loose-cruise", or "fighting-wing" formation at this time, not more than 100 ft apart, and they stayed that way. I fired the second Sidewinder at exactly the same track-crossing angle as the first one. I estimate that we had about 20 degrees aspect and about five degrees look-down on the MiGs.

'The second Sidewinder went down to the jet's altitude, appeared to level off, and then disappeared up its tailpipe. Nothing happened for a couple of seconds and then the whole aeroplane burst into a huge 100-ft wide ball of flame. Out of the forward edge of that ball of flame came the MiG-21, tumbling nose over tail. It did two tumbles and went into the ground with no ejection.'

When Dosé saw his second missile hit, he immediately pulled his nose into the lead MiG (MiG 2) and triggered his third Sidewinder, which guided to the MiG and detonated about ten feet behind, almost exactly as his first missile had done. Meanwhile, Hawkins had also fired two AIM-9s at the same aeroplane, and both missiles detonated just aft of and below the MiG. As Hawkins fired his third Sidewinder the MiG broke into it with a 90-degree angle of bank, giving the Phantom II pilot a perfect plan view of his target. The Sidewinder passed about 15 ft behind the MiG's tailpipe and detonated when it hit the ground.

When MiG 2 performed its breaking turn, it was doing an estimated 300 knots, and Hawkins about 550 knots. The VF-92 pilot initially pulled as hard as he could to see if there was any possibility of staying with the MiG. When it became obvious that he could not make the turn, he pulled back on the stick, shoved in rudder, and started doing high-G rolls up and around the MiG. He remarked to his RIO Tinker, 'Another 90 degrees of turn and this SOB is going to fly into the ground'. Hawkins was certain that the MiG was either going to crash or be forced to level his wings and give him another shot.

The engaged aircraft circled Kep airfield during the entire engagement, staying within about five nautical miles of the field. Dosé checked the sky above him and saw an overcast of 57 mm and 85 mm flak behind them, and also a third MiG-21 (MiG 3) at about two nautical miles, slicing down at Hawkins's 'five o'clock'. Dosé called his leader and suggested an immediate disengagement, telling him to 'Bug out', but Hawkins was now on a northerly heading, and did not want to disengage.

'No, I can get this guy', he told Dosé, and continued to press on after the second MiG-21. The third MiG closed so fast on the VF-92 jet that he passed right through Hawkins's 'six o'clock' in a lag pursuit and never presented a real threat. When Hawkins reached the southern end of the airfield, he disengaged vertically, went out, then rolled over. The second MiG pulled his nose back into Hawkins's general area and launched an Atoll. The missile, however, went ballistic and missed.

The section headed for the beach over the karst in full afterburner at just 50 ft, continuing to jink as they looked for MiG 3 in their 'six o'clock'. During their jinking manoeuvres, Hawkins and Dosé became separated, and each jet egressed alone. Hawkins exited south of Haiphong towards the 'hourglass' rivers, while Dosé exited north of the port city. They rejoined on the tanker and returned to their ship without further incident. Dosé later commented on his egress, 'If not a noble departure, it was at least a successful one at near Mach below 50 ft, with MiG-21s behind us firing Atoll missiles'.

After the flight, Austin Hawkins noted, 'The thing that I think could be learned from the engagement itself is that with the missile, look-down is the same as angle-off as far as tracking is concerned. It's something that's got to be remembered. I think something that's not stressed enough is the fact that a simple "six o'clock" shot is not good enough – you've got to know all the parameters. If you've got 200-300 knots overtake, pressing to three-quarters

Tactical Navy tankers provided a crucial lifeline to fighters during missions flown in 1972, when fuel was often used up at an alarming rate by crews that engaged afterburner for extended periods whilst chasing, or evading, MiGs, or attempting to avoid SAMs and AAA. This EKA-3B (refuelling two F-4Js from VF-92 in March 1972) was from CVW-9's VAQ-130 Det 1, and it shared the tanker duty within the wing with KA-6Ds from VA-165 and buddy tank-equipped A-7Es from VA-146 and VA-147 (*via Peter E Davies*)

of a mile or one mile, you're pushing it. The missile was guiding on the plume itself, plus the fact that it was a look-down shot as it went past the tailpipe, and the missile detonated directly below the aeroplane. I saw both of mine blow up the same way.

He also said, 'If I had it to do over again, knowing what happened to my Sidewinders, I'd make sure that I was at the same altitude as the MiGs before I'd shoot. I wouldn't shoot with any look-down. In this particular engagement a gun would have made all the difference due to the close range. It would have been no trouble at all to have achieved a

Curt Dosé uses his hands to describe to fellow VF-92 pilot Lt Cdr Gordon Williamson (back to the camera) how he manoeuvred in behind his MiG-21 before despatching it with an AIM-9G (*Aerospace Publishing*)

smooth gun-tracking position, as he was in a position where there was nothing he could do but turn. It seems that there have been so few times that I've launched on a hop where I ended up with eight missiles that I could use. You're always wondering, "When is that damned missile going to detune on me?"'

Dosé also made some telling comments following this engagement. 'The one big mistake I made was, as soon as we got out of there, and we knew that there were MiGs behind us, we should have jettisoned our tanks, and we never did. I never thought about it'. He also said that a gun would have made a difference in the engagement, perhaps adding another kill. 'I have no doubt in the world, especially with the unimaginative defensive tactics that the MiG was using, that if I'd had an M-61 cannon, I could have hosed him right out of the sky'.

But Dosé's most interesting comments are those relating to his Topgun experience, and its effect on his flying on this day. 'During the whole engagement I felt that I had been there before. We've done so much training in this environment that you look at an aeroplane with a certain closure, and a certain airspeed, and say "Let's come this way", because that's the way you have done it before, and you know that it works'. Without question, Dosé's dissimilar ACM training at Topgun enabled him to accurately evaluate the situation, and was a major factor in the success of the mission.

When the crews returned to *Constellation* it was clear that something big had happened. Dosé and Hawkins were summoned into 'Intell', and queried on what they had hit. *Red Crown* was reporting that all available MiGs were being moved to the Hanoi/Haiphong area, and that North Vietnamese air defences were 'running wild'. The truth was that the VPAF had been hit hard, losing four MiG-21s during the early morning hours, and the Air Force, which had conducted a simultaneous strike with the Navy, had downed North Vietnam's single most important road/rail bridge, the Paul Doumer, which spanned the Red River east of Hanoi.

Dosé and Hawkins had merely helped 'stir the hive', and now the VPAF was mad, and taking to the air just in time for the day's second Alpha strike.

McDevitt and Dosé pose with their plane captain in front of 'Silver Kite 211' (BuNo 157269). Accepted by the Navy at St Louis on 5 February 1970, this aircraft served for the first year of its flying career with VF-121. Transferred to VF-92 on 12 May 1971, it subsequently deployed with the unit on its *WestPac*/Vietnam cruise aboard CVA-64 on 1 October. Used to claim VF-92's sole MiG kill of the war, on 10 May 1972, the jet returned to Miramar with the squadron on 1 July. BuNo 157269 was then transferred back to VF-121, where it remained until 12 December 1972, when it joined VF-114. Undertaking a single *WestPac* with this unit (from 23 November 1973 to 9 July 1974), BuNo 157269 rejoined VF-121 for a third time on 16 May 1975. It left the Navy F-4 training squadron for its Marine equivalent on 17 June 1976, when the fighter was sent to VMFAT-101 at Yuma. The Phantom II returned to frontline flying in June 1977 with VMFA-235, which was initially based at Yuma, but then forward-deployed to Kadena, on Okinawa, Iwakuni and Kaneohe Bay. Flown to NARF North Island on 24 October 1979, the fighter was rebuilt as an F-4S and issued to VMFA-122 at Beaufort on 7 September 1980. BuNo 157269 returned to VMFAT-101 on 11 May 1983, and was eventually flown to AMARC on 26 February 1986. Stricken from the Navy's inventory on 14 June 1993, it still languishes in storage at Davis-Monthan today (*Curt Dosé via Peter E Davies*)

Several hours after the first Alpha strike had recovered back aboard CVA-64, the aircrews of CVW-9 found themselves back in action again over the skies of North Vietnam. At approximately 1148 hrs, *Constellation* turned into wind and started launching her 32 aircraft for the strike. It would be almost 30 minutes before the strike was formed and ready to head north.

VF-96's Lt Michael J 'Matt' Connelly and RIO Lt Thomas J J Blonski (in BuNo 155769, call sign 'Showtime 106') manned one of the jets that comprised the two TARCAP sections supporting a major Alpha strike against the Haiphong railway sidings and the Hai Duong and Cam Pha railway bridges. The overall attacking force included strike groups from three carriers, totalling 70 strike/MiGCAP aircraft, as well as the usual supporting tankers and ECM jets.

This strike was *Constellation's* second of the day, and due to the exploits of Dosé and Hawkins, as well as the downing of the Paul Doumer Bridge, it would be opposed by more MiGs than any other mission of the war.

Also participating in this strike were Randy Cunningham and Willie Driscoll (in BuNo 155800, call sign 'Showtime 100'), and their usual wingmen, Lts Brian 'Bulldog' Grant and Jerry Sullivan. They were escorting an A-7E 'Shrike bird', flown by Lt Norman Birzer, as was Lt Steven Shoemaker and his RIO, Lt(jg) Keith V Crenshaw (in BuNo 155749, call sign 'Showtime 111'). Finally, flying MiGCAP were the XOs from both VF-92 and VF-96, Cdrs Harry L Blackburn (in BuNo 155797, call sign 'Silver Kite 212', with RIO Lt Stephen Rudloff) and Dwight Timm (BuNo 157267, call sign 'Showtime 112', flying with Lt Jim Fox).

The TARCAP F-4Js were each armed with four AIM-7E-2 Sparrows and four AIM-9G Sidewinders, plus a 600-gallon centreline tank.

The two TARCAP sections escorted the strike group to a 'feet-dry' position at the 'hourglass' rivers (south of Haiphong), then headed north up the Red River to the target area. Connelly and Blonski were off to the left of the force while the other TARCAP section was positioned to the right. As the strike group began hitting the target, the strike leader, CVW-9 CAG Cdr Lowell 'Gus' Eggert, called 'Play ball! Play ball!' At once, each TARCAP section made a level cross-turn, passing the other section in combat-spread. Connelly and his wing headed south, establishing a barrier against MiGs from Bai Thuong. They soon began to receive MiG calls from *Red Crown*.

The first call Connelly heard was from an A-7 pilot screaming that there were MiGs on his tail, and for somebody to come and get them off. The pilot was so excited that he neglected to give his position, and Connelly had to radio, 'Where are you?' Looking down, he saw an A-7 (flown by Lt Birzer) at his 'three o'clock', low, at about three nautical miles, with two MiG-17s right behind it. The lead MiG was firing 37 mm rounds at the Corsair II but was not pulling lead.

Connelly called 'Tally-ho' and then commanded a 6G break turn to engage the bandits. As soon as he pulled G, his RIO Blonski hollered 'We just lost the damned radar! We've got a black scope'. Connelly tried desperately to maintain visual contact with the MiGs, and eventually lost his wingman – the two remained separated throughout the rest of the engagement. Apparently having seen Connelly roll in, MiG 2 immediately broke to the right.

The pilot of 'Showtime 106' continued to pursue the lead MiG, sliding into a position about 8000 ft behind it and 30 degrees angle-off. Birzer's A-7 then started to roll wings-level, with the MiG right behind it. Although Connelly felt he was out of the firing envelope for his Sidewinders, he decided 'I've got to shoot now to get that guy off Birzer's tail', and he squeezed the trigger. The AIM-9 launched with good tone, but it didn't seem to guide. The MiG 'driver' must have seen it coming and broke hard enough to nearly meet the F-4 head-on.

Using the same kind of hand gestures as those employed by Curt Dosé in the photograph seen on page 34, VF-96's Lt 'Matt' Connelly shows his squadronmates exactly how he destroyed two MiG-17s in quick succession over Hai Duong. Looking on is his RIO, Lt Thomas Blonski (*via Robert F Dorr*)

Connelly then came right back into the MiG and found himself at the bottom of a large dogfight with VPAF jets 'all over the place'. He offers his thoughts on the engagement that followed;

'To come back and try to reconstruct what followed after that on a blackboard is impossible. I don't even know if the first MiG I shot down was the same guy that I initially shot at. I don't think it was, but everything was so confusing, and there were so damned many of them! They were all over the place! If you were chasing one, and looked over and saw another one that was less angle-off, and you had less degrees to pull to get at his "six", you just went after him.

'The whole thing transpired at about 7000 ft or so. I had enough energy to maintain the bottom of the fight, and control it pretty well. I didn't want to go up with the other F-4s because I could pick the MiGs up easily. They were always about 1000 ft above me when I picked them up, and I had plenty of altitude over the ground, so I wasn't worrying about it that much.'

After turning back into the lead bogey and finding a sky full of MiGs (as many as 20), Connelly, now in full afterburner, locked his eyes onto another MiG-17 (MiG 3), which was in a right turn at about 300 knots. The MiG's pilot apparently did not see Connelly, who was then slightly off of his tail and manoeuvring. Realising that he was closing too fast, Connelly pulled the power back to idle and popped his speed brakes.

As MiG 3 started to roll wings-level, Connelly brought the speed brakes back in, drifting in behind his target. Obtaining a good tone, he squeezed the trigger, loosing an AIM-9 off the rails and sending it straight up the MiG's tailpipe. The VPAF jet exploded in a huge ball of fire. Although he did not realise it until after he returned to the carrier, Connelly must have fired this missile just seconds after deciding to retract the speed brakes, for the weapon's exhaust burned a hole in his left brake!

Connelly remembers that the MiGs seemed to 'jump on aircraft that were arcing around the sky'. He was not really threatened because he was either chasing a MiG or rapidly switching from one to another. Picking up another MiG-17 (MiG 4) in a right turn, Connelly made an attack similar to the one which had resulted in his first kill.

As he and Blonski started drifting towards its 'six o'clock', MiG 4 reversed left, putting Connelly on the inside of its turn. Then, apparently not seeing the F-4, the MiG rolled out to a wings-level position. 'I had a really good tone', Connelly said, 'and I took my time because I only had three Sidewinders (all that had been loaded). I had wasted the first one. The second worked, and I really wanted to make the third one work too'.

At about 4000-5000 ft, Connelly triggered another missile, but just as he fired the tone dropped off. The AIM-9 departed, made a corkscrew, and detonated alongside the MiG. Connelly thought that he had missed, but his RIO Blonski called, 'Wait a minute, his tail's gone'. Smoke then started streaming from the aeroplane, and the MiG rolled left and the pilot ejected.

An F-4 passed less than 1000 ft over the top of Connelly while he was watching MiG 4. The next thing he saw was a MiG-17 (MiG 5) sitting about 30 ft out at his 'nine o'clock'. This MiG was almost flying wing on Connelly, with both aircraft at 220 knots. 'He was co-speed and I was at 220 knots', Connelly noted. 'I thought, "You almost had your ass shot off!" I don't know what the hell I was doing or how we got that way. If you lined up ten "Gomers" tomorrow, I could recognise that SOB. He wasn't flying with an oxygen mask. I was looking at him and he was looking at me'.

To counter the VPAF pilot, Connelly performed a slow-speed roll over the top of MiG 5, which put it in his 'three o'clock'. He felt confident that he could perform a rolling scissors and thought 'That's the only thing I can do right now'. MiG 5 followed him through the manoeuvre, but then for no apparent reason its pilot dumped the nose and disengaged. Connelly noted, 'He (MiG 5) wouldn't have had to do too much of anything if he had continued his slow fight until he got behind and started to pepper us. For the life of me I can't figure out why he broke off'.

Despite having fired all of his Sidewinders, and with his radar unserviceable (leaving him without the ability to employ his four Sparrow missiles), Connelly nevertheless set off in pursuit of two more MiG-17s (MiGs 6 and 7). 'I used the old philosophy "it's easier for me to chase them than to have one of them behind me". I chased one of them (MiG 6) around for a while, and he was pulling pretty hard. He finally dropped his nose and started diving for the deck.

'I thought he was going to go home, so we started to make a turn towards the beach. Then another one (MiG 7) flew right in front of me. He was turning to the left and I just followed him. He did the same thing as the other one, and I don't think he ever saw me. I was right behind him, and just chasing him around. I could have been in an excellent gun position – all I would have had to do was add a little more power and catch them'.

Most of the aircraft were starting to exit the area, so Connelly made another full-circle sweep before heading out. As he checked the area, he saw an F-4 (belonging to Cunningham and Driscoll) with a MiG-17 (MiG 8) pulling up below him. Connelly called, 'F-4 heading 180 degrees. You've got a MiG-17 coming up behind you. Unload, full 'burner – you can outrun him'. But the F-4 did not respond. Connelly started pulling his nose towards MiG 8 and selected radar as he repeated the call. Cunningham finally heard Connelly's warnings and unloaded in full afterburner.

At a distance of about two nautical miles, and a 20-degree aspect angle, Connelly put his pipper on MiG 8. With his radar scope still black, but the missile select lights on, he squeezed the trigger, hoping to force the MiG to break off its attack. 'I was really appalled at the missile', Connelly later remarked. 'Normally a Sparrow comes out and starts doing ballistic trajectories. This one came off and started going right at him. The trouble is, before the Sparrow got to the guy I pulled my nose away from him and headed for "feet-wet". The second that the thing came off the rail and travelled a hundred yards, the MiG just snapped right off Cunningham's F-4. All of a sudden the guy was nose down, diving away, and we had resumed our heading out towards the beach'.

Unfortunately, the Sparrow passed right over the MiG as it turned to disengage and missed. Connelly then egressed and headed back to the carrier. He later added, 'An interesting side note was the fact that there was plenty of gas (tankers) in the air but we couldn't find it. We stayed on strike frequency for a while and got the run around. We decide, "That's not going to work", and went to Marshall, and they said, "Standby". Finally, we went to Tower and he said "We've got a tanker I'm launching two right now"'.

By then Connelly was within 30 nautical miles of the ship, and he realised that he had enough fuel to make it. He landed with just 700 lbs remaining in his tanks.

Connelly told the *Red Baron* interviewers that 'Neither of the MiGs manoeuvred while the missiles were in flight. Neither had a wingman. They were out there by themselves. Every guy we engaged was single, aside from the first two'.

In contrast, the American crews were much better trained and disciplined. 'The most significant thing was the section integrity. Sections were made and dissolved in seconds. We maintained mutual support. The whole fight was contained within about a four-mile area, and you could see the other black-nose aeroplanes. You'd see a guy with a MiG behind him, and you would come on the radio and say, "Keep pulling to port". I heard a lot of that on the radio. Sections were made and dissolved in just seconds with that kind of quick mutual support'.

A three-ship formation of F-4Js from the 'Black Falcons' release their Mk 82 bombs (six apiece) over North Vietnam in the spring of 1972. Closest to the camera is CAG jet BuNo 155800 – a future triple MiG killer (*via Peter E Davies*)

Connelly says that the MiG's camouflage helped the VPAF pilots escape once they committed to disengaging. 'When the MiGs disengage, they all dump their noses and go right down to the deck. That damned camouflage – you get them in that rice paddy and you lose them. You can have them locked up visually, but as soon as they get down there in those rice paddies, you can't see them'.

As to the F-4's lack of guns, Connelly also said, 'There's no doubt in my mind that if we had had gas and guns, we probably would have bagged five that day. It would have been easy'. Blonski reiterated this, stating that 'To have a fighter without a gun is just asinine'.

The RIO said of the engagement, 'If all the MiG "drivers" that day had the benefit of the training that we've had, and if they had had a chance to fly against an aeroplane comparable to the F-4, it might have been disastrous, because we made mistakes. We've never experienced that many MiGs in a confined area at one time'. Blonski also said that the North Vietnamese had 'set up a flak trap that bagged one F-4 before the MiGs arrived. He (Cdr Blackburn) flew into their flak trap and was blown out of the sky. He was really set up for it'.

But Connelly and Blonski's kills were just the beginning of the fight.

Two of the VF-96 crews participating in this second mission were tasked with providing flak-suppression for CVW-9's strike on the Hai Duong marshalling yard south-east of Hanoi. Armed with Rockeye cluster bomb units (fitted to bulky triple ejector racks), four AIM-9 Sidewinders and two AIM-7 Sparrows, the jets were crewed by Randy Cunningham and Willie Driscoll, as lead, and Brian Grant and Jerry Sullivan in the wing slot.

During their ingress to the target area, the Phantom II crews encountered two SAMs and heavy AAA. Fortunately, neither missile tracked well, and the mission proceeded normally until the A-6s of the strike package missed the target due to overcast skies and had to be called back. In the resulting confusion, all of the strike aircraft ended up making their bombing runs from the same direction.

Cunningham later commented, 'The mistake that everybody made was that their runs were all from west to east, and they looked like a line of ants

Arguably the most famous Navy Phantom II of them all, 'Showtime 100' is seen patrolling over the Gulf of Tonkin on 29 March 1972. BuNo 155800 was accepted by the Navy at St Louis on 17 October 1968 and issued new to VF-96 two days later. One of the first F-4Js sent to the unit in place of its war-weary B-models, the fighter participated in its first war cruise, aboard USS *Enterprise* (CVAN-65) between 6 January and 2 July 1969. BuNo 155800 ventured to sea once again with VF-96 aboard USS *America* (CVA-66) on 10 April 1970, when CVW-9 conducted a Vietnam cruise with the Atlantic Fleet carrier that lasted until 22 December. The jet's third *WestPac*/Vietnam deployment commenced on 1 October 1971, aboard the *Constellation*. As with its previous two cruises, BuNo 155800 was marked up as VF-96's CAG jet. On 10 May 1972, 'Duke' Cunningham and 'Willie' Driscoll used 'Showtime 100' to down three MiG-17s, thus making them the first American aces of the Vietnam conflict. Later in the mission the aircraft was badly damaged by a SAM which exploded beneath the fighter, and the crew was forced to eject just beyond the North Vietnamese coastline when BuNo 155800's hydraulic systems failed. It had completed 1813 flight hours up until its final, historic, sortie (*via Robert F Dorr*)

going down a hill. One F-4, right across the circle from my wingman and I, circled around to the north following the same flight path as the A-6s and A-7s after they had rolled in. An 85 mm cannon barrage hit him (Cdr Blackburn). Flying in the same airspace just vacated by previous aeroplanes not only cost him his life and caused his RIO (Steve Rudloff) to become a PoW, but also resulted in his wingman (Rod Dilworth and Gerry Hill) being hit by the same barrage and losing an engine'.

Although the day was clear and there was AAA all over the sky, Cunningham and Grant could not pick up muzzle flashes to pin-point the gun locations for targeting with their Rockeyes. This left them with little option but to switch from the flak-suppression role and go after their secondary target – a long red storage building. A SAM was launched at them during their attack, but after a small break it did not track, and the Phantom IIs continued in on their run.

Cunningham had pulled off and rolled back right to observe his Rockeye 'walking' through the target when Grant called, '"Duke", you've got MiG-17s at "seven o'clock"'. Flying at a speed of just 380 knots, Cunningham quickly reversed and saw three MiG-17s (MiGs 1, 2 and 3) closing rapidly, about 3000 ft away. In Cunningham's words, 'My instinctive reaction was to break into the MiGs, but I knew that if I did, they would rendezvous on me. I thought, "I'm slow, so I don't have that many possibilities. I can't go up, and to use the MiG-17 disengagement manoeuvre when he's got closure is asinine. He'll just run right up my tailpipe"'.

Cunningham then put his nose low, stood on the rudder pedals and pulled back on the stick. The first MiG (MiG 1) overshot slightly under and in front of him. Stabbing his right rudder pedal to the floor, he reversed back to the right, then began a reversal.

'Just as I picked him (MiG 1) up', Cunningham later related, 'his two wingmen pitched up and rolled in on me. The MiG-17 "driver" (MiG 1) didn't keep any angle-off, and it was a zero-deflection shot. His tailpipe was sitting right there in front of me. He was still in afterburner, and he had his nose down, which allowed me to accelerate. As I reversed, I selected 'burner, nosed down and got a tone while I was unloading. I was pushing forward-stick and squeezing the trigger at the same time. The missile hit him, and this was one of the few MiGs that I had hit that only had little pieces knocked off. The MiG went out of control and smashed into the ground.

Seen in more peaceful surrounds at NAS Quonset Point, Rhode Island, in the summer of 1971, a recently-resprayed 'Showtime 100' was visiting the east coast air station as a participant in its base open house (*via Robert F Dorr*)

Hoping to drag the two MiGs in front of Grant's F-4, Cunningham was surprised to hear his wingman call, 'I can't help you, One'. Cunningham looked back and saw four more MiG-17s attacking Grant. 'At this point', Cunningham related, 'our mutual support degraded a little bit'. Using a disengagement manoeuvre, he pulled out just ahead of the two MiGs. Grant, too, also used this manoeuvre, and was quickly back on Cunningham's wing.

Both pilots had now dropped their centreline tanks. The triple ejector racks, however, were a different story. Cunningham would have liked to jettison them to reduce drag, but if they went, so did the remaining Sidewinders, which were being carried on the same weapons stations.

Cunningham called, 'Okay, cross-turn, Two. We're going back in'. They now had good airspeed, and were about 5000 ft above the fight. As they returned, Cunningham saw three F-4s in a 350-knot defensive wheel (Lufbery) with eight MiG-17s. 'Everything was in slow motion', he recalled. 'On one side you'd see MiG-19s climbing, and over there you'd see a MiG-17 going down in flames. In slow motion you'd see F-4s zooming and you'd see MiGs after them. I thought something was the matter with me. At that point in the fight I was probably very vulnerable to something coming up my "six o'clock".

Then Cunningham saw four more MiG-17s join in the Lufbery for a total of twelve, with four MiG-21s above the fight not engaged. There were also two MiG-19s about three nautical miles off his right wing.

Cunningham intended to make a supersonic pass through the Lufbery. 'I'm engaged, you're free', he called as he rolled in. Grant replied, 'One. I'm caught again'. Looking back, he saw more MiG-17s swarming all over his wingman – these were not part of the 12 in the Lufbery. 'I don't know where they came from', Cunningham remarked, 'but there were enough MiGs for everybody. That's the point where you realise there's really not a tooth fairy!'

At about the same time Grant called that he was engaged, another VF-96 jet in a left turn in the Lufbery came belly-up to Cunningham. The Phantom II was being flown by XO Dwight Timm (with RIO Jim Fox) at about 350 knots, and he had a MiG-17 firing from 3000 ft behind him, a MiG-21 about 4500 ft back on the inside of his turn and a second MiG-17 (MiG 4) 300 ft away from him on his belly side. Cunningham called, '"Showtime", reverse starboard', but Timm did not see MiG 4 and continued his turn. Finally, Cunningham shouted, 'Turn your aircraft and unload or you'll be dead'. At this call, Dwight Timm reversed, saw MiG 4, unloaded and started accelerating away – Cunningham then positioned for a Sidewinder tone.

He was trying to stay in a lag-pursuit position on MiG 4, which was chasing Timm, when the two MiG-19s at his 'three o'clock' rolled in on him. There were also four MiG-17s behind Cunningham on the in side of his turn and four MiG-21s 5000 ft overhead. He described the subsequent events;

'The MiG-17s behind us were dropping back, but every time Timm would arc they would rendezvous on me. At one time they got to about 2000 ft away. The MiG-17s would close, and I'd have to go back to the lag-pursuit position at 500 knots and pull up. At this time the MiG-19s rolled in on us and I broke up hard into them, which actually helped me because

135

it resulted in a lag-pursuit roll to the outside of the MiG-17 (MiG 4).'

Timm and Fox started to use the disengagement manoeuvre, but for some reason the XO put the G back in and the MiG-17 rendezvoused on him again. As Cunningham continued to manoeuvre into position on MiG 4, the MiG-19s went out to his 'six o'clock' and pulled their noses up into a loop, tangent to his circle. He never saw them again. Cunningham now had three MiG-17s ahead and four behind him, four MiG-21s about 5000 ft above and the two MiG-19s that had just disappeared at his 'three o'clock'.

'We were lucky after this', he continued. 'Timm's F-4 unloaded again and walked away from the MiG-17s. The MiG-21 (that was inside of the XO's turn) broke off for some reason and I never saw him again'.

Cunningham now had MiG 4, which was in afterburner, centred in his windscreen, with a good tone on his AIM-9G. As soon as Cdr Timm came out of 'burner, Cunningham squeezed the trigger. The Sidewinder tracked to the MiG and detonated. 'I almost hit the pilot', he recalled. 'He had on little Gomer goggles and a little Gomer hat, and he had boots laced up to the knees. The guy didn't even wave'.

Following his second kill of the day, Cunningham looked around and saw MiGs everywhere, but did not see any other friendlies. He therefore started to egress and head for the carrier. As Cunningham left, he picked up a dot on the horizon about 20 degrees to the right, and quickly identified it as a MiG-17 (MiG 5). He decided to play a game of chicken with the MiG, as he had often done to rattle other pilots at Miramar, and turned into it. As the two closed head-on, the MiG started firing.

'It didn't even dawn on me that he was going to shoot at me', Cunningham later recalled. 'It was something I'd practised and practised against A-4s, and there's a saying "You fight like you train". I'd made a mistake in not visualising the actual weapons capability that the MiG had in that situation because the A-4s I flew against didn't have guns. So I smartly moved out to the side and he still kept shooting short bursts. The 23 mm cannon shoots out a flame about a yard long. No exaggeration – it's scary'.

Cunningham still had plenty of fuel (an unusual situation in an F-4), and he decided to engage the MiG-17. 'All the other MiGs that I saw would either run or they'd turn horizontally – they were all plumbers. So, when I met him (MiG 5) I pitched straight up. I was going to get another easy kill and then bug out. I expected to see him in the horizontal, running, about three miles away. As I rolled back up and started bringing my head back, looking for the horizon, what I least expected to see was the MiG canopy-to-canopy with me, but there he was, about 400 or 500 ft away from me, going straight up'.

A short burst from the MiG forced Cunningham to quarter-turn out of the plane of fire. He then pulled towards the MiG's 'six o'clock' and they entered a rolling scissors manoeuvre. 'I got the advantage when he put his nose down for airspeed', Cunningham stated. 'As soon as his nose went low, I started putting my nose down. All of a sudden his nose came up so fast it was amazing. As my nose went down, I went out a little bit in front. The fight was going advantage-disadvantage, and then it started going disadvantage-disadvantage'.

More 'talking hands', as 'Randy' Cunningham 'holds court' in the VF-96 ready room at 1920 hrs on the evening of 10 May. Just a few hours earlier, he and RIO 'Willie' Driscoll had been fished out of the Gulf of Tonkin by a SAR HH-3A and flown to the Marine helicopter assault ship USS *Okinawa* (LPH-3). From there, they had been transferred back to the 'Connie' by a Marine Corps CH-46. Having downed three MiG-17s in eight minutes to 'make ace', and then been shot down by a SAM, Cunningham certainly had a few tales to tell! The pilot at the extreme right of the photograph, with his face turned towards 'Duke' Cunningham, is Cdr Dwight Timm, XO of VF-96 (*via Robert F Dorr*)

Flying straight up in the vertical, Cunningham disengaged from the rolling scissors. When the MiG-17 had its nose high, he kicked rudder, pulled to the MiG's 'six o'clock' and gained separation, then he pitched back into the fight. 'I didn't have the knots', Cunningham said, referring to his speed, 'and I almost got bagged – he rendezvoused on me'. The American again unloaded and picked up a good airspeed, before turning once more into the MiG.

'I pulled it through as hard as I could, but it was to the point that I couldn't meet him head-on. What really surprised me was that little MiG-17 zoomed with me up there. I expected his nose to fall off, but it didn't. It ended in a carbon copy of the first engagement – a rolling scissors – but again I disengaged in the same manner.'

Each time Cunningham went out in front, the MiG's cannon would fire. 'I'm not going out in front this time', Cunningham told Driscoll. 'This time we're going to get where I know I can at least meet him head-on'. Obtaining the energy level he desired, Cunningham zoomed and the MiG once again went into the vertical with him. Then, chopping his throttles, he went to idle power with speed brakes extended.

Cunningham continues. 'Here I am, sitting behind a MiG-17, nose up. As soon as I saw relative motion stop, I went back into full 'burner and locked about 1000 ft behind him, but he would hold angle-off. I was on the rudders, just sitting, and I thought, "Boy, what a stupid decision you just made. You're really in great shape, 1000 ft behind a MiG-17, 170 knots, slowing". The only thing is, I always had the feeling that I could disengage any time I wanted to'.

The MiG-17 had been operating in afterburner for about five minutes, and was evidently now down to a critical fuel state because he tried to disengage and made a run for Kep. The VPAF jet did a slow-speed reversal, went almost 45 degrees nose down and started rocking his wings as if he had lost sight of Cunningham. As he headed towards Kep, the MiG stopped wing-rocking and dived for the deck.

'I guess he thought he could outrun me', said Cunningham. 'I started pushing forward on the stick, trying not to bury the nose, and I actually

137

had to stand on the rudder a little bit to hold the nose up. I unloaded and squeezed the trigger as I got the tone. It knocked off a little piece of the tail but didn't alter his flightpath at all, and I thought he was going to get away. He was still running. I followed him down and started to squeeze again when a little fire erupted'. Cunningham continued to watch as the MiG descended into the ground. No ejection was seen.

Whilst following the fleeing MiG, four other MiG-17s and a single MiG-21 had fallen in behind 'Showtime 100'. The MiG-17s were about a mile astern, with the MiG-21 some distance further back. Cunningham was warned of this new threat by fellow VF-96 pilot Lt Michael J 'Matt' Connelly. On his advice, Cunningham went to afterburner and accelerated away from the MiG-17 behind him, then pitched up into another MiG-17 which was attacking him from 'two o'clock'. At this point Connelly fired an AIM-7E-2 into the MiGs and they scattered, departing the area.

As Cunningham and Driscoll were egressing, they heard SAM calls. The pilot remembers looking to his right and seeing a missile. However, just as he started to turn, the missile went off about 500 ft above him – the VPAF have maintained that 'Showtime 100' was hit by an Atoll missile fired by a MiG-21, as was the VF-92 jet of Blackburn and Rudloff. The F-4 shuddered a little, but all gauges appeared normal and Cunningham continued his climb out. At 25,000 ft, the aircraft gave a hard pitch to the left and the pilot realised that he had lost both the utility system and the PC-1 hydraulic system, with PC-2 starting to fluctuate.

'I came out of 'burner and left it at 100 per cent, and then the nose went straight up on me. It was not very violent though – it just started a climb, and I pushed the stick full forward, but nothing happened. I remember kicking bottom rudder and I thought, "Okay, roll this SOB out". We started rolling, and the thought went through my mind not to bury the nose because I'd never get it out with rudder. As soon as the nose started approaching the horizon, I stood on the opposite rudder and tried to slice

Clutching their flight gear and helmets, 'Randy' Cunningham and 'Willie' Driscoll return to CVA-64 minus 'Showtime 100'. Note that Driscoll seems to have lost his flying boots during his hasty evacuation of his crippled jet. Minutes after this photograph was taken, Cunningham and Driscoll were surrounded by well-wishers. 'Everyone knew we had gotten three MiGs to become aces, but the statement that moved us the most was made by one of the enlisted troops. He walked up to me and said, "Mr Cunningham, we are glad you shot down three MiGs today and became aces, but we're even happier that you're back with us!" That statement really brought home to me the importance of the team effort that allowed us to shoot down those MiGs. Every one of the men on the "Connie" deserves credit for our victories. Their efforts made them possible', 'Duke' Cunningham later said (*via Robert F Dorr*)

the nose through. Once I had got the right wing up, I stood on the right rudder and got the nose climbing again. It sounds smooth, but it was violent as hell'.

About this time Willie Driscoll looked out and said 'We're on fire'. Cunningham recalled, 'We lost a wing tip, and luckily the fire had blown our radios too. I'm glad now, because on the tape you can hear guys screaming at us to eject. The aeroplane was on fire, part of the wing was missing, and they said it looked like a blow torch going through the sky. The cockpits were all right. There wasn't any smoke – there wasn't anything except a lot of anticipation. We kept rolling the aeroplane for some 15 miles like that'.

Soon after Cunningham went 'feet-wet' the utility system failed completely and the aircraft entered a spin. Both crew members ejected successfully and were recovered from the sea by two of the three HH-3As from HC-7 that had been waiting off the coast, performing the Combat Search and Rescue role. They were flown back to USS *Okinawa* (LPH-3), and then onto the *Constellation* by a Marine Corps CH-46 later that same day.

Following the events of 10 May, Randy Cunningham discussed the engagement with *Red Baron* investigators;

'Probably the most important thing that came out of the whole fight was that if we had had a gun in the aeroplane, I would have three more MiGs today. We flew up behind three MiG-17s flying straight and level, and filled the windscreen full of MiG before we had to pitch off. We couldn't manoeuvre because of MiGs chasing us, and couldn't shoot because we were inside minimum (missile) range.'

MORE KILLS FOR VF-96

The final MiG kill credited to VF-96 on 10 May fell to ex-*Blue Angels* pilot Lt Steven Shoemaker and his RIO, Lt(jg) Keith V Crenshaw (in BuNo 155749, call sign 'Showtime 111'). Like Cunningham and Driscoll, they were assigned as an escort for the A-7E *Iron Hand* aircraft flown by Lt Norman Birzer, which was in turn providing ECM protection for the Alpha strike on the Hai Duong marshalling yards.

The mixed section headed in-country to the left of the strike group, towards the bottom tip of the 'hourglass' rivers, then turned north and headed for the target area. The section was operating at an altitude of 12,000-14,000 ft, and cruising at about 350 knots, with Shoemaker and Crenshaw escorting from a modified wing position on the A-7. Shoemaker weaved back and forth between 1000 and 1500 ft above Birzer, covering his own 'six o'clock', and maintaining sufficient speed to keep the big fighter manoeuvrable.

Looking every inch the fighter ace in his dress whites, an immaculately groomed Lt 'Randy' Cunningham is interviewed by the world's press in Saigon on 11 May 1972. Such news conferences were dubbed the 'Five O'Clock Follies' by the naval crews that participated in them (*via Peter Mersky*)

The Honourable John W Warner, Secretary of the Navy, pins the Navy Cross on Lt(jg) 'Willie' Driscoll at NAS Miramar on 14 October 1972. Standing to the right of Driscoll, already wearing his medal, is Lt 'Randy' Cunningham. This presentation took place during the establishment ceremony for the Navy's first two F-14 Tomcat units, VF-1 and VF-2 (*via Peter Mersky*)

About halfway to Hai Duong, the A-7 pilot pre-emptively fired an AGM-45 Shrike towards a SAM site located south of Hanoi. The firing represented a new tactic for the Americans, for the North Vietnamese had been firing SAMs without guidance, then turning on their radars at the last minute. This tactic reduced the opportunity for the Shrikes, which were being launched in direct support of the strike force.

As a result of this change made by the communists, the Navy had adopted a 'nav-loft' tactic, which meant that the Shrikes would be launched into an area of probable SAM activity from about 25 miles out, and, crucially, before the missile controller began transmitting. When the radar did come on, the Shrike was ready to pounce.

As Birzer manoeuvred the A-7 to launch his second Shrike, the section heard *Red Crown* call, 'Bandits, *Bullseye*, 030 degrees, 26 miles, heading 220 degrees, altitude unknown'. The section was at 090 degrees at 30 nautical miles from *Bullseye* (Hanoi) at the time, and it turned north-east to head for a second SAM site. Moments later someone yelled, 'Hey, there's MiGs on the strike group. There's MiGs attacking the strike group'.

Since the MiGs were located at his 'six', Shoemaker called for the section to come left and head for the strike group. If the MiGs should attack, he wanted them to come at the section's front, not its tail. Shoemaker takes up the story;

'I turned him (the A-7) left, and he said, 'Okay, I've got an F-4 at my "two o'clock", and I replied "No sweat. That's me". That's the last time I saw the A-7, because as I looked up I saw a MiG coming our way. I don't know what happened to the A-7. He got the hell out and never said anything. I had just started heading towards the strike group, and it was really getting wild then. About this time another A-7 pilot came up and yelled, "I got one on my ass". He was screaming "Somebody get that SOB off of me". The MiG-17 chased him all the way to the coastline, and he was screaming all the way!'

The MiG-17 passed to the left of Shoemaker, about 2000 ft out, level, and kept going – no attempt was made by either aircraft to attack. The next thing Shoemaker saw was a large dogfight involving Connelly/Blonski and Cunningham/Driscoll. RIO Crenshaw said of the distant dogfight, 'Man, it was a massive "hassle". It was as if someone said, "I'll meet you over San Clemente (an island off San Diego over which much West Coast fighter training took place) with my six F-4s and you get your eight F-8s out here and we will have at it". Aeroplanes going up and around, missiles going off and 'chutes in the air. I saw 'chutes and heard beepers. It was mass confusion'.

Shoemaker also talked about his view of the 'furball'. 'My main thought was, "God, I'm out here alone and I don't have a 'wingy' protecting 'my six'", so I had my RIO turn around. He was nearly unstrapped looking over that ejection seat, and I was really moving the aeroplane. I figured that with as many MiGs as there were flying around, chances were that I would surely fly in front of one of them. It really made me nervous. I didn't think I needed to coax my RIO to look around behind us because it was his rear end on the line too'.

The next thing that caught Shoemaker's attention was an F-4 with a MiG-17 'camped on its six', with another F-4 chasing the MiG with

The last kill to be credited to VF-96 on 10 May was claimed by ex-*Blue Angel* Lt Steven Shoemaker and Lt(jg) Keith Crenshaw. Although they actually downed their MiG-17 four minutes prior to Cunningham and Driscoll 'bagging' their third kill of the mission, the crew of 'Showtime 111' did not see their MiG either being struck by the Sidewinder that they had fired, or the stricken jet hit the ground. 'We came on this MiG-17 to the south-west of the "furball" over Hai Duong. He appeared in front of us, and he seemed to be trying to get out of the fight. We didn't make any big turn. We just dived on him, and I heard "Shoe" call, "We got good tone", then he fired the Sidewinder. After that we had to pull up, as we were getting too close to the ground. We lost sight of both the missile and the MiG. We got some altitude then rolled over, and on the ground was what was obviously an aeroplane burning, giving off thick black greasy smoke', explained RIO Crenshaw. Although initially listed as a probable, this MiG-17 was subsequently credited to the crew as a confirmed kill. Keith Crenshaw had not seen a MiG 'in the flesh' up until this sortie. 'Previously, we had agreed that if we hassled with MiGs I would search aft of the wing line and "Shoe" would search forward of it. I had been looking behind, and one of the vivid memories I have of that fight is the sight of a canopy as a MiG-17 suddenly appeared and rolled over the top of us! It was very close, about 500 ft away – the first MiG I had ever seen. I said, "Er, 'Shoe', there's a MiG just gone over the top of us . . .' He replied, "Jesus, Keith, look around!" I glanced forward and there were MiGs all over the place, two of them in flames. We went whipping by a guy swinging on a parachute' (*via Peter Mersky*)

80-90 degrees angle-off. He remembers thinking, 'That poor SOB is going to get killed'. As Shoemaker watched, the F-4 swung around in front of him, with the MiG following behind, and firing.

'I'll just "hose" one off', Shoemaker thought, 'and scare the hell out of that MiG driver. If nothing else, hopefully he will make a mistake and the other F-4 can get into position for a good shot'. Shoemaker rolled out, put his pipper on the MiG and fired a Sidewinder from about 90 degrees angle-off, without tone, from a range of about 1500 ft. The missile went over the top of the MiG's left wing, about halfway between the wing tip and the wing root. 'I don't even know whether my missile had any effect on the MiG', Shoemaker later said of the launch.

'I didn't have a valid shot. I wanted to scare him and make him break off, or make a mistake. The next thing that happened was that I almost had a mid-air with the second F-4! He was chasing that guy and I was watching where the missile went when he pulled right up in front of me. I broke left, with them still in their happy little gaggle. I figured I'd better get out of there – they could handle it by themselves. I wasn't going to get involved in that one again. I guess they got rid of him right after that'.

Shoemaker then broke off and made a full circle turn, during which he saw two square 'chutes with red circles on them, heard beepers going off and watched another F-4 (probably Connelly and Blonski) down a

141

MiG with a missile. Worried about a MiG sneaking up behind him, Shoemaker talked continually to his RIO Crenshaw, and repeatedly asked, 'How's our "Six"?'

Heading out at 8000 ft, Shoemaker saw two F-4s egressing, the second in trail with the first, about 2-3 nautical miles south-west of the target area. A MiG-17 (MiG 3) was 3000-4000 ft behind them, low, at their 'six' position. Before Shoemaker could transmit a warning, the MiG started an easy left turn, 20-30 degree angle of bank. Shoemaker headed for the MiG and flew over it with a separation distance of some 2000 ft. When the VPAF jet started descending, he began spiralling down in hot pursuit. Shoemaker describes what happened next;

'We were descending all the time. I probably started at 5000 or 6000 ft, and it seemed to me we went around twice, or maybe a turn-and-a-half. He (MiG 3) wasn't diving for the deck. He was spiralling straight down, over a point, and I just fell in behind him. I don't think he ever saw me. I wasn't really pulling hard to get there, but was diving with my nose about 300 degrees below the horizon. I arrived at a position on him – about 10-20 degrees off, pipper on him, good tone, inside his turn about 2000 ft back – and I fired.

'He was then at a height of about 1000 ft, and I was at 1500-2000 ft. The missile came off the rail and I broke hard to starboard to clear my "six". I'd been concentrating on getting behind this guy, and somebody could have easily slipped up behind me, as I was in a steady turn. I rolled it back to the left again, but the MiG was gone. Then I looked at the ground right down below me and could see black smoke. Right then my RIO yelled, "We've got a MiG at our 'eight o'clock'". I rolled out and a MiG-17 (MiG 4) slid over to my "eight o'clock", about 2000 ft away'.

In what must have been a strange moment of war, the two pilots stared at each other for a few seconds. Then, after dipping its left wing as it was going to turn away, the MiG started rolling towards Shoemaker. He then rolled out, unloaded, hit afterburner and, with negative-G, immediately started walking away.

As Shoemaker recalls, 'The thing that really struck me about this engagement is that they always said that the MiG-17 had a slow roll-rate, but this guy was rolling so slowly it was ridiculous. The guy started rolling really slowly, and got his nose up a little bit. I was in 'burner, going like a streak, well out of gun range. We walked away from him like a Cadillac going away from a Volkswagen.'

Although Shoemaker and Crenshaw separated from the MiG without difficulty, during the engagement the crew had lost all of its compass systems except the 'whiskey' compass.

Shoemaker was now down to a low fuel state, and he had to disengage. He describes his conclusion of the engagement, 'I ended up going every which way. Did you ever try to make yourself fly straight and level to read the wet compass knowing that you're the last guy in there? I had a SAM shot at me at 500 ft when I was heading towards Haiphong, trying to find my way out of there. I finally ended up finding one of the "hourglass" rivers, and I followed it out and went "feet-wet" with about 800 lbs of fuel left. I think trying to get out of there was almost more interesting than the MiG engagement'. After successfully egressing the area, the crew returned to their carrier without further incident.

Shoemaker said that during the engagement he 'didn't see any two MiGs that looked like they were together. They were all over the place'. Moreover, the MiG pilots seemed to be ill-suited to flying tactically. 'Almost all the MiGs that I saw were in a tight turn, on the inside, going towards someone's "six", and all horizontal'. He added, 'I sure wouldn't have any instincts if all I flew were intercept hops. If all you ever did was turn horizontally, that's all you're going to be able to do'.

'SCREAMING EAGLE 111'

Constellation's Phantom IIs were not the only Navy F-4s battling MiGs on 10 May. Concurrent with the VF-92 and VF-96 engagements, F-4Bs from *Coral Sea's* VF-51 were flying MiGCAP support for a major Alpha strike on the Hai Duong Railway Bridge between Haiphong and Hanoi.

Although the fighters' pre-planned station was to have been over Phantom Ridge, north-east of Haiphong, *Red Crown* (on this occasion their controller was Radarman First Class Nalwalker) assigned them to a CAP station just south of Haiphong.

Flying as wing to Lt Cdr Chuck Schroeder (and his RIO, Lt(jg) Dale Arends), Lt Kenneth L 'Ragin Cajun' Cannon and RIO Lt Roy A 'Bud' Morris Jr (in BuNo 151398, call sign 'Screaming Eagle 111') held on their assigned station at 10,000 ft, 'feet-wet'. During their orbit, *Red Crown* moved the location. 'Your new CAP station is 280 degrees at 60 miles', which repositioned them at a point about 20 nautical miles south of Hanoi.

As the Phantom IIs headed 280 degrees, they started a descent to just 100-200 ft. Cannon related, 'Our thoughts were that we could either dodge SAMs or look for MiG, and we chose to look for MiGs down low. We decided to get down on the deck to avoid being detected by the SAMs' Fan Song radar. We both had fully-up systems'.

As they went 'feet-dry' in a combat-spread formation, the crews began receiving MiG calls from *Red Crown*, but due to a radio problem, Cannon only picked some of these transmissions. Thus, he was aware that the section was on some sort of MiG vector, but he did not know the location of the MiGs.

About 30 nautical miles inland, the VF-51 crews saw a solid white parachute pass between them. They noted that the man hanging below the canopy was of small stature, and surmised that he was a VPAF pilot who had been shot down.

They had a brief glimpse of a possible MiG-21 at their 'three o'clock', but after a couple of check turns returned to their original degrees vector. About a minute later the Phantom IIs, now about 40 nautical miles inland, picked up a plan view of a MiG-17 at 1000 ft,

One of the last units to transition onto the Phantom II, VF-51 had a 'hardcore of ex-F-8H fighter jocks' within its ranks when it discarded its much-loved Crusaders for combat-weary F-4Bs in 1971. The eight 'gunfighters' that stayed on with the 'Screaming Eagles' following the conversion are seen together at NAS Miramar in the late spring of 1971. They are, from left to right (standing), Lt Ken Cannon, squadron XO Cdr 'Tooter' Teague, squadron CO Tom Tucker, Lt Dave Palmer and Lt Don Scott. And in the front row (left to right), Lt Rick Bradley, Lt Cdr Chuck Schroeder and Lt Cdr 'Devil' Houston. Cannon, Teague and Houston would all down MiGs the following year. The transition from the F-8 to the F-4 was not all plain sailing, as 'Devil' Houston remembers, 'We had been single-seat F-8 pilots, and as such we'd ridiculed all multi-crewed aircraft, especially the "Phantom phlyers". No we were becoming some of, well . . . *them*! Our hardcore philosophy going in was that there wasn't then, nor would there ever be, an NFO we'd rather have than an extra 500 lbs of fuel and the 20 mm cannons we were sacrificing by leaving the F-8s. Word of how we felt soon got about at Miramar, and it was with a great deal of reluctance that F-4 pilots and NFOs accepted orders to VF-51' (*Jerry Houston*)

just two nautical miles away in their '11 o'clock' position, heading due north at an estimated 350 knots.

The F-4s turned slightly left 'to put the MiG on their nose'. Apparently, the MiG pilot saw the Phantom IIs and started a right turn, slightly nose high, into them. 'He could have pulled that aircraft hard enough to meet us head-on', Cannon said of the MiG, 'but he didn't choose to do that'.

Cannon gave this description of the preliminary moves in the engagement. 'We were looking at him at about 90 degrees off, and Schroeder more or less became the engaged fighter. He started pulling his nose up and I pulled my nose higher and started climbing to a cover position on him. At this time, Schroeder looked like he was in good shape on him. He started to turn with him, and he had a tone after 45 degrees of turn. The engagement lasted through 270 degrees of turn, and I would say that the MiG probably climbed to 2000 ft.

'I was on the inside of the turn, topping out at about 7000 ft. I was sitting on my back, directly above the fight, trying to get separation on the guy. During the whole engagement I had a nice planform view of the top of the MiG-l7'.

Taking advantage of the Phantom II's superior speed, Schroeder closed on the MiG with a 150-knot overtake. After about 90 degrees of turn, the VPAF pilot performed a high-G, square-corner type barrel-roll-underneath manoeuvre, and ended up at Schroeder's 'six o'clock'. The VF-51 pilot called, 'Okay, he's at my "six". I'm extending 180 degrees'. However, the MiG was not a big threat at that point for he was not shooting, and was more than 3000 ft behind the lead F-4.

Once Schroeder started to extend and accelerate, the MiG pilot wasted no time in chasing him. He lit his afterburner for about two seconds and made a 180-degree, nose low left turn back in the direction of Hanoi. From his position overhead, Cannon saw the MiG's manoeuvre and called to Schroeder, 'He's breaking off, headed 360 degrees – bring it back to port'. Then Cannon rolled over the top and let his nose fall through. He repeated this call, but Schroeder still did not receive it, and continued to extend out of the fight. Cannon takes up the story;

'As soon as I got my nose on the MiG and put him in my gunsight, I got a beautiful tone. He was in a reversal from his hard port turn to a starboard turn. It looked like a slow-motion roll at that speed and altitude. He didn't have the control response to really whip it over, and

Coral Sea's commanding officer, Capt Bill Harris, got to congratulate his 'MiG killing' fighter crews no less than five times on the flightdeck of his carrier during the vessel's 1971-72 *WestPac*. This photograph was taken on the third of those occasions, on 10 May, when VF-51's Lt Ken Cannon (helmet off) and RIO Lt Roy Morris (extreme right) downed a MiG-17 20 miles south of Hanoi. This kill was the last of 11 MiGs destroyed by American fighters on 10 May 1972. Eight of these victories were credited to Navy F-4s (*Jerry Houston*)

that's where I caught him, right at his "dead six". I fired with 1G on the aircraft, and I doubt he had 2G on the MiG-17, because he was in this roll trying to reverse to starboard. I estimated the distance to be 3000 ft when I pulled the trigger.

'It seemed like an eternity before the missile came off the rail, but finally it powered away. It was a beautiful shot. The missile exploded right in his tail and parts of it started falling off. He began a slow roll back to port and slowly nosed over, impacting the ground in a near vertical dive. I had closed to 1500-1000 ft, and thought somebody was after me when I flew through all the debris coming down on both sides of the canopy.'

With the MiG now gone, the two F-4s rejoined and proceeded 'feet-wet'. Keeping down on the deck, Cannon jinked until he got back over the water, then rejoined Schroeder and headed for a tanker. Because of the heavy MiG activity, *Red Crown* had originally intended to refuel the Phantom IIs and return them to the area. However, the action quietened down just before they came off the tanker, so the VF-51 crews returned to their ship.

Cannon remembers, 'We seemed to have had problems hearing one another in MiG engagements. I think one of our big problems was the Sidewinder tone. We had discussed the possibility of having the tone in the front seat only so the RIOs could hear a little better'.

Again, experience played an important part in this victory, for according to Cannon (an ex-*Have Drill* pilot with personal experience of flying against a MiG-17 in the US), 'from what I saw, the MiG's manoeuvre was basically the same manoeuvre used against the F-4 and F-8 in 'Drill. With one of our aircraft at his "six", the high-G, square-corner manoeuvre that he did was basically the same thing that I saw in *Have Drill*.

'I think the way *Have Drill* helped me the most was by simply exposing me to the MiG-17. You can sit around and talk at the bar all you want about the "square corner" the MiG-17 can turn, but until you've seen it with your own eyes, you can't visualise the way this thing can turn. It wasn't that big a surprise to me. I was expecting the MiG-17 to do that, and it looked the same as it did in *Have Drill*, where I initially saw it.'

Cannon added, 'Our training had a lot to do with our success, because the manoeuvres we flew all came more or less automatically to us. Nothing much was said, but we did end up in the classic fighter-cover, two-on-one situation. I fought using the same tactics that I had been taught during *Have Drill*, except for the fact that we were at a much lower altitude.'

'Bud' Morris voiced the following opinions in the wake of this engagement. 'From past experience, I was convinced there had to be another MiG-17 there. Therefore, I never stopped looking until we were feet-wet. I never did see another MiG, but I was looking. The only time I changed that aft lookout doctrine was when I saw the Sidewinder come off the rail, and I did it to see if the missile would hit. As far as the RIO goes, I can't stress enough how important it is for him to be looking outside being defensive while the pilot's being offensive'.

During the climactic air battles of 10 May, a total of 294 sorties were flown against North Vietnam by the Navy, with a further 120 by the Air Force. These aircraft were met by at least 39 VPAF MiGs – 14 MiG-17s, eight MiG-19s and 17 MiG-21s.

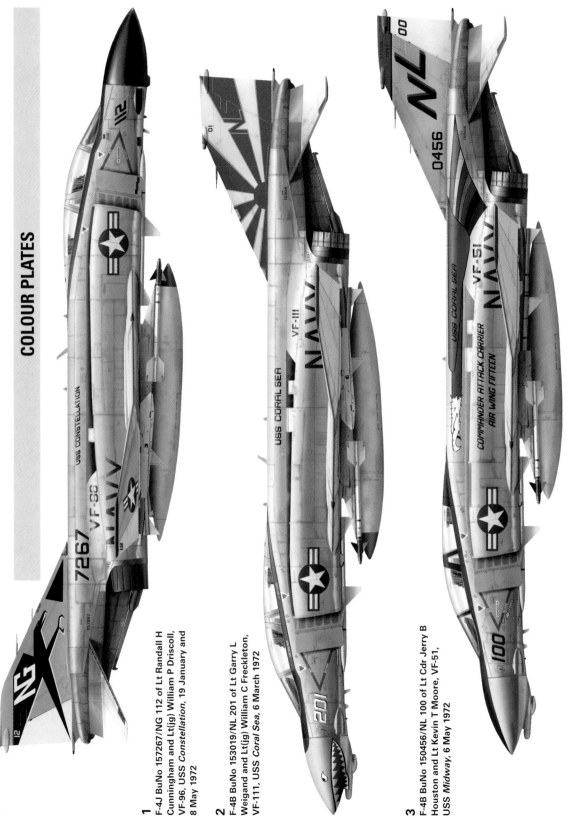

COLOUR PLATES

1
F-4J BuNo 157267/NG 112 of Lt Randall H
Cunningham and Lt(jg) William P Driscoll,
VF-96, USS *Constellation*, 19 January and
8 May 1972

2
F-4B BuNo 153019/NL 201 of Lt Garry L
Weigand and Lt(jg) William C Freckleton,
VF-111, USS *Coral Sea*, 6 March 1972

3
F-4B BuNo 150456/NL 100 of Lt Cdr Jerry B
Houston and Lt Kevin T Moore, VF-51,
USS *Midway*, 6 May 1972

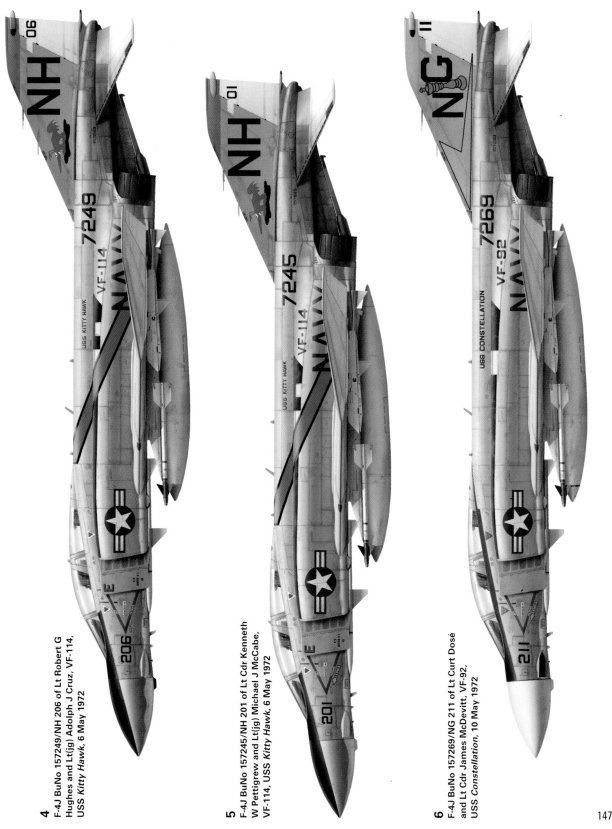

4
F-4J BuNo 157249/NH 206 of Lt Robert G
Hughes and Lt(jg) Adolph J Cruz, VF-114,
USS *Kitty Hawk*, 6 May 1972

5
F-4J BuNo 157245/NH 201 of Lt Cdr Kenneth
W Pettigrew and Lt(jg) Michael J McCabe,
VF-114, USS *Kitty Hawk*, 6 May 1972

6
F-4J BuNo 157269/NG 211 of Lt Curt Dosé
and Lt Cdr James McDevitt, VF-92,
USS *Constellation*, 10 May 1972

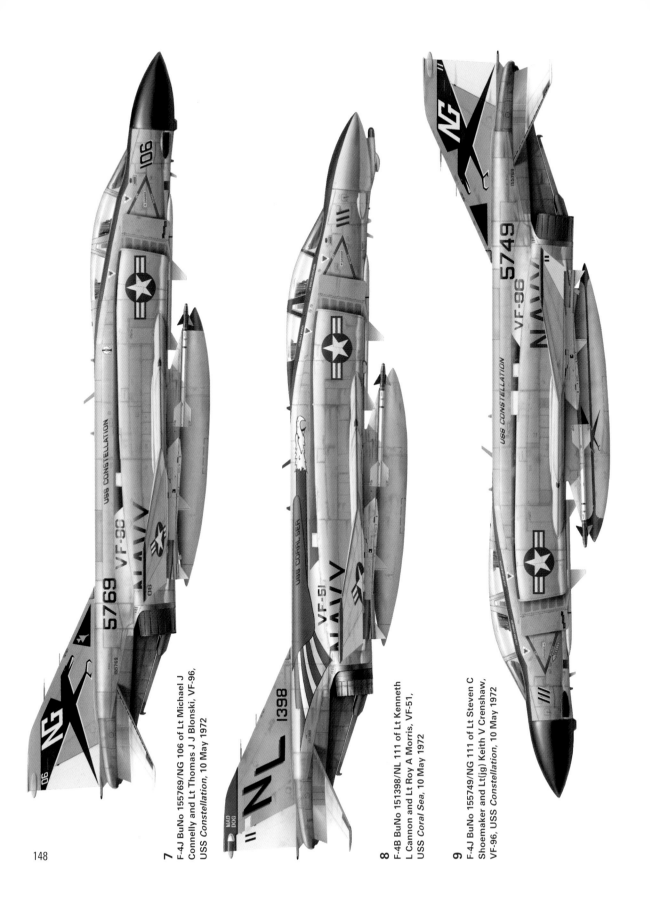

7
F-4J BuNo 155769/NG 106 of Lt Michael J
Connelly and Lt Thomas J J Blonski, VF-96,
USS *Constellation*, 10 May 1972

8
F-4B BuNo 151398/NL 111 of Lt Kenneth
L Cannon and Lt Roy A Morris, VF-51,
USS *Coral Sea*, 10 May 1972

9
F-4J BuNo 155749/NG 111 of Lt Steven C
Shoemaker and Lt(jg) Keith V Crenshaw,
VF-96, USS *Constellation*, 10 May 1972

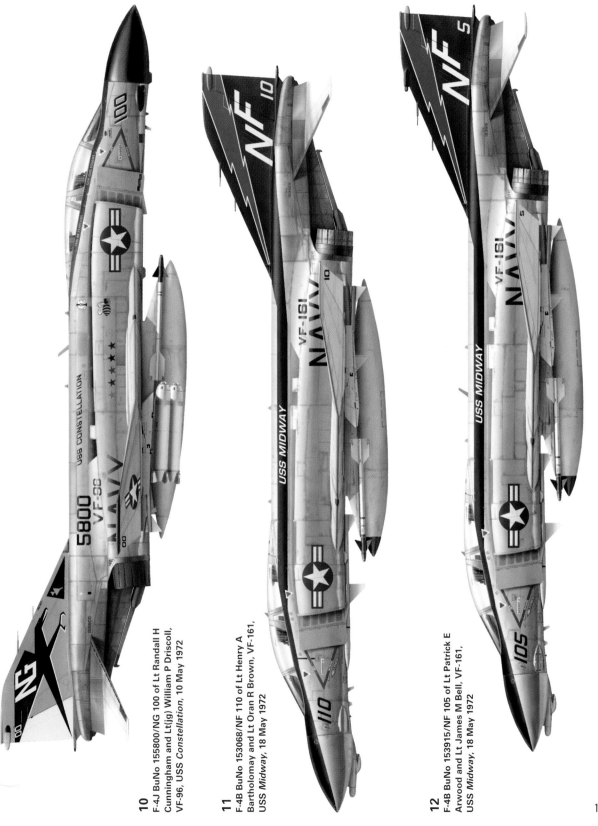

10
F-4J BuNo 155800/NG 100 of Lt Randall H
Cunningham and Lt(jg) William P Driscoll,
VF-96, USS *Constellation*, 10 May 1972

11
F-4B BuNo 153068/NF 110 of Lt Henry A
Bartholomay and Lt Oran R Brown, VF-161,
USS *Midway*, 18 May 1972

12
F-4B BuNo 153915/NF 105 of Lt Patrick E
Arwood and Lt James M Bell, VF-161,
USS *Midway*, 18 May 1972

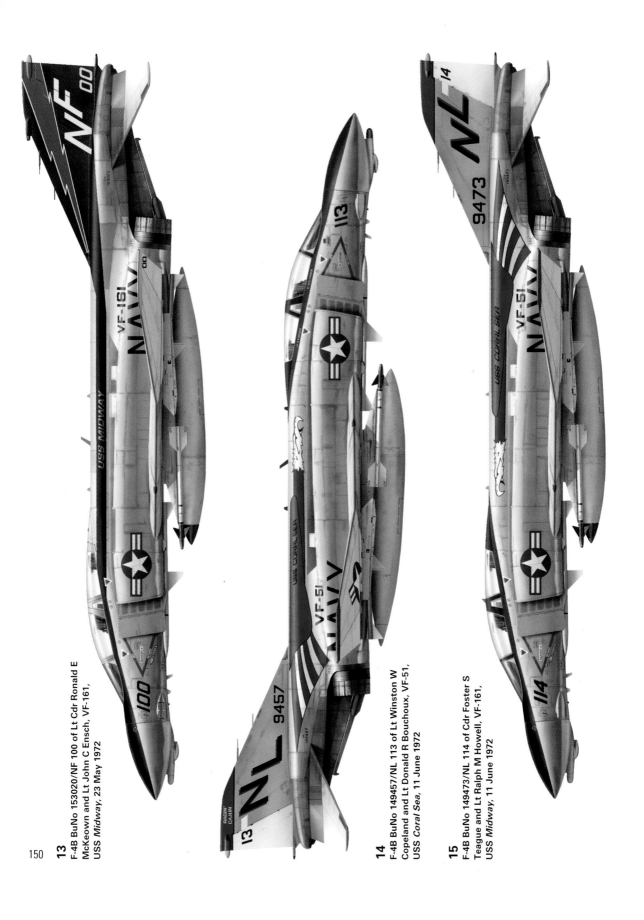

13
F-4B BuNo 153020/NF 100 of Lt Cdr Ronald E
McKeown and Lt John C Ensch, VF-161,
USS *Midway*, 23 May 1972

14
F-4B BuNo 149457/NL 113 of Lt Winston W
Copeland and Lt Donald R Bouchoux, VF-51,
USS *Coral Sea*, 11 June 1972

15
F-4B BuNo 149473/NL 114 of Cdr Foster S
Teague and Lt Ralph M Howell, VF-161,
USS *Midway*, 11 June 1972

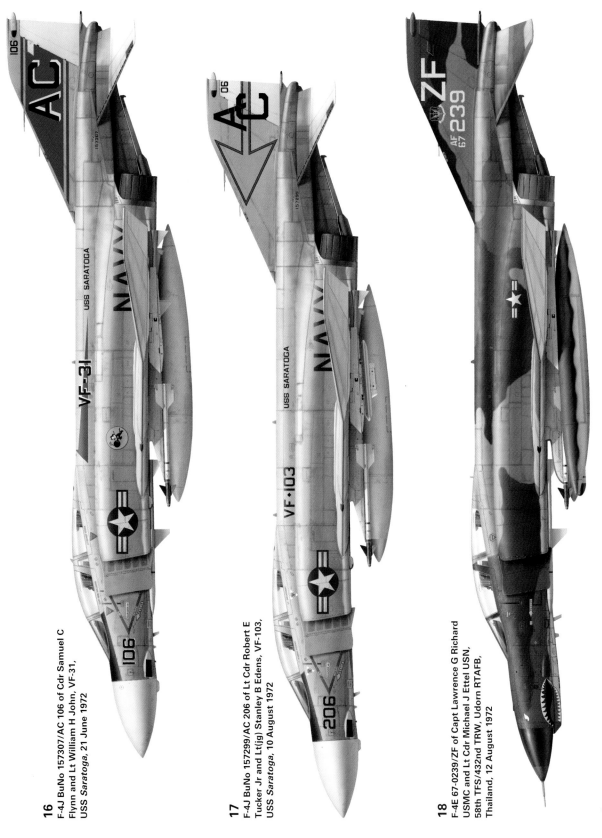

16
F-4J BuNo 157307/AC 106 of Cdr Samuel C
Flynn and Lt William H John, VF-31,
USS *Saratoga*, 21 June 1972

17
F-4J BuNo 157299/AC 206 of Lt Cdr Robert E
Tucker Jr and Lt(jg) Stanley B Edens, VF-103,
USS *Saratoga*, 10 August 1972

18
F-4E 67-0239/ZF of Capt Lawrence G Richard
USMC and Lt Cdr Michael J Ettel USN,
58th TFS/432nd TRW, Udorn RTAFB,
Thailand, 12 August 1972

151

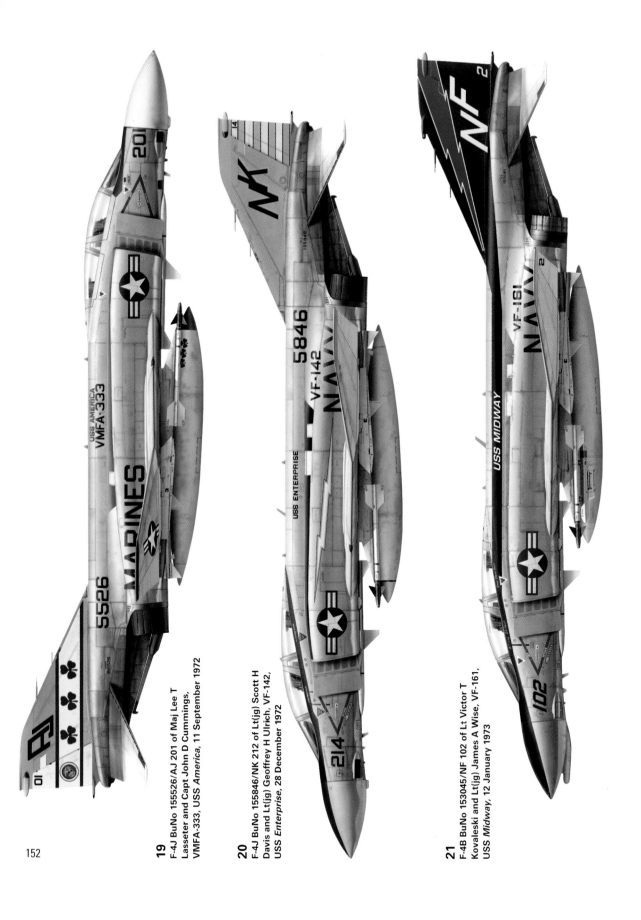

19
F-4J BuNo 155526/AJ 201 of Maj Lee T
Lasseter and Capt John D Cummings,
VMFA-333, USS America, 11 September 1972

20
F-4J BuNo 155846/NK 212 of Lt(jg) Scott H
Davis and Lt(jg) Geoffrey H Ulrich, VF-142,
USS Enterprise, 28 December 1972

21
F-4B BuNo 153045/NF 102 of Lt Victor T
Kovaleski and Lt(jg) James A Wise, VF-161,
USS Midway, 12 January 1973

1

2

3

4

5

6

7

8

9

10

11

12

13

14

15

16

17

18

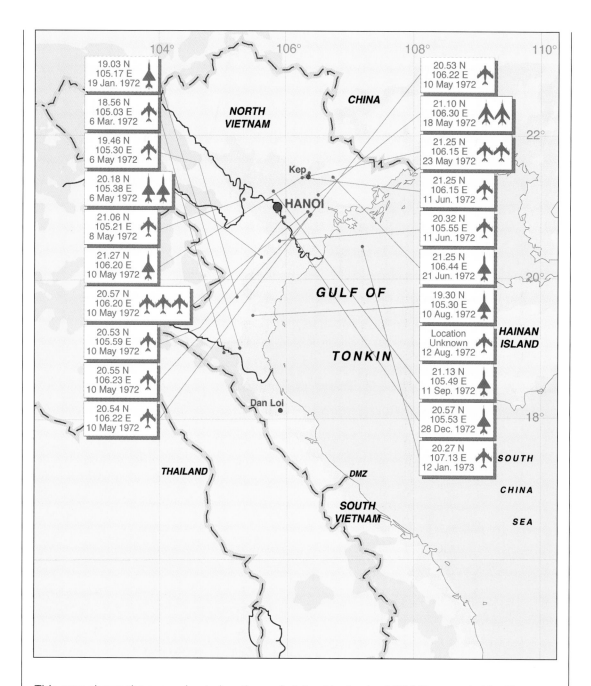

This map shows the approximate locations of all the *Linebacker* MiG kills recorded by Navy and Marine Corps crews flying from aircraft carriers or on exchange duty with the USAF. The vast majority of these victories were claimed around the Hanoi area

LINEBACKER I
IN FULL EARNEST

Although the intensity of the aerial action of 10 May 1972 would never again be repeated, two more engagements later that month would result in a further four MiG kills for Navy F-4s.

Two of these victories occurred on 18 May during a large Alpha strike on the Haiphong highway and rail bridge. The MiGCAP support for the strike consisted of two F-4Bs from VF-161, embarked in USS *Midway* (CVA-41). These aircraft were crewed by Lts Henry A 'Bart' Bartholomay and Oran R Brown in the lead jet (BuNo 153068, call sign 'Rock River 110') and Lts Patrick E 'Pat' Arwood and James M 'Taco' Bell flying wing (in BuNo 153915, call sign 'Rock River 105'). The strike force was made up of eleven A-7Bs, four F-4Bs and three A-6As, all with mixed bomb loads, plus the normal supporting aircraft.

Following the launch from *Midway*, the two F-4Bs tanked off shore. The original plan called for the escorts to coast in north of Hon Gai, then follow a ridge of hills to their CAP station five miles south of Kep. This route offered radar cover from the ridge, and also put the jets in an area where few SAM sites were located. But Bartholomay experienced problems with his basket during tanking, and now the only way for them to arrive on-station on-time was to fly straight up the Red River, over Haiphong and then on to Kep.

When Bartholomay and Arwood finally reached their assigned CAP station, they were in combat-spread, with 'Rock River 105' on the right. During their ingress, RIO Bell busied himself studying the radar scope, looking for signs of a contact. But as soon as they received a 'bogey' call from *Red Crown*, Bell pulled his head out of the cockpit and started looking for MiGs outside.

As they continued their orbit, Bartholomay looked to his right to check his wingman and saw two sun-flashes low against a ridgeline at his 'two o'clock' position at an estimated range of 7-8 nautical miles. Recognising these flashes as potential 'bogies', he immediately called for a right turn, lit his after-burner and turned into Arwood. While crossing to Bartholomay's left side, Arwood also acquired a tally-ho. The section accelerated to about 650-675 knots and closed up.

In a rare example of inter-air wing operability, three F-4Bs from VF-161 drop their Mk 82s alongside a trio of A-7Cs from VA-86, assigned to CVW-8 aboard the *America*. The aircraft are conducting a Loran (Long range navigation) attack on a target 'up north', bombing through a moderate undercast (*via Angelo Romano*)

159

Bartholomay soon identified the two contacts as MiG-19s, then called that he was going to go 'shooter' and directed Arwood to go 'protective cover'. The MiGs (from the 925th Regiment) were just entering into the break on their approach to their airfield at Kep following a flight from China. The chase took the section directly to the VPAF base. Bartholomay begins his account;

'They appeared to see us about a mile west of Kep, as they started a port turn, still in trail. I was at 300 to 500 ft AGL (Above Ground Level), crossing the northern edge of the runway. The MiGs were level with me, and I told Arwood that I was going to push them around to port. Moments later I saw both their tanks come off simultaneously.'

The MiGs stayed in a level 3-4G turn for 360 degrees as Bartholomay maintained a lag-pursuit position about 1.5 nautical miles behind. Bartholomay continues;

'To let Arwood and Bell get out of phase with me and come in for a shot, I started a lag-pursuit at about 550 knots, pushing them around. Two or three times in the first 180 degrees of turn I tried to pull my nose up to them for a shot, but they recognised it and added another G or two and spoiled my solution.'

As the two F-4s completed the first 360-degree turn, the MiGs were close together in front of them. Arwood was about 3000 ft high, to the inside of the turn, with a good sight-picture of the lead MiG. Here, he describes what happened next;

'I had my pipper on him and was at a range of about 4500 ft, but I couldn't get a tone, so I kept trying. He was almost wings-level, with maybe a little right turn. I felt like I was almost "dead six". I was closing on him, so I fired the missile anyway.'

When the AIM-9 was fired, the lead MiG broke hard left as its wing continued right. Bartholomay commented, 'I felt that guy really laid on the G when Arwood shot his missile. He almost pulled the wings off'. The missile went ballistic and passed about 190 ft behind the MiG. Arwood estimated his speed at 400-450 knots, with about 50 knots of closure, at the time the missile was fired.

The MiGs immediately separated after Arwood fired his Sidewinder. Bartholomay followed the trailing MiG as it turned right, while Arwood

The crew of F-4B 'Rock River 105' (BuNo 153915) top off their tanks from a buddy store-equipped A-7B of VA-93 prior to heading into North Vietnam on a CAP mission. This aircraft downed a MiG-19 on 18 May 1972 whilst being flown by Lts 'Pat' Arwood and James 'Taco' Bell. Accepted at St Louis by the Navy on 30 November 1966, BuNo 153915 initially remained on site in Missouri with McDonnell undertaking research and development flights. On 10 March 1967 it was transferred to VF-121 at Miramar, and the fighter served with the unit until 13 July, when it was issued to VF-161. Completing two *WestPac/* Vietnam cruises with the 'Chargers' aboard the *Coral Sea* (7 September 1968 to 19 April 1969) and *Midway* (23 September 1969 to 1 July 1970), the jet then spent 16 months in NARF North Island being overhauled. Emerging from its lengthy maintenance period, BuNo 153915 returned to VF-161 and headed for the war zone, again on CVA-41, on 10 April 1972. Arriving back at Miramar on 3 March 1973, the F-4B switched coasts and joined Oceana-based VF-41 just 11 days after departing the *Midway*. BuNo 153915 was transferred to VMFAT-101 at Yuma prior to VF-41 deploying to the Mediterranean, and the jet served with the Marine training unit from 23 August 1973 through to 1 January 1975. Despatched to NARF North Island the following month, BuNo 153915 returned to fleet service with VF-111 in March 1976 as an F-4N. It remained (continued on page 67)

with the 'Sundowners' until the unit deployed on a Mediterranean cruise in October 1976, BuNo 153915 staying in California when it was sent to MCAS El Toro and VMFA-314. The jet flew with the Marines through to February 1982, when it returned to NAS North Island for overhaul. Back in fleet service eight months later, BuNo 153915 joined VF-154 at Miramar, and participated in the unit's final cruise with the Phantom II the following year. Deploying aboard the *Coral Sea* in March 1983, the 'Black Knights' completed a world cruise with the veteran carrier that lasted until 12 September. On 4 November the fighter participated in a flypast at Miramar which marked the retirement of the last US-based frontline Navy Phantom IIs. Sent to NARF Pensacola 13 days later, BuNo 153915 was administratively stricken (having amassed 4376 flight hours) within 24 hours and transferred to the Naval Aviation Museum at NAS Pensacola. It is presently displayed within this facility as VF-154's NK 101. When VF-161's double 'MiG killer' Jack 'Fingers' Ensch first saw the Phantom II displayed in the museum in 1991-92, he pointed out the jet's historical wartime significance to the museum curator, making a case that it should be repainted in the same VF-161 scheme that it wore when it got its MiG-19. 'I think my suggestion fell on deaf ears. I was told that the aircraft was painted in a VF-154 scheme because that was the last squadron it had been assigned to, and that it carried former *Blue Angel* CO Larry "Hoss" Pearson's name beneath the cockpit because he had also been CO of VF-154. When my suggestion was disregarded, I never brought the subject up with the museum again. If they didn't see the historical significance of the aircraft being a "MiG killer", I figured "the hell with them" – so much for historical accuracy! To me the historical significance of the aircraft being a "MiG killer" should have taken precedence over what squadron it was last assigned to, or who might have been that squadron's former CO' (*via Angelo Romano*)

pitched up into a nose high, left turn to follow the lead jet. Continuing his account of the engagement, Arwood said, 'The lead MiG was heading in a south-easterly direction, and I was high above him, coming down. As he continued his extension manoeuvre, he was rolling his aircraft from a 90-degree left to a 90-degree right bank. He was not really changing his flightpath any, but was rolling in an attempt to regain me visually'.

The lead MiG suddenly made a hard left turn, which caused Arwood to momentarily lose sight of it. He continued his left turn, however, and regained visual contact whilst still in a lag-pursuit position behind the MiG. The jet briefly continued its left turn, then pulled its nose up slightly and started reversing to the right. Arwood was now in a good tracking position behind the lead MiG, and he could see Bartholomay closing on the MiG ahead of him.

Just as the lead VPAF jet pulled its nose to the right, Arwood fired off his second Sidewinder. The missile tracked and exploded about five feet behind and to the right of the MiG. A split second later, Arwood saw part of the aircraft come off, followed by a bright flash in the tailpipe. The MiG then went out of control and the pilot ejected.

When the MiGs had split after Arwood fired his first missile, Bartholomay had gone to the belly side of the second MiG. Here, he recalls his opponent's reaction. 'He gave a "flip-flop" of his wings about three times and padlocked me at his "5.30" as I was pulling my nose up to him. As soon as he saw me, he pulled 6-7G and gave me a beautiful plan view, then extended'. Returning to lag-pursuit, Bartholomay made another attempt to pull his nose up to the second MiG, and was again met with a 7G turn.

Since his tactics were not working, Bartholomay unloaded and extended about two nautical miles to the west. He accelerated to 550 knots, picked up his nose about 20 degrees and pulled hard left into the MiG while it continued its left turn. Describing his actions, Bartholomay said, 'I lost sight of him (the second MiG) for about five to ten seconds, but my RIO still had him. He said, "Okay, he's at your 'nine o'clock' going to your '8.30'". So I said, "We're going to cause an overshoot here – call my turn". My RIO watched him go back to about "seven o'clock" and said, "Pull up now". I pulled up high into him and rolled to his outside and there he was, overshooting. It worked'.

Bartholomay continued his roll, but the second MiG countered by pulling up in front of him and rolling to the outside. 'As we both completed our rolls', Bartholomay recalled, 'I was looking at him at about "ten o'clock" some 1000 ft above me, both of us getting slow. I'd say he was at about 250 knots and I was doing about 220 knots, because he was still giving me nose-to-tail separation'.

While Bartholomay was in this slow-speed fight with the second MiG, the leader (who was being chased by Arwood and Bell) reached a position about two nautical miles behind 'Rock River 110'. Bartholomay then became concerned about his situation. Not wanting to slow down on his MiG while the lead MiG was closing at his 'five o'clock', he decided to unload. 'As it turned out, the (second) MiG had some hairy idea of dragging me out or trying to get away, because we simultaneously lowered our noses and started to extend.

'We went from about 220 knots to 400 knots, maintaining the same position and accelerating together. He was 1000-2000 ft in front of me

From the left, Lts Oran Brown, 'Bart' Bartholomay, Pat Arwood and 'Taco' Bell celebrate downing the Navy's only MiG-19 kills of the Vietnam War. They had achieved their success during a late afternoon MiGCAP mission mounted near Kep airfield on 18 May 1972. In claiming a kill, Pat Arwood achieved the unique distinction of downing a MiG on his first mission over North Vietnam, as his RIO, 'Taco' Bell, explains. 'I was flying RIO with "nugget" (new guy) Pat Arwood. He had only about 150 hours of flying time in the F-4 when we arrived on *Yankee Station*. I had two previous combat cruises, but on each of them we had only worked in Laos and South Vietnam. During our first week on station, Pat and I only flew BARCAPs, and until the day we got our MiG, neither of us had flown over North Vietnam!' (*via Peter Mersky*)

and I was in a lag-pursuit. My nose was behind him and I couldn't really pull it up'.

As they accelerated to about 400 knots, Bartholomay and Brown started gaining on the second MiG. 'I know he didn't see me back there', Bartholomay commented, 'for he started pulling up, and my RIO was calling the other MiG back about a mile-and-a-half, and closing. At this time Arwood shot his second missile and my RIO told me, "He got it – he got it". I said, "Great, we're in fat city". Just about ten seconds after that I pulled up and hosed my MiG with an AIM-9. It looked like the guy had gone into afterburner, and it apparently hit him in the tail because he spewed fuel or something. Then he pitched nose-up and went into a flat spiral'.

The entire engagement had taken place within three to five nautical miles of the runway at Kep airfield at altitudes between 150 and 6000 ft. No AAA activity was seen by Bartholomay and Arwood during the fight, even though the engagement lasted for a considerable time.

Both crews were surprised that they had not encountered any flak or SAMs during the engagement, or for that matter any other MiGs. Feeling somewhat lucky, the two joined up and headed 'feet wet' to tank, then back to the carrier. They were later told that two MiGs had given chase, and had come as close at ten miles before breaking off.

The *Red Baron* evaluators were critical of the engagement, noting that Bartholomay and Arwood had 'violated basic combat-spread principles when they separated for one-on-one attacks. The absence of other threats in the area allowed their split section to operate successfully'. Yet, this may well have been factored into the moment by the crews, who knew the situation in the air.

Like Cunningham before him, Bartholomay credited the success of his mission to the training he had received at Topgun, and the influence the school had had on overall fleet tactics. 'Our (VF-161) ACM training was a direct result of Topgun's influence on re-defining fighter tactics, and our squadron's insistence on spending more hours training its aircrews in these tactics than other squadrons did'.

A DOUBLE HAUL

Five days later, on 23 May, another crew from VF-161 tallied two more MiGs. This time, the Phantom IIs were part of a MiGCAP force supporting an Alpha strike sent to bomb a petroleum storage area to the north-east of Haiphong.

The strike force consisted of seven A-7Bs, three A-6As and five F-4Bs, carrying a mixed load of bombs, plus the normal supporting aircraft. Lead for the MiGCAP was flown by Lt Cdr Ronald E 'Mugs' McKeown and

Lt John C 'Jack' Ensch (in BuNo 153020, call sign 'Rock River 100'), with Lt Mike Rabb and Lt(jg) Ken Crandall on their wing. Their assigned MiGCAP station was north of Hai Duong over the western edge of the ridge line approaching Kep, about 40 nautical miles from Hanoi.

McKeown and Rabb coasted in over Cam Pha (some 80 nautical miles from Hanoi), turned west and then headed down the karst ridges towards their CAP station, taking the same route flown by Bartholomay and Arwood a few days earlier. Ingress was at 7000 ft at 480-500 knots.

When the MiGCAP package reached a position due north of Haiphong, *Red Crown* (operating that day from the guided missile frigate USS *Biddle* (DLG-34)) radioed a warning of bandits at 280 degrees and 35 nautical miles, then vectored the F-4s towards the contacts. But McKeown was having no success in establishing radar contact and Rabb's radar was inoperative, the latter having gone 'down' during the coast-in. Yet *Red Crown* continued updating the bandits' position with relative bearing calls.

When the two F-4s were about halfway between their initial vector point and Kep, *Red Crown* called, 'They're low, they're low'. McKeown and Rabb then descended to about 4000 ft to improve their radar search coverage.

As McKeown passed about two nautical miles north-east of the Kep runway, he called, 'I've got two "bogies" on the nose at about five miles'. Rabb then called a 'tally-ho'. Ensch immediately got a radar paint on the MiGs, but could not acquire radar lock due to ground clutter. McKeown added this account of the engagement. 'We were trying to lock them up to get some idea of closure. The next thing we knew they were on us, flying right between the section. The only thing we could do was cross-turn'.

As the two MiG-19s passed between them, the F-4s started a cross-turn, with McKeown going high. 'As we got high', McKeown remembers, 'I looked around and it was "raining"| MiG-17s on us. There were MiG-17s everywhere, and I think all of us thought that we were "up to our ass in alligators". Loose-deuce tactics from that point seemed to break down. There was no isolating any one MiG'.

As the section completed the first quarter of its cross-turn, four MiG-17s attacked from about 1000 ft, and Rabb was immediately engaged. He recalled, 'The two that turned on me (the second section of MiG-17s) had already achieved a high deflection-type shot following an almost 90-degree turn. It seemed like they were on a pedestal turning through the sky. I initiated a break-turn into the closest MiG-17 and he rendezvoused on me. I'd say within the next 270 degress of the turn he achieved a really fine firing position. He was not much more than 500 ft away, pulling lead and firing.

Still wearing their sweat-soaked flightsuits, Jack Ensch (left) and 'Mugs' McKeown (centre) give a light-hearted debriefing of their double 'MiG-killing' mission in the VF-161 ready room soon after returning to CVA-41 on 23 May 1972. CVW-5 CAG, Cdr 'CE' Myers, looks on with amusement (*via Angelo Romano*)

'I remember having it run through my mind whether or not I should continue the hard-as-possible break into this guy or attempt the roll-away manoeuvre. My instinct was to keep turning into him'.

Rabb then entered a 7G, nose-low spiral and descended to about 50 ft. During the spiral, the MiG-17 slid slightly outside and high on Rabb. Meanwhile, McKeown had come around into the fight after his cross-turn. 'I had expected them to fight horizontally', he said, 'but they weren't. They were fighting mostly in the vertical'.

Seeing a MiG-19 low, McKeown started pulling for it. 'As I was pulling', he continued, 'I looked up and saw the belly of a MiG-17 coming right down at us, head-on. I thought, "Oh, Jesus, we're going to have a mid-air". We missed him by about 25 ft'.

As soon as the MiG-17 passed, McKeown pulled back into it as hard as he could. 'We were in a hard, nose-high turn, 30 degrees nose up, pulling around hard to the right in heavy buffet. It was classic for the F-4. The stick started lightening on me, I kept pulling, and then the jet went out of control. It rolled back left over the top about two rolls. As soon as I got over on my back, I pushed full forward-stick. The F-4 completed about one-and-a-half more rolls and came out inverted.

'I got it into to my head that we were going to spend the night in this little valley, eat pumpkin soup and have our name on a bracelet. All these things flashed through my mind, but as soon as the F-4 popped out at 1800 to 2000 ft, it was "right back into the fight and kill somebody".'

When McKeown recovered from his departure, he looked up and saw a MiG-17 in front of him. He pulled in behind the VPAF jet, got a good tone and fired an AIM-9G. 'All of a sudden he really cranked it around', McKeown remembers, 'and the target went from being a "dead six" to about a 90-degree shot, just like that. He was in 'burner, and the missile seemed to guide by him. It went right by his tail'.

By now McKeown had seen Rabb and Crandall with a MiG-17 directly behind them, firing its deadly 37 mm cannon shells in their direction.

Photographed by an RF-8G photo-recce pilot from CVW-5's VFP-63 Det 3, two clean F-4Bs from VF-161 cruise at altitude over the Pacific soon after embarking on the *Midway* at the start of the unit's sixth, and last, wartime *WestPac*. This deployment would last for 205 days, and see VF-161 fly 2322 sorties. Led by Cdr Wayne 'Deacon' Connell (his assigned jet – BuNo 152243 – is seen in the foreground of this photo), who placed great emphasis on ACM training for his crews, VF-161 would enjoy unparalleled success on this cruise, downing five MiGs and winning the Adm Joseph Clifton award as the best fighter squadron in the Navy (*Mike Rabb via Jack Ensch*)

'Extend and take him out', McKeown called, as he manoeuvred behind the MiG. Firing a single Sidewinder (which missed), McKeown continued to pursue the enemy jet across the circle as it worked its way down to about 200 ft. When the MiG picked up its nose and started to climb, he got a good tone and loosed off another missile, which tracked directly to the MiG. The missile tore pieces of the jet's tail and the VPAF fighter flipped over on its back and went down.

As McKeown started to leave, Ensch called, 'We've got one at "4.30", and he's gunning'. They could see the MiG's belly, and the 37 mm cannon rounds were passing in front of them. McKeown continues, 'He was pulling lead on us and working. I'd heard reports that guys broke into a MiG forcing the overshoot. We had pretty good airspeed – about 400+ knots – so we tried it and made a hard turn into him. I broke really hard into him and hell, he had read the report! He dug inside our turn and started rendezvousing on us. All of a sudden it hit me. I shouted, "He can't see me! The bastard can't see me!"'

Because the MiG pilot was pulling such a large amount of lead, McKeown knew his Phantom II was in his opponent's blind spot. He went on to say;

'As soon as it hit me that he couldn't see us, I pushed negative-G, unloaded, came out of 'burner and watched him turn inside of us. He flew right by the starboard side. When we didn't fly out in front of him, he broke back to the left with that really slow roll rate synonymous with the MiG-17. He was nose high, and we just rolled in behind him. I got behind him, had a good tone, fired a Sidewinder and that one went right up the tailpipe. It blew up and the guy ejected.'

Immediately after McKeown and Ensch's second kill, the two Phantom IIs joined in combat-spread and exited the area without further incident.

McKeown estimated that all of his AIM-9G firings were at a range of 3000 ft or less, looking right up the tailpipe of the MiG with very little track-crossing angle.

McKeown and Rabb's flying was outstanding that day, especially considering the four-to-one odds each crew faced. In early August McKeown received orders to report to Topgun to take over as CO of the Navy Fighter Weapons School. Jack Ensch, however, remained with the 'Chargers' aboard *Midway*, and he was shot down (in their MiG killing jet, BuNo 153020) on 25 August by a SAM, becoming a PoW for the war's duration. Ensch was badly injured in this action, and his pilot, Lt Cdr Michael Doyle, failed to survive the shootdown.

As May came to an end, the Navy's F-4 force tallied 16 MiGs (eleven MiG-17s, two MiG-19s

A highly experienced two-tour combat veteran by the time he 'bagged' his two MiG-17s on 23 May 1972, Lt Jack Ensch is seen climbing aboard a 'Chargers' F-4B on the *Midway* in mid-1972 (*Jack Ensch*)

On 25 August 1972, Jack Ensch and his pilot Lt Cdr Mike Doyle were shot down by a SAM. Ensch was badly injured in the high speed ejection that followed, but survived as a PoW. Doyle was killed. On 29 March 1973 Ensch was returned to US authorities at Hanoi's Gia Lam airport, where this photo was taken. He was amongst the last group of PoWs to be released (*Jack Ensch*)

and three MiG-21s), and had endured the most serious aerial fighting of the war. And while the Navy had officially suffered no losses in air-to-air combat, an F-4 from VF-92 had been downed by AAA and a VF-96 jet destroyed by a SAM – both on 10 May.

THE RAIDS CONTINUE

Early June 1972 saw a downturn in activity from the previous month due in part to President Nixon's visit to Moscow. Indeed, from 25 May through 5 June, bombing was forbidden within a ten-mile radius of Hanoi as a political gesture towards the Soviets while Nixon prepared to discuss the Strategic Arms Limitations (SALT) Agreements with Premier Leonid Brezhnev. It was not long, however, before the Navy Phantom II crews were repeating their successes of the previous month.

On 11 June, two F-4Bs from VF-51 were part of a MiGCAP force from the *Coral Sea* supporting an Alpha strike of 14 A-7s, five F-4s and three A-6s on the Nam Dinh Thermal Plant and army barracks. Cdr Foster S 'Tooter' Teague and his RIO, Lt Ralph M Howell, crewed F-4B 'Screaming Eagle 114' (BuNo 149473), while Lts Winston W 'Mad Dog' Copeland and Donald R Bouchoux manned 'Screaming Eagle 113' (BuNo 149457) as their wing.

Teague, an ex-F-8 pilot, was Commanding Officer of VF-51, and he was regarded by all who knew him as a 'colourful' character! Copeland, a Topgun graduate, had been 'in hack' (restricted to his stateroom for an infraction), and had to be given special permission to fly this sortie.

'It seemed as if I lived in hack while in that squadron – three times in 18 months!' Copeland remembered years later. 'I was in hack on 11 June 1972 because a few days earlier I had flown a Phantom II from the boat to NAS Cubi Point, in the Philippines, to swap it out with another aeroplane on the beach. The RIO who flew with me went home on emergency leave, and I had to bring the replacement jet out to the ship two days later. I couldn't find a RIO on base, so I flew from Cubi Point back to the *Coral Sea*, on *Yankee Station*, single-seat (without a RIO), and by myself (a single aircraft versus a section, with a wingman).

'I calculated the charlie time (pre-planned landing on time) and caught a three-wire. As I was passing out mail in the ready room, the captain of the boat called "Tooter" Teague and asked him why I had landed single-seat on his boat! "Tooter" went a little crazy and sent me to my stateroom. No sense of humour! As a result, I lost my section leader qualification, and I could only fly with "Tooter", "Blackjack" (squadron XO Cdr Jack Finley), "Devil" (Lt Cdr Jack Houston) and Chuck Schroeder – thus I got to fly the best hops!'

Prior to the MiG-killing mission, Copeland and Bouchoux had not flown together before – Copeland's normal RIO, Lt(jg) Dale Arends, had flown the previous night and was exhausted. 'Mad Dog' had already made one Vietnam cruise with VF-151 aboard *Midway*, and had been transferred to VF-51 when it transitioned from Crusaders to Phantom IIs in mid-1970 to help with the evolution of squadron tactics against the MiGs

The two F-4Bs crossed the beach into North Vietnam at about 5000 ft, and 420 knots, and proceeded to their assigned MiGCAP station approximately 190 degrees and 25 nautical miles from *Bullseye*. Once on CAP, the two established a combat spread figure eight weave orbit at 3000 ft.

The Phantom IIs had been on station for about five or six minutes when *Red Crown* called, 'Bandits, 049 degrees at eight nautical miles'. Neither crew heard the controller due to radio difficulties, but the message was relayed by a nearby A-6.

Teague and Copeland had been on vector for about 90 seconds when Howell called 'tally ho' on four MiG-17s. The MiGs were at 800 ft in a 20- to 30-degree left bank, some 2.5 nautical miles off in their 'one-o'clock' position. The first section was about 500 ft apart in a loose fighting-wing formation. The trailing MiGs (numbers three and four) were separated by about 2000 ft to the right. Copeland then moved to the right of Teague and acquired a visual at his 'eleven o'clock'.

According to Teague, the MiGs did not yet see the VF-51 jets. 'I'm sure they didn't see us, and were looking up for us. We started an easy left turn into them. At about that time I think they saw us, because the formation started disintegrating'. Teague and Howell then started after the third MiG. 'The number one and number two MiGs came hard left, and the number three MiG went straight ahead, with the number four in a sort of gentle right turn. The number two MiG reversed right over the top of my canopy, and I told my RIO (Howell), "Watch that guy – he's going to our six". Teague continued, 'About that time he exploded right over the top of us!'

Copeland and Bouchoux had already pulled up to a cover position following their tally-ho. The pilot of 'Screaming Eagle 113' remembers, 'I pulled up and to the left a little bit, waiting for the leader of the first section to present his "six" to me for a belly shot. At that time he (MiG 2) saw Teague and Howell and began to roll over him. I was looking at the MiG about ten degrees off, 200 ft high, and approximately 2000 to 3000 ft in trail. I was closing at about 100 knots, so I tried to get my shot off as soon as I could. I knew I was going to be at minimum range shortly.

'I fired my Sidewinder and it seemed to take a week to get off the rails. It really only took about eight-tenths of a second, but time stood still. The missile went abruptly to the right, then immediately cut back towards the MiG. At first I thought it was going to miss, but it struck the MiG at the wing root and caused an immediate fireball. I had to pull up to miss it'. The MiG-17 then fell away in flames and hit the ground at high speed.

Copeland's evasive move put him and Bouchoux at a height of about 1000 ft, from where he saw the two remaining MiGs about 3000 ft in front of him 'in a fairly tight section formation'. But Copeland had now lost sight of Teague. He immediately scanned the skies and sighted his leader about 2000 ft off in his 'five o'clock' position. Copeland then tried to re-acquire the two fleeing MiGs, but they had quickly disappeared into a scattered cloud layer.

Capt Bill Harris 'pressed the flesh' with 'MiG killers' from VF-51 for the last time on 11 June 1972 after the 'Screaming Eagles' downed their final two victories of the war. Amused by their captain's congratulatory comments are, from left to right, VF-51 CO Cdr 'Tooter' Teague and Lts Ralph Howell, 'Mad Dog' Copeland and Don Bouchoux (*US Navy*)

VF-51's entire flying staff for its 1971-72 *WestPac* deployment pose on and in front of their CAG jet (BuNo 150456) aboard the *Coral Sea* soon after departing Alameda, California, on 12 November 1971. This was the aircraft that 'Devil' Houston (sat on the windscreen) and Kevin Moore used to down their MiG-17 on 6 May 1972. Delivered to the Navy from St Louis on 6 December 1962, it completed two combat deployments to Vietnam, seeing action with VF-161 from the *Coral Sea* between 26 July 1967 and 6 April 1968, and with VF-51 between 12 November 1971 and 17 July 1972. BuNo 150456 returned to the Gulf of Tonkin in 1973, again with VF-51 and CVA-43, and flew bombing missions over Cambodia. Upgraded into an F-4N, the fighter's next operational deployment was with VF-41 to the Mediterranean aboard USS *Franklin D Roosevelt* (CVA-42) in 1975. Transferred back to Miramar in July 1976 for service with reserve-manned VF-301, BuNo 150456 had flown with this unit for only a matter of months when it was sent to NARF North Island for overhaul. It next joined the Marine Corps reserve unit VMFA-321 at NAF Andrews, in Maryland, on 11 April 1977. Replaced by an F-4S in November 1984, the jet was duly sent to NARF Cherry Point, where it was converted into a QF-4N target drone. Issued to the Naval Weapons Center at China Lake, in California, in February 1986, BuNo 150456 was finally expended as a missile target on 27 January 1989. By then the fighter had accrued an impressive 5600 flying hours (*J Houston*)

Although Copeland missed Teague's encounter, Teague described it as follows from the point where he saw the explosion of MiG 2;

'The MiG that I was after (MiG 3) was still in a very gentle right turn, maybe 5-10 degrees angle-of-bank, but not pulling. We went through a little puffball cloud and I lost sight of him temporarily. When we came out, he was still in the gunsight. I could not get a tone on my first missile (an AIM-9). I could either go back in the cockpit and re-select another missile or fire that one off, hoping that I just had a bad tone system. I fired and it went ballistic. I immediately got a good tone on the next one and squeezed the second missile off. The second one went right up his tailpipe. He exploded and tumbled out of the sky.'

Teague then pressed his attack on MiG 4, which was still to the right at his 'one o'clock'. Teague and Howell turned, got a good tone, then launched their third AIM-9. Teague reported, 'About the time I squeezed the trigger, MiG 4 started into a hard, right turn with the missile in flight. He broke right, as only a MiG-17 can at about 350 knots, and the missile went ballistic. He went down our right side and had already completed about 90 degrees more turn than I had. We ended up at my wingman's deep "seven o'clock", streaking south with no MiGs in sight'.

It was at this point that the two MiGs reported by Copeland flew under the F-4Bs, heading north. Because the two Phantom IIs were experiencing radio problems, Teague was not able to call Copeland, and the MiGs disappeared.

As the two F-4Bs rejoined, the crews made a quick sweep of the area, seeing no MiGs. However, according to Copeland *Red Crown* reported that two MiG-21s had been vectored into their area, and the two Navy crews decided to 'bug out'. Both F-4s egressed a low altitude (about 50 ft above minimum level, and at nearly 550 knots), trying to avoid SAMs and the approaching MiGs. Copeland described this effort;

'We were jinking pretty hard – as much as we could without bleeding off too much airspeed. Seven miles from crossing "feet-wet", we had a port engine fire light illuminate in the cockpit. We hadn't felt any hits.'

Copeland said that he brought the port engine to idle, but the light refused to go out and the aeroplane continued to stream smoke. 'We debated briefly whether we should eject, but we were not real keen on spending time in Hanoi. So we decided to test our luck. As soon as we crossed "feet wet" I started a gentle climb at about 350 knots, shut down the left engine and took the right engine out of afterburner because I didn't want to be in 'burner with that fire back there. "Tooter" came over and told us that we had a fire around our left engine'.

When he reached the carrier, Copeland was waved off on his approach because the fire had apparently started again. The carrier then told the pilot to hold until the remaining strike aircraft had recovered. As Copeland and

Bouchoux climbed, the fire finally went out. However, they continued to trail smoke, and the two argued with the 'boat' as to whether to eject. Copeland finally won the day, making a single-engine landing. It was later discovered that their F-4B had taken two small-arms rounds just outboard of the left auxiliary-air door, which had severed fuel lines and an oil line, causing fuel to seep into the hot section of the left engine.

Winston Copeland went on to become an instructor at *Topgun*, and later continued his flying career as a CAG of CVW-1 (in 1986-88) and then captain of USS *America* (CV-66). He eventually reached the rank of rear admiral, and commanded the USS *Theodore Roosevelt* (CVN-71) Battle Group during Operation *Allied Force* over Kosovo and the former Yugoslavia in 1999.

ONE F-4 DOWN AND ONE MiG KILL

On 18 June, F-4J BuNo 157273 of VF-213, embarked in the *Kitty Hawk*, was lost when it was struck by 23 mm AAA whilst overflying Hon Nieu island. Its crew, Lt Cdr Roy Cash (a 'MiG killer' with VF-33 on 10 July 1968) and Lt R J Laib, were flying a BARCAP mission in support of a dawn attack on a merchant ship at the time. The jet was struck in the port wing and a fire erupted. Cash managed to fly the aircraft some 100 miles back towards his carrier before he and Laib were finally forced to eject. Both men were quickly picked up by a Navy helicopter.

Three days later VF-31 avenged this loss when squadron XO Cdr Sam Flynn and Lt(jg) Bill John 'bagged' a MiG-21. They were flying MiGCAP for a 21-aeroplane Alpha strike against the Co Gian SAM assembly area, the Doan Lai storage area and the Hai Dong marshalling yard at approximately 1215 hrs. Their F-4J (BuNo 157307, call sign 'Band Wagon 106') was armed with four AIM-9G Sidewinders and four AIM-7E-2 Sparrows, plus a 600-gallon centreline tank.

While maintaining their station, the section received a call from *Red Crown* that there were 'Blue Bandits,

Its glory days over, 'Screaming Eagle 113' sits in a forgotten corner of the NARF North Island facility in the mid-1970s, its once immaculate paint scheme now faded and streaked. As the MiG-17 silhouette on its splitter plate denotes, this machine was used by 'Mad Dog' Copeland and Don Bouchoux to claim VF-51's final kill of the Vietnam war on 11 June 1972. One of the oldest F-4s to see action in the *Linebacker* campaign, BuNo 149457 had been delivered to the Navy as an F4H-1 on 11 June 1962. A veteran of three combat cruises and a spell in-theatre with the Marines, it was retired by VF-51 in September 1973. Currently stored by the Naval Aviation Museum in Pensacola, BuNo 149457 had been displayed in front of the nearby Naval Aviation Schools Command for many years (*via Angelo Romano*)

VF-31's future 'MiG-killing' F-4J (BuNo 157307) heads north-east on a bombing mission with A-6As from VA-75 in mid-1972 (*via P Mersky*)

Tucked up beneath the wing of their leader, the crew of 'Bandwagon 106' (BuNo 157307) keep a watchful eye on the photographer as they head for the *Saratoga* at the end of yet another uneventful BARCAP in the autumn of 1972. Accepted by the Navy at St Louis on 18 December 1970, this F-4J served with VF-31 until September 1975, during which time it completed three Mediterranean cruises and a Vietnam deployment. Transferred to VF-33 six months later, it visited the Mediterranean with the unit aboard USS *Independence* (CV-62) from October 1975 to April 1976, and then moved to VF-74 in May 1977. BuNo 157307 undertook its fifth Med deployment (aboard the *Forrestal*) between April and October 1978. In September of the following year it moved once again, joining VF-103 and heading for the Mediterranean aboard the *Saratoga* in March 1980. BuNo 157307 joined fleet replacement squadron VF-171 at Oceana in October 1981, and stayed with this unit until sent to NARF North Island in April 1983 for upgrading to F-4S specification. The jet returned to service on 27 December 1983 when it was posted to VMFAT-101 at Yuma. Transferred to VMFA-232 at Kaneohe Bay in May 1987, the fighter was replaced by an F/A-18A in November 1988. BuNo 157307 was duly flown to Dulles International Airport, in Washington DC, on 29 November and transferred to the National Air and Space Museum, Smithsonian Institution, for eventual restoration and display (*via Peter Mersky*)

030 degrees at 17 nautical miles'. The two F-4 pilots immediately steered onto their new heading and accelerated to 400 knots at 11,000 ft. Flynn's wing, Lt(jg) Nick Strelcheck and Lt Dave Arnold, sighted the MiG-21s first, high in their 'one-o'clock' position at a range of four nautical miles. The MiGs were in a line-of-bearing formation, with the second MiG in trail about 40 degrees from the lead jet.

Neither MiG apparently saw the Phantom IIs at first. However, as soon as the two F-4s turned into them, the MiGs separated, with the lead bandit going high and the trailing MiG going low. Flynn then called tally-ho, and indicated that he was taking the high MiG. Strelcheck manoeuvred to provide cover. According to the *Red Baron* report, the engagement proceeded like this;

'MiG 1 went into a high yo-yo manoeuvre, followed by what looked like a rudder reversal into a steep nose-down 180-degree turn. In this manoeuvre, John attained a full-system radar lock-on. Flynn attempted to fire an AIM-7 at a range of two-and-a-quarter nautical miles. However, no missile came off the aircraft. Flynn looked into his aircraft and checked his switches. Noting that the aim-dot was just outside the ASE (Allowable Steering Error) circle, he squeezed again, but still could not get an AIM-7 to launch. By this time the lead MiG was starting to meet him head on, so he pulled up high, rolled onto his back, and pulled back towards the MiG.'

Cdr Flynn continues the description of the action;

'I saw him get his nose down – really steep down – and I was going to try the old "roll in at six" trick. I left my nose up and went into 90 degrees of bank and came down on him. I switched to "heat" and got a tone on him, looking down. When he saw me there, he levelled his wings and hauled ass right into the clouds, heading south. I actually got a growl on him but couldn't track long enough to get a Sidewinder off. He started opening on me right after I got the tone, and gave me an opening velocity of 100 knots or better. Then John came up and said, "There's one on 02's rear".'

The second MiG, which had separated low, had rejoined the fight and was now camped at about 3000 ft behind Flynn's wingman. The XO hollered at Strelcheck to 'keep turning', just as the MiG fired an Atoll missile. Flynn said, 'I knew it wasn't guiding and I didn't really sweat it. The Atoll went a good 1000 ft behind Strelcheck. I think that's when he unloaded, because I saw him start opening, and I breathed a sigh of relief'.

Flynn had expected the MiG to start pulling its nose forward on his wing for a guns pass, but instead it continued in a lag-pursuit course. As Strelcheck began to accelerate away from the MiG-21, the bandit 'yo-yoed' off, giving Flynn the opportunity he needed for the kill.

Flynn obtained a good tone, then triggered an AIM-9 from about two miles. He commented, 'I wasn't

very happy with the range of the first Sidewinder. After that first shot, he bent it into me so hard that I was 90 degrees off. For some reason or other he eased off his turn, and when he did, I got a good growl. I shot the second Sidewinder and I told John, "We got him this time"'. But Flynn's missile passed just aft of the MiG and 'apparently did not fuse'.

Flynn pulled his nose back onto the MiG and loosed off his third Sidewinder. This one, however, found its target. 'It didn't even matter if it fused or not', Flynn said, 'because it went right up his tailpipe'. The MiG went into a flat spin and the pilot ejected at about 2000 ft. Although a third MiG-21 circled above Flynn's section, it chose not to join the engagement. The XO called, 'Let's get out of here – keep your "six" clear', as the two Phantom IIs joined in a combat spread and exited the MiGCAP area.

Following this engagement, the *Red Baron* report noted that Flynn had benefited considerably from having flown the MiG-21J simulator at NASA. Commenting on this, the XO stated, 'I flew the NASA-operated MiG-21J simulator, where I learned that they (MiG pilots) were not flying the aeroplane on the ragged edge of the envelope. Instead, they were flying the aeroplane the way a relatively raw nugget or a returnee from a desk job would fly it'. *Red Baron* concluded that this training 'greatly enhanced Flynn's ability to effectively engage the MiG-21'.

The Navy's three MiGs in June raised its total to 21 VPAF aircraft in 1972 for the loss of just one F-4 in air-to-air combat. Given the successes of the Navy aircrews against MiGs, the VPAF refused to tackle Navy F-4s unless they had a distinct advantage. Indeed, following these June MiG engagements, the Navy would down only two more MiGs through to the end of *Linebacker I* in October, while losing two F-4s to MiGs.

As XO of VF-31, 'MiG killer' Cdr Sam Flynn had his victory silhouette applied to the splitter plate of his assigned aircraft, 'Bandwagon 102' (BuNo 157293). This in turn has led aviation historians to erroneously state that he was flying this machine when he claimed his MiG-21 on 21 June 1972 (*via P Mersky*)

Cdr Flynn applies the finishing touches to a MiG-21 kill marking on BuNo 157307, watched by his RIO, Lt(jg) Bill John (*via P Mersky*)

LINEBACKER I COMES TO AN END

id-summer saw a dramatic change in the North Vietnamese air defences. In April and May, American air forces had encountered significant MiG activity and heavy AAA and SAM fire. US losses from MiGs during that period totalled 24 aircraft (for all three services), plus many others from AAA and SAMs. Now, North Vietnamese air defences were severely damaged and depleted, the communists having expended much of their ordnance in the early days of *Linebacker I*.

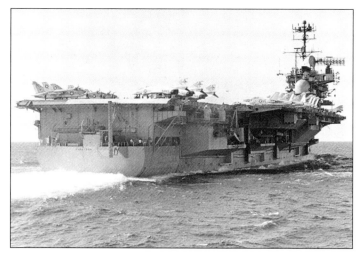

Moreover, because the Americans had mined the North Vietnamese ports and heavily bombed the railways running from China to Hanoi, the North Vietnamese were unable to import Soviet or Chinese weaponry and ammunition, and thus were without replacements.

Despite these shortages, on 10 July the Navy lost another Phantom II to VPAF MiGs when a CAP flight of F-4Js from VF-103, embarked in USS *Saratoga* (CV-60), was engaged by several MiG-17s from the 923rd Fighter Regiment over Kep. BuNo 155803 (call sign 'Clubleaf 212'), crewed by Lts Robert Randall and Frederick Masterson, was hit by cannon fire whilst dogfighting with a MiG flown by Hanh Vinh Tuong. The aircraft caught fire and the crew ejected – both men were quickly captured. Minutes later Tuong himself was killed by an air-to-air missile, although official US records fail to list any claims for this date.

USS *Saratoga* (CV-60), embarking CVW-3, was hastily sent to the Gulf of Tonkin in April 1972 when the *Linebacker* campaign moved into top gear. An east coast carrier more used to patrolling the waters of the Mediterranean, 'Sara' performed just one combat cruise with Task Force 77. The vessel arrived on *Yankee Station* on 18 May 1972, and completed its seventh, and last, spell on the line on 8 January 1973. In that time its two Phantom II units had claimed two MiG-21s destroyed, but CVW-3 had in turn lost seven aircraft to AAA, five to SAMs and one to a MiG-17. A further four machines were lost in operational accidents (*via Peter Mersky*)

VF-103's CAG jet during its 1972-73 combat cruise on the *Saratoga* was F-4J BuNo 155826. CVW-3 was commanded at the time by Cdr Richard 'Deke' Bordone, who 'Sluggers' 'MiG killer' Lt Cdr Gene Tucker described as being 'one of naval aviation's top tacticians of that time' (*via Brad Elward*)

VF-103 had to wait until 10 August to avenge this loss, when it claimed one of the Navy's few night kills. That evening, two F-4Js were performing single-ship off-shore MiGCAP in support of a 12-aeroplane Alpha strike launched from the *Saratoga* at dusk. Intelligence had told the crews that it believed an operational MiG-21 had been seen at Vinh (one of the VPAF's southernmost airfields) that day. Lt Cdr Robert E 'Gene' Tucker Jr and Lt(jg) Stanley B 'Bruce' Edens of VF-103 were flying the lead MiGCAP jet (BuNo 157299, call sign 'Clubleaf 206').

At 2018 hrs, *Red Crown* detected a bandit track south of Vinh, and immediately vectored Tucker's wing south-west to intercept. As the lead F-4J ingressed, Tucker's wing advised *Red Crown* that he was unable to locate the bandit with his radar. The controller recalled the jet, and vectored Tucker and Edens toward the 'bogey' instead. Their wing remained offshore, flying a route parallel with the coast.

Tucker and Edens approached the bandit, now confirmed as a MiG-21, on a south-westerly heading, and at 8000 ft. Tucker called 'Judy', which meant that the RIO, or pilot in the case of single-seat aircraft, had got total control of the intercept, including positioning for missile launch. It signified that the ground controller, or airborne intercept controller, should continue monitoring the intercept, but remain quiet while the RIO/pilot continued the intercept to missile launch, visual identification or whatever the rules of engagement required.

Having received clearance to fire from *Red Crown*, Tucker and Edens kept the MiG locked up. It was now ten degrees off their port side at just eight nautical miles. The pilot banked his Phantom II to the right on a 340-degree heading and fell into a trail position with the MiG, then increased his closure speed to 300 knots. The two held their pursuit for three minutes until Tucker lost his lock-on when the MiG-21 dropped to just 200 ft off the ground. At this point in the engagement, Tucker and Edens were about 130 nautical miles from Hanoi.

Tucker tried desperately to regain his lock on the MiG, descending to 3500 ft. Just after jettisoning his TERs and centreline tank, he reacquired the MiG dead-ahead, and low at six nautical miles. Tucker closed to within two nautical miles and centred his aim-dot, then triggered two AIM-7Es at four-second intervals. Both missiles guided and explosions were seen. At once, the contact dropped from both Edens' screen and from *Red Crown's*. Although neither crew member was able to locate the wreckage, the kill was officially confirmed two days later.

Seen ashore at NAS Oceana in the spring of 1973, this F-4J (BuNo 157305) features the kill marking of its assigned crew, squadron Operations Officer Lt Cdr Gene Tucker and RIO Lt(jg) Bruce Edens. As previously mentioned in this chapter, the crew were actually flying 'Clubleaf 206' (BuNo 157299) when they destroyed their MiG-21 on the night of 10 August 1972 (*via Brad Elward*)

With an empty TER just visible beneath the wing leading edge slats, 'Clubleaf 205' (BuNo 157303) nears the greasy deck of the *Saratoga* at the end of a bombing mission during *Linebacker I*. VF-103 and sister-squadron VF-31 were equipped with some of the newest F-4Js in the fleet just prior to their 1972-73 *WestPac* (*via Brad Elward*)

This engagement validated the tactic of flying a single-ship interception whilst undertaking a MiGCAP, as the authors of *Red Baron* explain;

'The tactics employed by *Red Crown* in directing this engagement were outstanding. The decision to immediately recall Tucker's lead when he was unable to establish radar contact enabled Tucker and Edens to conduct a successful intercept. *Red Crown's* foresight in directing Tucker's wing along the coast, parallel to the engagement, was another indication of excellent planning.

'The use of single-ship sorties at night is tactically sound. This procedure essentially created a free-fire zone for the attacker, while providing a viable back-up for the committed aircraft.'

Significantly, this engagement resulted in the Navy's sole AIM-7E Sparrow MiG kill of the entire *Linebacker* campaign.

EXCHANGE SUCCESS

Two days after this night kill, exchange pilot Capt Lawrence G Richard USMC and his RIO, Lt Cdr Michael J Ettel USN, scored a kill while flying Air Force F-4E 67-0239 (call sign 'Dodge 01') out of Udorn, Thailand, with the 58th Tactical Fighter Squadron/432nd Tactical Reconnaissance Wing.

The two naval aviators had sortied as the flight lead for a mixed formation of three F-4Es and an RF-4C on a weather reconnaissance mission in advance of *Linebacker* strikes scheduled for later that day. The mission called for photo-passes to be made over two targets – one just south-west of Yen Bai and the second on the Northeast Railway – coupled with the real-time collection of weather information using the RF-4C's high frequency radio.

The flight passed through the 'Gorilla's Head' then proceeded north across the Red River, about 115 nautical miles south-east of Yen Bai. As the flight crossed the river, *Red Crown* called, 'Bandits airborne out of *Bullseye*, heading 180 degrees'. However the flight proceeded on its mission 'to the middle of Thud Ridge at an altitude of 17,000 ft and at 450 knots, in fluid-four formation'.

Again, *Red Crown* called 'Bandits heading 210 degrees – turning to 360 degrees', then '"Blue bandits" (MiG-21s), bearing 180 degrees at 30 miles, accelerating at medium altitude'. The flight then slowed its speed to 300 knots, jettisoned its centreline tanks and accelerated back up to 450 knots. The flight began a left, descending turn, rolling out on a heading of 180 degrees. The MiGs were now directly ahead of the Phantom IIs, at 20 nautical miles. Closing, the flight selected minimum 'burner to conserve energy and reduce smoke trails. *Red Crown* then called, 'MiGs bearing 120 degrees at nine miles'. Capt Richard recounts what happened next;

'We spotted them at four miles just as they were starting their stern conversion on us. They were supersonic, while we were at 0.92 mach. I don't think they had acquired us visually, so they had to be relying on their GCI controller. The lead MiG-21 was silver, and his wingman was a mottled green camouflage – a really pretty aeroplane. I called tally ho, and we blew off our wing tanks as my element began a slice turn down into their inside. The MiGs had begun a slow port turn, which they hoped would put them at our "six o'clock". Our other element went high to protect my "six".

'At two miles I got a radar lock on the lead MiG-21. I don't think they had seen us yet, as their manoeuvres were not in the least bit evasive. As we closed to a mile-and-a-quarter, I fired a Sparrow. The missile came off the aeroplane and started leading out in front toward the MiG. I was about 20-30 degrees off his tail, and something must have told him to look back just then. He got the surprise of his life, because the Sparrow was about halfway to his aeroplane when he spotted it, and that big plume of smoke that it trails must have really gotten his adrenaline going. He reefed it right into me, and the missile went over the top of his aeroplane. I couldn't tell if it was really as close as it looked – if it was, then the fuse must have malfunctioned, because it didn't detonate.

'He passed me, canopy to canopy, no more than a couple of hundred feet away, rolled around my "six" and dove out of sight. As he did this,

Seen in November 1971, this 308th TFS/31st TFW aircraft was the sister-ship of 'MiG-killing' F-4E 67-0239, which was used by naval aviators Capt Lawrence Richard (USMC) and Lt Cdr Michael J Ettel (USN) to 'bag' a MiG-21 on 12 August 1972. Delivered to the USAF in May 1968, 67-0239 was initially issued to the 15th TFW at MacDill AFB, Florida, on 5 June 1968 as part of the wing's upgrade from the F-4C/D. On 16 January 1970 the fighter moved to the 560th TFS/ 4531st TFW at Homestead AFB, again in Florida. Nine months later, on 15 October, the 4531st was replaced by the 31st TFW. The 560th TFS was re-designated the 308th TFS (which formerly served with the 4403rd TFW) on 30 October. The squadron deployed (along with 67-0239) to Udorn Royal Thai Air Force Base on 1 May 1972 to operate on TDY (Temporary Duty) with the 432nd TRW. During its time in-theatre, 67-0239 was flown primarily by crews from the 308th until the squadron was replaced by the 307th TFS on 29 July. The F-4Es remained in-theatre, however, and it was used by an exchange crew from the 58th TFS to down a MiG-21 on 12 August 1972. The 58th was itself attached to the 432nd from the 33rd TFW! 67-0239 returned to Homestead on 31 October, and continued to serve with the 31st TFW post-war. In January 1980 it was one of 35 F-4Es taken from the 31st TFW and supplied to the Egyptian air force as part of Operation *Peace Pharoah*. 67-0239 still serves today with the 222nd Tactical Fighter Brigade at Quahira-West air base (*via Dave Menard*)

I unloaded my aeroplane, picked up some more speed and locked onto the wingman, who was still in his turn. His leader had just left him in the turn, and my high element assured me that the first MiG was smoking for home, and was no threat to me.

'I had pretty much the same parameters for firing at the second MiG, and I shot off another Sparrow. It came off the rail, smoked out in front of us, pulling lead on the MiG, and finally hit him just forward of the vertical fin. The MiG snapped up and rolled over into a spin as the tail fell off. I didn't see any big fireball or plume of smoke, and as I pulled up I lost sight of him.

'One of the funny aspects of the mission was that the recce pilot on my wing had no idea that we were going to engage the MiGs. When we turned around, he thought that we were just smoking for home. He had good reason to think so too, for recce flights were often chased out of North Vietnam by MiGs. The first indication that he had that things were not as he thought they should be was when wing tanks began coming off aeroplanes, and we went to full 'burner in a high-G turn. He was just hanging on for dear life, trying to keep from getting spat out of the rear end of the fight, and ending up on his own.

'Until he saw the Sparrows come off my aeroplane, he didn't know we were in a fight. He was as a happy with the results as I was though, and being a recce pilot, he took great delight in putting half a star on his intake ramp after the mission.'

MiG KILL

August was not all good for the Phantom II force, however, for on the 26th F-4J BuNo 155811 was lost to a MiG-21. At 1126 hrs, two F-4Js from Nam Phong-based VMFA-232 were flying BARCAP south of Hanoi is support of a large 101-aeroplane strike on the Xuan Mai military complex. What had started as a straightforward intercept quickly deteriorated when the fighters' radar control facility (codenamed *Teaball*, which was a newly-activated site not known for its reliability) failed as the F-4s closed on the MiGs. Problems were further exacerbated by a faulty radio in one of the Marine jets.

By the time *Red Crown* could pass radar vectors to the BARCAP, the MiGs had passed the F-4s, and six-kill ace Lt Nguyen Duc Soat of the 927th Fighter Regiment fired off an Atoll at 1Lts Sam Cordova and D L Borders in a 'high-speed, one-pass' attack. The Marine jet was struck in the tail by the AA-2, and it was quickly consumed by fire.

Both crewmen ejected, and although 1Lt Cordova communicated with other aircraft in the area on his survival radio, he was killed either during or after capture. 1Lt Borders enjoyed better luck, however, being rescued by a USAF HH-53 helicopter.

Lt Cdr Mike Ettel and Capt Larry Richard and their sharkmouthed F-4E 67-0239. Just how a crew of naval aviators got to down a MiG in a USAF jet is explained by Larry Richard. 'I was on exchange duty with the 58th TFS, out of Eglin AFB, Florida. We deployed to Udorn RTAFB for six months under what was termed the "Summer Help Program" in mid 1972. My backseater was Lt Cdr Mike Ettel, who had been attached to the Air Force's 10th Weather Squadron at Udorn as a pilot. When the unit closed down operations, he was left without a job, so he went around to the various squadrons hoping to get assigned. Our squadron agreed to fly him in the back seat until he got current in the F-4, and he flew with me most of the time until he was qualified as an aircraft commander. That worked out well, since we were both on exchange duty with the Air Force.' Lt Cdr Ettel joined newly-formed adversary unit VF-43 at NAS Oceana in 1974, but his tenure with this unit did not last long, as double 'MiG killer' 'Mugs' McKeown explains. 'Mike Ettel was killed on 18 November 1974 when he had an engine flame out in TA-4J BuNo 154317 and couldn't get it restarted. When he tried to eject, the seat wouldn't fire, and he couldn't get the canopy to come off so he could get out manually. Mike just rode it in, broadcasting very calmly over the air to his wingman just before the jet went in the water, "Well, that's it. I'll see you guys"'

Aside from the crucial radar failure, another contributing factor that led to this loss were the poor tactics employed by the lead Marine jet. 1Lt Borders said;

'All through the intercept, after about 20 miles' range, I just wanted to get the hell out. It was obvious that if we engaged we would be extremely lucky to even get out, much less bag a MiG. When lead went into a shallow, left descending turn, I knew that if the MiGs saw us, we were definitely on the defensive, and at a big disadvantage. Our flight failed to do the basics – we didn't punch tanks, no AB (afterburner),

poor communications, lack of aggressiveness etc. We entered the fight on the defensive rather than on the offensive.'

Just two weeks later, though, VMFA-333 restored some pride to the Marine Corps when two F-4Js intercepted two MiG-21s over Phuc Yen, destroying one and damaging the other. The squadron was operating with CVW-8 aboard the *America* at the time, its participation in this *WestPac* cruise marking the first time that a Marine F-4 squadron had deployed aboard a Navy carrier.

On 11 September, Marine Corps Topgun graduates Maj Lee T 'Bear' Lasseter (VMFA-333's XO) and Capt John D 'Lil' John' Cummings were flying lead in BuNo 155526, call sign 'Shamrock 201', with Capt 'Scotty' Dudley and 1Lt 'Diamond Jim' Brady in BuNo 154784, calls sign 'Shamrock 206, as their wing. They were part of a four-ship MiGCAP sortied to protect an Alpha strike sent to bomb the Co Giam SAM assembly area about 50 nautical miles north-east of Hanoi.

The remainder of the strike package consisted of seven A-7 Corsairs and four A-6 Intruders, each carrying Mk 82 500-lb 'iron' bombs, four *Iron Hand* A-7s and four F-4Js configured for flak suppression. Each of the MiGCAP Phantom IIs were armed with four AIM-7E-2 Sparrows and four AIM-9G Sidewinders, plus a 600-gallon centreline tank.

According to official reports, the MiGCAP crews had been briefed to perform a pre-strike weather check of the primary and secondary target areas, then relay their findings before the strike package crossed the beach. As part of this MiGCAP, Lasseter and Cummings and their wing were in the process of tanking when *Red Crown* noted that the strike package was just six miles away. The section was immediately instructed to disengage and commence their run, preceding the main force to their coast-in point. Lasseter and Cummings were at 6000 ft, and their wing was at 9000 ft.

Upon reaching the coast in point, Lasseter's section was vectored, 'Bandits, 290 for 61'. The pilot of 'Shamrock 201' noted after the mission, 'We came west to 290 degrees and started a nice descent which ended up at about 3500-4000 ft'. The two contacts – MiG-21s – were orbiting near Phuc Yen airfield at approximately 12,000 ft.

The only MiG kill credited to a Marine Corps crew in a Marine Corps jet fell to VMFA-333 during the unit's 1972-73 *WestPac* aboard the USS *America* (CVA-66). This photograph shows a number of 'Shamrock' crews relaxing between sorties in the unit's ready room aboard the carrier. All of these men each had over 200 landings on CVA-66 to their names when this shot was taken in late 1972. Standing at the extreme left is Maj 'Bear' Lasseter, XO of the unit (later promoted to CO after Lt Col John Cochran had to return to the US for hospital treatment after ejecting from his battle damaged F-4 on 23 December 1972), and the pilot who 'bagged' VMFA-333's MiG. His RIO on this mission, Capt 'Lil' John Cummings, can be seen kneeling (right) (*via Peter E Davies*)

Red Crown called again, 'Bandits at 268 degrees for 28'. Now, a second group of bandits appeared (two-to-four MiGs) coming out of the north-west towards Phuc Yen. Lasseter added, 'At this time we began to realise that this was not an average day. We were going into a big trap. We were looking right into the sun, and the "bogies" were repeatedly changing altitudes. We had numerous contacts with the MiGs, but couldn't get a lock-up because as soon as they turned head on, we lost them'.

When *Red Crown* called the bandits at 12 nautical miles, the two F-4 pilots selected afterburner and continued on their attack vector.

When the section reached a position a few miles to the east of Phuc Yen, Capt Dudley sighted two MiG-21s at his '11 o'clock', some seven nautical miles away. The trailing MiG, painted light blue, was out to the left and high on the lead MiG, which was unpainted. Lasseter also saw the MiGs and started an attack. As he later recalled, 'I picked up the lead MiG and locked him up. As soon as I had done this, the wingman decided to leave'.

Cummings reported, 'As far as the radar goes, this guy was in orbit, and that ruled out pulse Doppler radar, so everything was in pulse. We don't have an automatic angle track for boresight in our particular aircraft, just an extended switch. This really helps out because you just slap it down and you're in boresight. As soon as you get a lock-on, just slap it back up again, and you have angle lock. We locked the MiG up with this technique.

'At three nautical miles, locked-up with a clearance to shoot from *Red Crown*, we committed one missile. I waited too long for the missile to come off and committed another. We lost two AIM-7E-2s right there. The missiles came off and started toward the MiG. It looked like good guidance, but the MiG made a square corner. He

'Shamrock 203' forms up with its strike lead and heads for North Vietnam in the summer of 1972. The aircraft's offensive weaponry consists of six Mk 82 500-lb low drag bombs, four AIM-9G Sidewinders and two AIM-7E-2 Sparrows. The clean appearance of this aircraft suggests that it was photographed soon after CVA-66 arrived on the line on 14 July 1972 (*via Robert F Dorr*)

Less immaculate than the jet seen above, a storeless 'Shamrock 207' is connected to waist catapult three in preparation for launching. Note the *Mickey Mouse* head that adorns the splitter plate of the VF-74 jet secured to waist catapult four (*via Peter E Davies*)

rotated from a rear quarter to a beam aspect, just like that. That, of course, put our speed-gate into the ground clutter, and that's where, I presume, our missiles locked-on. The missiles never saw him when they came off the aircraft.'

Through four to five turns, both Phantom IIs and the MiG leader maintained full afterburner in a maximum rate, left, descending ('graveyard spiral') turn. Pulling between 4-7G, Lasseter was trying to manoeuvre on the MiG by using the vertical plane to lag-roll to the outside in preparation for another missile shot. He achieved a position at the MiG's 'six' at an altitude of 3000 ft, and less than a mile range, and triggered an AIM-9G. However, the missile detonated about 1000 ft in front of his aircraft.

'It (the missile that detonated early) damned near cost me a quarter of a turn on the MiG', Lasseter noted. 'I continued using the vertical and watching him – I didn't take my eyes off the MiG. Any time we got into a really good position to shoot, from here on out we'd get SAM-launch indications. My RIO was pumping out chaff as fast as he could, and we were turning as hard as we could'.

Still having a full-system lock-on, Lasseter triggered off a second AIM-9G. 'I shot a Sidewinder which went ballistic, although it was fired in parameters. We were just fixing to break away and go home because the MiG was in a left turn, just above the tree-tops, and there was no way to get him now. I committed two more Sparrows, however, with a high-clutter environment'.

When the lead MiG pilot saw that these two missiles had missed, he reversed his turn and allowed Lasseter to fire a third AIM-9G from the 'six o'clock' position, level, at an altitude of about 1000 ft, with one-half to three-quarters of a mile separation. This missile detonated in the MiG's tailpipe and severed its aft section just behind the canopy.

As Lasseter passed over the MiG's fireball, he looked up and saw a black-nosed MiG-21 (his victim's wingman) making a high, descending pass on Dudley. Lasseter quickly called for Dudley to 'break', which caused the MiG to overshoot. Dudley then reversed and Lasseter fired an AIM-9G from the MiG's 'six o'clock'. Seconds later, the VPAF jet took evasive action by dispensing a decoy flare. Lasseter said the flare was 'about half the intensity of a Mk-45 (a standard US night flare)'.

'The Sidewinder had no hesitation at all', Lasseter explained. 'It went straight to the MiG. It did not go for the decoy flare'. This missile hit the MiG's aft fuselage area, causing the jet to smoke. The MiG disengaged, then made a gradual high-speed, descending turn to depart the area. Dudley, now reaching a critically low fuel state, fired a final AIM-7E-2, but by then the MiG was out of range.

'Lil John' Cummings and 'Bear' Lasseter pose with their weapon of choice the day after downing their MiG-21 on 11 September 1972. These two individuals formed *the* crack F-4 crew within CVW-8 during CVA-66's combat cruise. Both men had already completed combat tours in Vietnam with land-based Marine Phantom II units, and had first crewed up as instructors in 1969 when assigned to the Marine Air Weapons Training Unit. Cummings had gone on to receive the USMC Naval Flight Officer of the Year Award in 1971 for developing 'Aircrew coordination techniques which allow the F-4 RIO to virtually fly the aircraft through directions to the pilot, when the pilot is visually unable to acquire the target', as well as 'Tactics which allow fighter aircraft to approach enemy aircraft undetected with all weapons simultaneously brought to bear'. Cummings had also published numerous articles on fighter tactics, which were considered 'The 2nd Marine Aircraft Wing's basis for the tactical deployment of the F-4 on long-range escort, night escort, BARCAP and TARCAP missions'. Together, Lasseter and Cummings led VMFA-333's ACM effort. Described by RIO Cummings as a 'gentle warrior', 'Bear' Lasseter passed away during routine surgery in 1981 (*via Robert F Dorr*)

Seen at MCAS Beaufort in early 1970, BuNo 155526 was the F-4J used by Lasseter and Cummings to destroy their MiG-21. Accepted by the Navy at St Louis on 8 February 1968 and transferred to VF-103 six days later, the fighter served with the 'Sluggers' for just a matter of weeks, for on 25 March it left Oceana and headed south to Beaufort to join VMFA-333 – the unit was in the process of replacing its F-8Es at the time. BuNo 155526 participated in two cruises with the unit aboard the *America*, the first of these being a Mediterranean deployment in 1970. On 5 June 1972 VMFA-333 once again joined up with CVA-66 and headed for Vietnam. On 11 September it claimed one MiG-21 destroyed and a second example damaged, before being lost to a SAM (*via R F Dorr*)

Cummings and Lasseter with the two MiG kill symbols that were applied to the replacement 'Shamrock 201' (BuNo 155852). Unofficially they were allowed 1.5 kills, but officially just one (*via Peter E Davies*)

As the section began egress, Lasseter called for a fuel check – he had 2200 lbs while Dudley reported, 1700 lbs. Lasseter advised Dudley to 'Keep it leaned out'.

During their egress, both crews heard continuous SAM-launch and AAA warnings. Because they had expended all of their chaff during the MiG engagement, Lasseter and Dudley wanted to bypass as much of the heavy ground defences as possible. Therefore, the pilot of 'Shamrock 201' selected a route to the north of Ile Cac Ba.

Passing just north of Haiphong at 15,000 ft, the Phantom IIs turned onto a heading of 160-170 degrees to rendezvous with their tankers, which were about 25 nautical miles away. During this turn, Dudley saw a SA-2 pass about 20 ft below Lasseter and continue up to about 25,000 ft, where it detonated. He saw a second SAM about 300 yards to Lasseter's rear, which detonated within a few feet of his leader's tail.

Lasseter later declared, 'If you ever get hit by a SAM there's no doubt about it. It's a 500-lb bomb going off right at your tailpipe. We immediately had two fire lights, and everything in the cockpit was going ape. We lost all our hydraulic fluid, and we were on fire'.

Even though his jet was seriously damaged by the SAM, Lasseter was nevertheless able to maintain control of the F-4 by slowing down. He continued egress to about 15 nautical miles 'feet-wet'. During this time, an unidentified F-4 heading 150 degrees at 15,000 ft was sighted by the tankers – the tankers turned 150 degrees to rendezvous. This turn delayed the rendezvous with Lasseter's section such that when they reached the tanking point both were registering 'zero fuel remaining' readings.

Just as Dudley reported that 'Shamrock 201' was 'burning pretty bad', Lasseter lost control of his aircraft. 'I said, "Okay, let's go", took my hand off the stick, and reached for the alternate handle. That was a big mistake! The aeroplane departed into an inverted spin and we had about 4-6 negative G on us. We fought like SOBs to get out of that aeroplane. It was close to me not being here today.'

Following Lasseter's example, Dudley also ejected. All four crew members were recovered. A later study of the mission cockpit tape revealed that both Phantom IIs had been operating in maximum afterburner for just under six minutes. Both had about 9000 lbs of fuel at the time of afterburner initiation, which was consistent with the 2200 and 1700 lbs disengagement fuel readings. *Red Baron* pedantically concluded that both crews had erred in continuing their engagement until they had insufficient fuel to egress safely.

By October, the North had expended its supply of missiles, and was miserably short of anti-aircraft ammunition. American aircraft roamed at large, unmolested as they had in the last days of the war in Europe. But at the very point where the US had seemingly defeated the North Vietnamese, Operation *Linebacker I* was terminated. On 23 October, President Nixon called a bombing halt north of the 20th Parallel, bringing to an end the most successful bombing campaign of the war.

LINEBACKER II

Operation *Linebacker II* began on 18 December 1972 when negotiations at the heart of the Paris Peace Talks appeared to stagnate. Called the 'Christmas Bombings' by some, these raids saw the most intense air assault on North Vietnam of the entire war. Directed by the Joint Chiefs of Staff, the strikes were maximum effort missions intended to hastily force the North Vietnamese back to the negotiating table, where a cease-fire agreement could be signed.

The heaviest air strikes took place during an 11-day period in late December that saw both Hanoi and Haiphong bombed, although air activity continued below the 20th parallel until 16 January, when all bombing of North Vietnam was halted.

On 28 December, the Navy claimed its first MiG kill of the *Linebacker II* campaign, when an F-4J (BuNo 155846, call sign 'Dakota 214') from *Enterprise's* VF-142 downed a MiG-21 during an Alpha strike on the Hanoi Radio Station, six nautical miles south of the city. The total force consisted of 12 strike aircraft, supported by reconnaissance, CAP and *Iron Hand* sorties.

A section of two F-4Js from VF-142, one of which was crewed by Lt(jg)s Scott H Davis and Geoffrey H 'Jeff' Ulrich, was assigned MiGCAP duty in support of the strike. The Phantom IIs ingressed from the south, coasting in near Thanh Hoa, and proceeding north to their assigned CAP point some 30 nautical miles south of Hanoi. The MiGCAP was to refuel and ingress early to perform a weather reconnaissance prior to the strike force's arrival. However, a deck foul-up delayed the tanker and necessitated the flight's ingress without refuelling. The Phantom IIs had no more than 11,000 lbs of fuel when they passed Thanh Hoa, inbound.

The flight reached its assigned CAP orbit with only light defensive reactions (some generally inaccurate 85 mm AAA), and began orbiting the CAP point at 10,000 ft and 350 knots. After two to three turns in the

No photographs of Scott Davis and Jeff Ulrich's 'MiG-killing' F-4J (BuNo 155846) have so far come to light, although this shot of 'Dakota 205' (BuNo 155764) shows how VF-142's Phantom IIs were marked for the unit's seventh, and last, Vietnam deployment. This photo was taken at NAS Miramar soon after the unit had returned home in June 1973. The Battle Efficiency 'E' and Safety 'S' worn on the jet's splitter plate were applied to all squadron aircraft after VF-142 had arrived back in southern California (*via Brad Elward*)

pattern, *Red Crown* called that a 'Blue Bandit' (MiG-21) was launching out of Hanoi.

A subsequent call placed the MiG five nautical miles east of Hanoi, at which time Davis's lead requested an intercept vector from *Red Crown*. However, no vectors were issued (*Red Crown* did not have radar contact with the bandit). The fighter controller called again, now indicating that the MiG was seven nautical miles north of the inbound strike group. Davis's section was then directed to a new heading of 010 degrees. The strike group was now north of the CAP point, and between the two F-4s and the approaching MiG.

As the Phantom IIs accelerated to the north at 10,000 ft, retaining their empty centreline tanks, RIO Ulrich began searching for the MiG with his radar. 'It was a hopeless situation', Ulrich commented. 'We were painting about ten aeroplanes (the strike force) on every sweep, and there was no way of telling which one might be the bandit. Finally, I gave up any hope of a long-range radar shot and just went 100 per cent visual'.

Davis takes up the account. 'In just a few seconds, I picked up a MiG-21 about 10,000 ft high and three to four miles out. He was in the rear quadrant of what appeared to be an F-4, and the sun was glinting off his canopy. I called for my lead to turn left, and I too started left after the MiG'. Interestingly, Davis's lead heard the call, but did not understand it. But when he saw his wingman turning left, he followed him in fighting-wing formation.

'As I turned left, the MiG turned left toward me, still in pursuit of the other F-4, but apparently unaware of us. We continued the climb at 376 knots in military power and, as we approached about 90 degrees angle-off on the bandit, he reversed his turn to the right. He rolled out right in front of me! I put the pipper on his tailpipe and got a good tone on the Sidewinder.'

Davis then noticed that he was right in the middle of several F-4s. 'The F-4s were weaving, and the MiG was jinking back and forth, trying to get into position. I was afraid to fire for fear of hitting a friendly. In my line-of-sight, the MiG was superimposed on an American aircraft. It seemed that because of the difference in size, the friendly must have then been behind the bandit. I saw a missile come off one of the aeroplanes, but it didn't hit anyone. Then another missile came off and there was a huge explosion. I remember thinking, "That was no MiG blowing up – the explosion is too big"'.

What Davis did not know then was that the exploding aircraft was RA-5C BuNo 156633 of RVAH-13, also embarked in the *Enterprise*. Hit by an Atoll, the aircraft burst into flames, and only the pilot (Lt Cdr Alfred Agnew) succeeded in ejecting. This ill-fated Vigilante was the 90th, and last, US aircraft to be shot down by a VPAF MiG according to official American sources.

'I told *Red Crown* that someone had been downed, and a SAR was required, as I chased after the MiG in his left, descending turn to disengage', Davis added. 'It appeared obvious that he was headed for the cloud deck about five miles away'.

Remaining in military power, Davis (with his lead now in fighting wing) cut across the inside of the MiG's turn to close the range. 'I knew I had to get him to turn into me to prevent him reaching the clouds, so I put

'Dakota 201' (BuNo 155894) served as the CO's aircraft with VF-142 during the unit's 1972-73 *WestPac* aboard the *Enterprise*. 'MiG killer' BuNo 155846 was delivered to the Navy on 23 January 1969, just months prior to this particular aircraft. Issued to VF-121 on 12 February, BuNo 155846 joined VF-142 at Miramar 16 days later, the aircraft being transferred to the unit as a replacement for one of its war-weary F-4Bs. It completed single *WestPac*/Vietnam cruises with the unit, as part of CVW-14, aboard the *Constellation* (August 1969 to May 1970) and *Enterprise* (June 1971 to February 1972), before returning to TF-77 with CVAN-65 in September 1972. On 28 December BuNo 155846's 'nugget' crew of Scott Davis and Jeff Ulrich downed a MiG-21. The jet was destined not to survive its third *WestPac*, however, for on 3 May 1973 it crashed at sea after its crew suffered 'control problems' – there is no other information available on this accident. BuNo 155846 had completed 1395 flight hours by the time of its premature demise (*via Mike France*)

the pipper on him and fired an AIM-9 with about 75 degrees angle-off. The missile guided and blew up just behind the MiG. It apparently didn't damage him, but he sure pulled it back into me hard. We continued to spiral down the inside of his turn, and my RIO advised me that my lead was beginning to slide forward toward my "nine o'clock" low position. I looked out to the left, past lead, and saw another F-4 about a mile out, headed toward us. Just as I picked him up, he fired a missile'.

Davis assumed that the F-4 was firing at the MiG. Consequently, he was not concerned about the missile. Later, Davis learned that his lead's RIO had also seen the missile and called to his pilot to 'break'. Honouring the call, lead broke and lost sight of Davis. The missile passed between the two Phantom IIs. 'Seeing the MiG duck into a little hole in the clouds', Davis recalls, 'I plugged in the 'burners and pressed after him, popping into the clouds in about a 45-degree dive. We broke out of the bottom at about 100 ft and 640 knots.

'I reacquired the MiG almost immediately, about 40 degrees off to the left. I guess he saw us at the same time, because he pulled hard into us. I let the nose lag a little and then pulled it around toward his tail again. I'd just gotten the pipper back to his tail when he reversed back to the left.

'I got a good tone on him then, and squeezed off another AIM-9. This one was tracking okay, but the MiG went through a little wisp of low-hanging cloud and the missile lost him and went ballistic. We were down to about 50 ft by this time, and we just kept chasing him back and forth in a not-too-vigorous horizontal scissors.

'I was gradually getting more and more in phase with him, and the range was down to about 3000 ft. I eventually set myself up to where I had a good tone at the beginning of his reversal, and as he rolled right to reverse, I fired another AIM-9. When he turned far enough to be able to see the missile, he really pulled it hard, and the missile went off about ten feet behind him with no apparent damage.'

A few seconds after the missile went off Davis saw the MiG's nose yaw up about 20 degrees, hesitate, and then yaw down about the same amount. 'He oscillated again', Davis related. 'The nose came a little higher this time, hesitated, and then started back down. It continued to drop to about 50 degrees, and he just ploughed into the ground in a big ball of fire.

Little harm was done to 'Dakota 207' (BuNo 155888) when its pilot (Lt Bruyere) was forced to take the barricade after his jet suffered flak damage over North Vietnam on 3 November 1972. VF-142 did not lose a single jet to enemy action during its final wartime cruise, although 'MiG killer' BuNo 155846 was of course destroyed in an operational accident whilst operating over the Gulf of Tonkin on 3 May 1973 (*via Peter Mersky*)

Second only to VF-96 in the number of MiGs it claimed during the Vietnam War, VF-161 proudly marked all of its F-4Bs with the legend *THE MIG KILLERS* on their splitter plates, as well as a red silhouette of a MiG-17, onto which the number '5' had been sprayed – the unit's tally on its final cruise. One aircraft so decorated was 'Rock River 113' (BuNo 151453), seen here on the Miramar ramp following VF-161's return from Vietnam in March 1973 (*via Brad Elward*)

'We passed over the top of him about two miles south of Hanoi, and started receiving some really heavy 23 mm AAA. I came hard right and began to jink out at 50 ft and 600 knots, between 090 and 120 degrees. I called my lead, who was just about over our position on top of the clouds, and told him we were egressing. Passing the beach, we zoomed to about 16,000 ft and got vectored to the tanker. We hooked up with 2900 lbs.'

The two Phantom IIs rejoined on the post-strike tanker and the section returned to the ship without further incident.

FINAL KILL

On 12 January 1973, the Navy claimed its 57th and last MiG of the war when two F-4Bs from VF-161 engaged and shot down a MiG-17 over the Gulf of Tonkin, some 55 miles south-east of Haiphong.

At about 1330 hrs, Lt Victor T Kovaleski and his RIO, Lt(jg) James A Wise, were flying a routine fleet-defence BARCAP mission (in BuNo 153045, call sign 'Rock River 102') from the *Midway* when they were directed by *Red Crown* to intercept an unknown contact. Kovaleski's section complied, but was then ordered to 'break off' the engagement. A few moments later, the section was again vectored onto an unknown blip, only to again be ordered to break off the intercept.

As Kovaleski's centreline tank went dry, his section was again given an intercept vector. This time, however, *Red Crown* had a position radar contact, and vectored the two Phantom IIs onto a north-east heading. Immediately, Kovaleski's wing assumed a combat-spread formation, 1500 ft high and 3000 ft out, line-abreast of him.

As the range to the MiG closed, Kovaleski and Wise descended to 3000 ft and accelerated to approximately 450 knots. At a range of four nautical miles, the pilot of 'Rock River 102' called a visual contact of a dark-coloured MiG-17, heading north at 500 ft. Obtaining clearance to

fire, the section closed to less than one mile of the MiG's 'seven o'clock'. At that moment, the VPAF pilot broke hard to the left, then into Kovaleski and Wise. The section slid into the MiG's 'six o'clock' blind spot, but anticipating an overshoot, the MiG pilot reversed hard to his right.

Still maintaining good nose-tail separation, Kovaleski and Wise reversed right with the MiG, placing it within the piper. Kovaleski triggered a Sidewinder, which detonated behind the MiG, knocking off a section of its tail. But the fighter kept flying.

Kovaleski triggered a second Sidewinder, this one at a range of 3000 ft. The missile guided well, and just before its impact, the crew saw the North Vietnamese pilot eject. The MiG then exploded in a huge fireball and careened into the water. No 'chute was seen. Kovaleski said after the engagement that 'the MiG made it easy for me by reversing back to the right prior to my overshooting – he solved the problem'.

Red Baron's review of the engagement concluded, 'Good flight discipline, excellent control by *Red Crown* and missiles that performed properly, all combined to achieve this clean kill – the last kill in the Southeast Asian air war. Shit Hot!' The report ended, 'We finally got it right'.

VF-161's kill was indeed the 167th and last MiG victory of the war. It was also *Midway's* fifth MiG of the *Linebacker* campaign.

In an interesting twist, Lt Kovaleski also held the dubious honour of piloting the last American aircraft to be lost over North Vietnam when he and his RIO, Ens D H Plautz (flying F-4B BuNo 153068, call sign 'Rock River 110' – this aircraft had been credited with a MiG kill on 18 May 1972), were downed by AAA over North Vietnam on 14 January while on a *Blue Tree* escort mission near Thanh Hoa. Both men were recovered by a Navy HH-3A SAR helicopter after ejecting over the sea.

US air operations in South-east Asia formally came to an end on 27 January 1973 following the signing of an armistice agreement by the North Vietnamese, the Viet Cong, South Vietnam and the Americans in Paris.

Linebacker had seen naval fighter crews unequivocally re-establish themselves as MiG masters. Indeed, the Navy's kill-to-loss ratio stood at a dramatic 12.5-to-1, with naval F-4s downing 25 VPAF MiGs for the loss of just two ship-based Phantom IIs. This obviously compared well with the overall service rate during the entire war of 2.13 MiGs downed for every aircraft lost to VPAF fighters. Clearly, Navy aircrews had reacquired the skills that they had once exhibited in the skies over the Pacific.

Parked alongside 'Rock River 113' at Miramar in March 1973 was the Navy's final 'MiG killer', F-4B BuNo 153045. Delivered on 17 August 1966, the jet initially served at NAS Key West with VF-101, where it remained until 30 November 1966. Then transferred to VF-74 at Oceana, it completed the unit's pre-Vietnam work-ups but was transferred to Miramar in June 1967. Without a unit until October, the fighter then joined VF-114, and participated in the unit's 1967-68 *WestPac*/Vietnam deployment aboard the *Kitty Hawk*. BuNo 153045 returned to TF-77 again aboard CVA-63 in December 1968, this cruise lasting until September 1969. In July 1970 the fighter transferred to VF-161, and it served with the 'Chargers' through to July 1973. In that time it completed two *WestPac*/Vietnam deployments aboard the *Midway*, the first between April and November 1971, and the second from April 1972 to March 1973. Placed in storage at NARF North Island in August 1973, the fighter was upgraded into an F-4N in 1974-75. BuNo 153045 was then issued to VF-301 at Miramar, and it continued to serve with the reserve unit until April 1981. Passed on to H&MS-41 'Det Dallas', which was parented by reserve-manned VMFA-112, the aircraft became permanently controlled by the 'Cowboys' in October 1981. Retired by the unit in September 1983 following VMFA-112's re-equipment with the F-4S, BuNo 153045 was administratively stricken on the 7th of that month, having completed 4213 flight hours. Its final disposition is unknown (*via Elward*)

APPENDICES

US NAVY/MARINE CORPS F-4 PHANTOM II MiG KILLERS 1972-73

Date	Squadron	BuNo	Crew	Carrier/Air Wing	Aircraft	Weapon
19/1/72	VF-96	157267	R Cunningham W Driscoll	*Constellation*/CVW-9	MiG-21	AIM-9
6/3/72	VF-111	153019	G Weigand W Freckleton	*Coral Sea*/CVW-15	MiG-17	AIM-9
6/5/72	VF-51	150456	J Houston K Moore	*Coral Sea*/CVW-15	MiG-17	AIM-9
6/5/72	VF-114	157249	R Hughes K Moore	*Kitty Hawk*/CVW-11	MiG-21	AIM-9
6/5/72	VF-114	157245	K Pettigrew M McCabe	*Kitty Hawk*/CVW-11	MiG-21	AIM-9
8/5/72	VF-96	157267	R Cunningham W Driscoll	*Constellation*/CVW-9	MiG-17	AIM-9
10/5/72	VF-92	157269	C Dosé J McDevitt	*Constellation*/CVW-9	MiG-21	AIM-9
10/5/72	VF-96	155769	M Connelly T Blonski	*Constellation*/CVW-9	MiG-17	AIM-9
10/5/72	VF-96	155769	M Connelly T Blonski	*Constellation*/CVW-9	MiG-17	AIM-9
10/5/72	VF-51	151398	K Cannon R Morris	*Coral Sea*/CVW-15	MiG-17	AIM-9
10/5/72	VF-96	155749	S Shoemaker K Crenshaw	*Constellation*/CVW-9	MiG-17	AIM-9
10/5/72	VF-96	155800	R Cunningham W Driscoll	*Constellation*/CVW-9	MiG-17	AIM-9
10/5/72	VF-96	155800	R Cunningham W Driscoll	*Constellation*/CVW-9	MiG-17	AIM-9
10/5/72	VF-96	155800	R Cunningham W Driscoll	*Constellation*/CVW-9	MiG-17	AIM-9
18/5/72	VF-161	153068	H Bartholomay O Brown	*Midway*/CVW-5	MiG-19	AIM-9
18/5/72	VF-161	153915	P Arwood J Bell	*Midway*/CVW-5	MiG-19	AIM-9
23/5/72	VF-161	153020	R McKeown J Ensch	*Midway*/CVW-5	MiG-17	AIM-9
23/5/72	VF-161	153020	R McKeown J Ensch	*Midway*/CVW-5	MiG-17	AIM-9
11/6/72	VF-51	149473	F Teague R Howell	*Coral Sea*/CVW-15	MiG-17	AIM-9
11/6/72	VF-51	149457	W Copeland D Bouchoux	*Coral Sea*/CVW-15	MiG-17	AIM-9
21/6/72	VF-31	157307	S Flynn W John	*Saratoga*/CVW-3	MiG-21	AIM-9
10/8/72	VF-103	157299	R Tucker S Edens	*Saratoga*/CVW-3	MiG-21	AIM-7
12/8/72	58th TFS/432nd TRW	67-0239	L Richard M Ettel	Udorn RTAB	MiG-21	AIM-7
11/9/72	VMFA-333	155526	L Lasseter J Cummings	*America*/CVW-8	MiG-21	AIM-9
28/12/72	VF-142	155846	S Davis G Ulrich	*Enterprise*/CVW-14	MiG-21	AIM-9
12/1/73	VF-161	153045	V Kovaleski J Wise	*Midway*/CVW-5	MiG-17	AIM-9

Editor's Note: Due to a restriction on space in this volume, the plates commentaries for the colour profiles appear in point form. Further information on most of these aeroplanes appears within the photo captions throughout the book.

1

F-4J BuNo 157267/NG 112 of Lt Randall H Cunningham and Lt(jg) William P Driscoll, VF-96, USS *Constellation*, 19 January and 8 May 1972
Delivered – 13 January 1970
Units served with – VF-121, VF-96, VF-114, VF-21, VMFA-232, VMFA-235, VMFA-122
Major modifications – upgraded to F-4S in 1979-80
Final fate – on display in the San Diego Aerospace Museum, California, since March 1990

2

F-4B BuNo 153019/NL 201 of Lt Garry L Weigand and Lt(jg) William C Freckleton, VF-111, USS *Coral Sea*, 6 March 1972
Delivered – 5 May 1966
Units served with – VF-213, VF-121, VF-111, VMFA-531, VF-201, VF-171
Major modifications – upgraded to F-4N in 1976
Final fate – gate guard at NAS Key West, Florida

3

F-4B BuNo 150456/NL 100 of Lt Cdr Jerry B Houston and Lt Kevin T Moore, VF-51, USS *Midway*, 6 May 1972
Delivered – 6 December 1962
Units served with – VF-121, VF-151, VF-161, VF-143, VF-51, VF-41, VF-301, VMFA-321
Major modifications – upgraded to F-4N in 1973-74
Final fate – expended as a QF-4N target drone in a missile test at the Naval Weapons Center at China Lake, in California, on 27 January 1989

4

F-4J BuNo 157249/NH 206 of Lt Robert G Hughes and Lt(jg) Adolph J Cruz, VF-114, USS *Kitty Hawk*, 6 May 1972
Delivered – 6 October 1969
Units served with – VF-114, VF-21, VMFA-212, VMFA-235, VMFA-122, VF-33, VF-103, VF-171, VMFA-115, VMFAT-101, VMFA-212
Major modifications – upgraded to F-4S in 1981-82
Final fate – stored since October 1986 in AMARC's Davis-Monthan facility

5

F-4J BuNo 157245/NH 201 of Lt Cdr Kenneth W Pettigrew and Lt(jg) Michael J McCabe, VF-114, USS *Kitty Hawk*, 6 May 1972
Delivered – 24 September 1969
Units served with – VF-114, VF-51, VMFA-212, VMFA-232, VF-121, VF-103, VMFA-251
Major modifications – upgraded to F-4S in 1980-81
Final fate – stored since August 1985 in AMARC's Davis-Monthan facility

6

F-4J BuNo 157269/NG 211 of Lt Curt Dosé and Lt Cdr James McDevitt, VF-92, USS *Constellation*, 10 May 1972
Delivered – 5 February 1970
Units served with – VF-121, VF-92, VF-114, VMFAT-101, VMFA-235
Major modifications – upgraded to F-4S in 1979-80
Final fate – stored since February 1986 in AMARC's Davis-Monthan facility

7

F-4J BuNo 155769/NG 106 of Lt Michael J Connelly and Lt Thomas J J Blonski, VF-96, USS *Constellation*, 10 May 1972
Delivered – 27 July 1968
Units served with – VF-154, VF-142, VF-121, VF-96, VF-194, VF-302
Major modifications – upgraded to F-4S in 1980-81
Final fate – crashed during landing roll-out at NAS Dallas, Texas, on 4 April 1983, both crewmen ejecting safely

8

F-4B BuNo 151398/NL 111 of Lt Kenneth L Cannon and Lt Roy A Morris, VF-51, USS *Coral Sea*, 10 May 1972
Delivered – 2 August 1963
Units served with – VF-101, VF-102, VF-32, VF-142, VMFA-115, VF-51, VF-161
Major modifications – upgraded to F-4N in 1972-73
Final fate – scrapped in Tucson, Arizona, in 1990

9

F-4J BuNo 155749/NG 111 of Lt Steven C Shoemaker and Lt(jg) Keith V Crenshaw, VF-96, USS *Constellation*, 10 May 1972
Delivered – 24 June 1968
Units served with – VF-21, VF-142, VF-96, VMFA-212, VMFAT-101, VMFA-235, VF-301, VMFA-321, VMFA-134
Major modifications – upgraded to F-4S in 1979-80
Final fate – converted into a QF-4S, the jet was lost during the annual Point Mugu airshow on 20 April 2002 whilst serving with the Naval Weapons Test Squadron. It crashed due to an apparent engine malfunction just before it was due to land after its demonstration flight. Both crewmen were killed.

10

F-4J BuNo 155800/NG 100 of Lt Randall H Cunningham and Lt(jg) William P Driscoll, VF-96, USS *Constellation*, 10 May 1972
Delivered – 17 October 1968
Unit served with – VF-96
Major modifications – none
Final fate – damaged by a SAM and crew ejected off North Vietnamese coastline on 10 May 1972

11

F-4B BuNo 153068/NF 110 of Lt Henry A

Bartholomay and Lt Oran R Brown, VF-161,
USS *Midway*, 18 May 1972
Delivered – 4 November 1966
Units served with – VF-74, VF-11, VF-213, the *Blue
Angels*, VF-161
Major modifications – none
Final fate – damaged by AAA and the crew
(including MiG-killing pilot Lt Victor Kovaleski) forced
to eject over the Gulf of Tonkin on 14 January 1973

12

F-4B BuNo 153915/NF 105 of Lt Patrick E Arwood
and Lt James M Bell, VF-161, USS *Midway*,
18 May 1972
Delivered – 30 November 1966
Units served with – VF-121, VF-161, VF-41,
VMFAT-101, VF-111, VMFA-314, VF-154,
Major modifications – upgraded to F-4N in 1975-76
Final fate – on display in the Naval Aviation
Museum at NAS Pensacola, Florida

13

F-4B BuNo 153020/NF 100 of Lt Cdr Ronald E
McKeown and Lt John C Ensch, VF-161,
USS *Midway*, 23 May 1972
Delivered – 27 May 1966
Units served with – VF-121, VF-213, VF-114, VF-92,
VMFA-314, VMFA-122, VF-161
Major modifications – none
Final fate – downed by a SAM and the crew forced
to eject over Nam Dinh on 25 August 1972. Pilot
killed and RIO captured

14

F-4B BuNo 149457/NL 113 of Lt Winston W
Copeland and Lt Donald R Bouchoux, VF-51,
USS *Coral Sea*, 11 June 1972
Delivered – 11 June 1962
Units served with – VF-121, VMF(AW)-314,
VMFA-513, VMFA-542, VF-51, VF-21, VF-142,
VF-143, VF-114, VMFA-122, VMFA-314, H&MS-33,
H&MS-11, VMFA-531,
Major modifications – none
Final fate – currently in storage with the Naval
Aviation Museum at NAS Pensacola, having
previously been displayed in front of the nearby
Naval Aviation Schools Command for many years

15

F-4B BuNo 149473/NL 114 of Cdr Foster S Teague
and Lt Ralph M Howell, VF-161, USS *Midway*,
11 June 1972
Delivered – 25 July 1962
Units served with – VF-102, VF-101, VF-14, VF-31,
VF-74, VF-32, VMFAT-201, VMFAT-101, H&MS-33,
H&MS-11, VF-51, Naval Missile Center
Major modifications – none
Final fate – destroyed as a range target at
Holloman AFB, New Mexico, in 1973-74

16

F-4J BuNo 157307/AC 106 of Cdr Samuel C Flynn
and Lt William H John, VF-31, USS *Saratoga*,
21 June 1972

Delivered – 18 December 1970
Units served with – VF-31, VF-33, VF-103, VF-171,
VMFAT-101, VMFA-232,
Major modifications – upgraded to F-4S in 1983
Final fate – currently on stored at the National Air
and Space Museum's Dulles International Airport
facility, Washington, DC

17

F-4J BuNo 157299/AC 206 of Lt Cdr Robert E
Tucker, Jr and Lt(jg) Stanley B Edens, VF-103,
USS *Saratoga*, 10 August 1972
Delivered – 24 November 1970
Units served with – VF-103, VF-11
Major modifications – none
Final fate – lost in a flying accident on 9 February
1977 whilst participating in a daytime ACM
training sortie from Oceana, the aircraft suffering
an in-flight fire within the fuselage. The crew
ejected safely

18

F-4E 67-0239/ZF of Capt Lawrence G Richard USMC
and Lt Cdr Michael J Ettel USN, 58th TFS/432nd
TRW, Udorn RTAFB, Thailand, 12 August 1972
Delivered – May 1968
Units served with – 15th TFW, 560th TFS/4531st
TFW, 308th TFS/31st TFW, 432nd TRW (TDY)
Major modifications – none
Final fate – supplied to the Egyptian air force as
part of Operation *Peace Pharoah*, the jet is still in
frontline service with the 222nd Tactical Fighter
Brigade at Quahira-West air base

19

F-4J BuNo 155526/AJ 201 of Maj Lee T Lasseter
and Capt John D Cummings, VMFA-333,
USS *America*, 11 September 1972
Delivered – 8 February 1968
Units served with – VF-103, VMFA-333
Major modifications – none
Final fate – damaged by a SAM and the crew
forced to eject over the Gulf of Tonkin on
11 September 1972

20

F-4J BuNo 155846/NK 212 of Lt(jg) Scott H Davis
and Lt(jg) Geoffrey H Ulrich, VF-142,
USS *Enterprise*, 28 December 1972
Delivered – 23 January 1969
Units served with – VF-121, VF-142,
Major modifications – none
Final fate – aircraft crashed at sea off South
Vietnam on 3 May 1973 after its crew suffered
severe control problems. Both men ejected
safely

21

F-4B BuNo 153045/NF 102 of Lt Victor T Kovaleski
and Lt(jg) James A Wise, VF-161, USS *Midway*,
12 January 1973
Delivered – 17 August 1966
Units served with – VF-101, VF-74, VF-114, VF-161,
VF-301, H&MS-41, VMFA-112

Major modifications – upgraded to F-4N in 1974-75
Final fate – withdrawn from service in September 1983, the jet's final disposition remains unknown

COLOUR SECTION

1
VF-96 'MiG killer' BuNo 157267 poses with the San Diego Aerospace Museum's MiG-17F (ex-Egyptian air force) at the General Dynamics plant in San Diego in October 1989. Five months later both jets were mounted on poles within the atrium at the museum in Balboa Park (*via Robert F Dorr*)

2
Matt Connelly and Tom Blonski's 'Showtime 106' (BuNo 155769) formates with a second jet from VF-96 in early 1972 (*via Peter Mersky*)

3
Steve Shoemaker and Keith Crenshaw's 'Showtime 111' was photographed on the Miramar ramp in late 1971. Converted into a QF-4S target drone, this aircraft was lost in a fatal crash at the Point Mugu airshow in April 2002 (*via B Elward*)

4
Formerly 'Showtime 112', dual 'MiG-killing' F-4J BuNo 157267 left VF-96 for VF-114 (via VF-121) in late 1972, and served with the 'Aardvarks' until April 1975 (*via Peter Mersky*)

5
'Linfield 201' (BuNo 157245) is seen with a suitably-marked travel pod mounted beneath its port wing. Photographed in 1971, this aircraft claimed a MiG-21 on 6 May 1972 (*via A Romano*)

6
VF-92's full complement of aircrew pose for a squadron photo in their 'Friday suits' whilst in the Gulf of Tonkin in 1972. Providing the backdrop to this shot is VF-92's CAG jet, BuNo 155799. All Navy units have these unofficial flightsuits made up in their squadron colours pre-cruise, but they are worn only on training flights (*via Peter E Davies*)

7 & 8
Seen at Miramar in August 1972, weeks after completing a gruelling Vietnam cruise, 'Screaming Eagle 110' shows clear signs of fatigue. This jet was used by Ken Cannon and Roy Morris to down a MiG-17 on 10 May. Ironically, it was assigned to Winston 'Mad Dog' Copeland (and his usual RIO Dale Arends), who downed a MiG-17 on 11 June in Cannon and Morris's 'Screaming Eagle 113' (BuNo 149457)! Wearing the modex 111 on cruise, the F-4B features Copeland's name spelt incorrectly on the canopy rail – it had been erroneously applied with an 's' at the end (*via A Romano and B Elward*)

9
An unknown pilot and RIO Lt Steve Brainerd strap into 'Rock River 110' (BuNo 153068) in August

1972. This aircraft had been used by 'Bart' Bartholomay and Oran Brown to destroy a MiG-19 on 18 May 1972 – their names appear on the canopy rails, and a kill marking is partially visible at the base of the splitter vane (*M Padgett*)

10
'Rock River 101' runs up in full afterburner prior to taking a 'cat shot' in mid 1972. Commenting on the jet's 'patch painting on the vertical fin', photographer Michael Padgett, who was VF-161's Corrosion Control Supervisor for this cruise, remembers 'Paint jobs were just maintained on the "boat". Whole aircraft painting, or even large section painting, was discouraged' (*M Padgett*)

11
The splitter plate kill markings applied to 'Mugs' McKeown and Jack Ensch's 'Rock River 100' (BuNo 153020) in the wake of their MiG-17 claims on 23 May 1972. This jet was subsequently shot down by a SAM on 25 August 1972 (*M Padgett*)

12
Wearing standard flightsuits, VF-161 aircrew pose for a cruise book shot in April 1972. They had been aboard CVA-41 just a matter of days when this photo was taken (*Mike Rabb via Jack Ensch*)

13
Michael Padgett painted the tail markings on most VF-161 jets in 1972, and he also decorated the door to the unit's ready room (dubbed *The "ROCK'S" Den*). 'I stood many a watch behind that door', he remembers (*M Padgett*)

14
VF-51 'MiG killer' BuNo 149457 was photographed in storage at NARF North Island on 13 November 1976. Assigned to the Naval Aviation Museum at NAS Pensacola since the late 1970s, the jet is presently in storage once again after having been displayed in front of the nearby Naval Aviation Schools Command for many years (*via R F Dorr*)

15
The assigned F-4J (BuNo 157293) of VF-31's Sam Flynn and Bill John wore their MiG kill symbol, although it was not a 'MiG killer' (*via B Elward*)

16
Three VMFA-333 F-4Js share the fantail on a rainy CVA-66 with other jets from CVW-8 (*via B Elward*)

17
Sister-ship to VF-142 'MiG killer' BuNo 155846, 'Dakota 213' is seen at Miramar in June 1973 (*via B Elward*)

18
Scorer of the final aerial victory to be claimed by an American aircraft in the Vietnam War, 'Rock River 102' (BuNo 153045) rests on the Miramar ramp in the spring of 1973 (*via A Romano*)